ONE TANK TRIPS
TRIPS
Road Food

To Bill, Jr.

Let's Eat!

11/6/99

ONE TANK TRIPS
Road Food

Neil Zurcher

GRAY & COMPANY, PUBLISHERS
CLEVELAND

This book is dedicated to several people:
First to Bonnie, my wife, my best friend, for her love and encourage-
ment, and her refusal to see the dark side of life.
My son, Craig Zurcher, who started out his life sharing my travels and is
now about ready to begin his own life's journey.
And to my newest grandson, Ryan Peter Luttmann, who now shares my
love of watermelon and cookies and who someday, I hope, will also
share my love for travel and the people you meet along the way.

Gray & Company, Publishers
1588 East 40th Street
Cleveland, Ohio 44103-2302
(216) 431-2665
www.grayco.com

This guide was prepared on the basis of the author's best knowledge at the time
of publication. However, because of constantly changing conditions beyond his
control, the author disclaims any responsibility for the accuracy and complete-
ness of the information in this guide. Users of this guide are cautioned not to
place undue reliance upon the validity of the information contained herein and
to use this guide at their own risk.

ISBN 1-886228-30-2

Printed in the United States of America

10 9 8 7 6 5 4 3 2 1

Contents

* The chapter numbers start with 85 because this is the third in a series of "One Tank Trips" books. Chapters 1–46 are in *Neil Zurcher's Favorite One Tank Trips* (Book 1); and chapters 47–84 are in *More of Neil Zurcher's One Tank Trips* (Book 2).

Throughout this book, I have cross-referenced chapters in these first two books so that you can find more fun things to do while making a "One Tank Trip" to one of the eateries described here.

Acknowledgments

No book is ever written without an enormous amount of help from a lot of people. I am particularly aware of this after writing three books. And I have a whole new appreciation for the opening pages of anyone's book—especially that page where they try to thank the people who have freely given of their time and expertise to make a book possible. It is no different with me.

I would have to start any list of people to whom I owe my gratitude with the name of Virgil Dominic, who gave me the opportunity more than 20 years ago to do the "One Tank Trips" series on WJW-TV. I am also deeply indebted to Mike Renda, the present vice president and general manager of FOX 8 TV, for his continued support of the series—now 20 years old and the longest-running local travel segment in television. Over the years I have been blessed with fine news directors to work for: Tony Ballew, Phyllis Quayle, Grant Zalba, Kathy Williams, and Greg Easterly. All continued the series down through the years despite changing tastes in television viewing, and all paid me the extreme compliment of allowing me to pick and choose where to wander each week. In truth, they often had no idea where I was. It is this kind of trust and cooperation that has made the series popular with viewers year after year.

I also wish to thank my traveling companions through the years: the FOX 8 photojournalists, Ali Ghanbari, Ron Mounts, Bill West, Bill Wolfe, Chris Reece, Jim Holloway, Herb Thomas, Greg Lockhart, Gary Korb, Ted Pikturna, Cragg Eichmann, Ralph Tarsitano, Roger Powell, Lorne Kruse, Cliff Adkins, Bob Begany, the late John "JP" Paustian, and Dave Almond. Their skills helped illustrate what I was talking about. Often their pictures far outshone my words, and I am deeply indebted to them for both their skills and their friendship.

Each week the final product that you see on television is the work of the video editor who takes my script and the photographers' pictures and weaves them together. Without him or her, there would be no "One Tank Trips." For the last several years Steve Goldurs has performed his magic to edit our segments. Others who have ably edited the series over the years have been Nancy O'Donnell, Terry Trakas, Kathy Smith, Maurice Sears, and Phil Knoftz. To each of them, thank you for often making me look better than I deserved.

There are many other people to thank, like my intern for the past year, Molly Randel, and the producers and directors who work to get the segment on the air each week.

I would also like to thank my family for all their ideas, love, and support: my number-one fan, my wife, Bonnie; my son, Craig; my daughters and sons-in-law: Melody and Ernie McCallister, and Melissa and Peter Luttmann. They first suggested many of the destinations you have seen and read about.

Lastly, I would like to thank three people who are the inspiration for many of the family destinations that I choose—my grandchildren, Allison and Bryan McCallister and Ryan Luttmann. I love you all.

— N.Z.

What This Book Is and Is Not About

Through the years, I have been accused by viewers and friends of visiting every ice-cream stand in Ohio and eight neighboring states. Of having the secret recipe of every hamburger place in the northeastern Midwest. Of scarfing up free meals at restaurants everywhere. And of ignoring my other work to find a really thick milk shake. To all of these charges I plead "not guilty." Well, to most of them, anyway.

I do enjoy food, though—especially finding and trying something or someplace new. That's what this book is about—food and fun.

But let me set the record straight on a few things.

First, I am a travel writer, not a food editor. I like food, and like most people I try to eat every day. Sometimes I care about what I eat; sometimes I eat just about anything that is placed before me, with little complaint.

So I would make a lousy food critic. My taste buds have long been trained to accept most any food that arrives in my mouth. I do not have a delicate palate that can perceive a faint wisp of tarragon or a breath of basil. Don't get me wrong, I love herbs. I use them every day, especially in recent months since I have been put on a salt-restricted diet. I am not too particular about food as long as it is fresh, well prepared, and decently cooked. That's about all I ask of a kitchen.

Now, I can admire a beautifully prepared presentation of, say, pecan-encrusted lamb chops with lightly steamed asparagus and a scroll of aspic as well as anyone, but it won't change the way the food tastes to me one whit. I could get just as excited about an overflowing cardboard box of fresh-cut French fries swimming in cheddar-jalapeno sauce with a side of malt vinegar. So, clearly I am neither a food critic nor a food snob. I just like food.

Second, I can't claim to know about *every* good restaurant in Ohio and surrounding states, either. Certainly, in the 20 years I have been doing "One Tank Trips," I have visited hundreds of places to eat. But let's face it, there are literally thousands more restaurants, taverns, cafes, soda fountains, diners, you name it, still left for me to try. No one could visit them all.

I don't want this guidebook to list places I have never visited or experienced. No one has paid a penny to be included in this book, and you have my word that I have personally visited every place that is listed in here at least once—some many times.

So, if you don't see your favorite place in here, don't jump to the conclusion that I didn't like it. More likely I just haven't gotten there yet.

Third, I do not claim these are the best places in Cleveland, Canton, Akron, or even Bucyrus. These are simply places I visited and enjoyed, places that have pleased my taste buds and my stomach. Will you like them? I hope so. I think so, or I wouldn't have included them. But I am also aware that food favorites can be very subjective. If you disagree, feel free to tell me so. (I also hope you will suggest other places that have pleased you that I may visit and possibly include in future updates.)

Like the "One Tank Trips" I take each week, the foods and places you will find in this book are very diverse. I have tried to take everyone into consideration. I have included restaurants and stores that sell foods for people who are on special or restricted diets (like I am). I have discovered and enjoyed vegetarian fare in the past few years, and I have included that, too. And for those who like to make sure they have the very best and freshest ingredients, I have included farms where you can go right to the source and pick your own.

The majority of the book, though, contains what I like to think of as "the common foods," foods that most of us share a delight in—hamburgers, hot dogs, ice cream, candy. I have included places that serve monster sundaes, ice cream cones, and even King Kong–sized hamburgers, just for fun.

Down through the years I have been on a quest for what I thought were the biggest, best, and quirkiest specimens that I could find. Because, let's face it, food should be more than just something to soothe our hunger: it should also be fun.

As with my other books, I urge you always to call first before you travel. It's especially important for this book, because the food industry is probably the most volatile field in the world. More businesses change hands, fail, and go out of business in this industry than any other. What is here today may not be tomorrow. Also, hours, menus, specials, and even management change frequently. So before wasting a tank of gasoline, spend a few cents on a phone call and save yourself some aggravation at the end of a long trip.

Now, I hope that you will read and enjoy.

—

About One Tank Trips

"One Tank Trips" was born in the spring of 1980. Virgil Dominic, who was then WJW-TV's news director, called me into his office one morning and said he would like to air a weeklong series of stories about places in northern Ohio that people would enjoy visiting on their vacation. That summer there was an oil embargo; prices for gasoline were skyrocketing across the country, and long lines were developing outside service stations. It looked like people would have to stay pretty close to home on their summer vacations. I had been working at WJW-TV since early 1967 and, for most of my career, had been doing feature stories—sometimes about people, sometimes about historic places, sometimes about interesting hobbies and fads. (Who can forget the mid-1970s when men wore leisure suits and had to be fitted with chest-hair toupees to look more masculine in their open-necked shirts?)

One thing I had not done was travel reporting, but I was familiar with several places around northern Ohio that my family enjoyed visiting. So I did five segments, which included Roscoe Village in Coshocton, Cedar Point Amusement Park in Sandusky, the Amish in Holmes County, and a riverboat in Marietta, Ohio. I didn't really give the whole matter much thought. It was just another assignment, albeit a fun one, and rather routine. Neither I nor Virgil Dominic anticipated the response. We apparently hit a nerve with our viewers. To this day I am not sure why, but letters poured into the station and our phone lines were filled with viewers' calls asking for more information about the five spots I had visited. Virgil decided to extend the series by making it a weekly feature on the Wednesday 6 p.m. news.

The problem I discovered, though, was that "One Tank Trips" is a misleading title. For one thing, everyone gets different gas mileage. And if I tried to cover only interesting things in Northeast Ohio, I would soon run out of destinations and have to do the same ones over and over again. I went to Virgil and asked if we could still call them "One Tank Trips" if I used the entire tank of gasoline just to get to a destination. He agreed, and I set out to destinations that would eventually take me to eight states and parts of southern Ontario, Canada.

Over the past 20 years we have discovered some wonderful destinations and exciting things to do, like riding a jet boat up the Niagara River into the Devil's Hole Rapids. I have had the quiet joy of watching a perfect sunset on the Ohio River, welcomed the sunrise over Lake Ontario, and once even traveled all the way to Alaska to view Mt. McKinley (that was a "One Tank Trip" in a jet airliner). I have stored up a thousand memories of people, places, and food.

Ah yes, the food. I have been given a golden opportunity to sample food I might not otherwise have tasted in my lifetime: the wonderful cheeses of Ohio's Little Switzerland; the homemade pies of the Amish area; exotic-sounding things like pierogies, bratwurst, schnitzels, and babaganouj; and food with names that I can't even spell. It has been an adventure. I was able to sample the favorite fried chicken of the president of the United States. I even tried to learn to like Cincinnati Chili (which I am told is an acquired taste). I have "borrowed" a squash from the personal garden of the governor of Ohio—it ended up on my dinner table. I have sampled prime-rib cuts so big they looked as though they had been cut from a T-Rex in prehistoric times. And I have been introduced to vegetarian fare so good that I considered giving up meat. Then there was the ice cream, flavors of my childhood come back to haunt me—even (I had to pinch myself) getting paid to hunt for the biggest ice-cream cone in Ohio!

When I am out in public, usually one of the first questions I get is about food. It took a while for me to realize that perhaps it was time to sit down and write about food—wonderful "One Tank Trips" Road Food—to share with all of you some of the extraordinary bounty we have here in the Buckeye State and in some of our neighboring areas as well.

Food Days

Congress has too much time on its hands. The first time I heard that Congress had ordained a day to commemorate a food—say, pickles—I thought it was kind of cute. You know, taking a moment to recognize the importance (if any) of pickles to our way of life. But frankly, after seeing the vast number of foods that our government has decreed days, and even weeks and months, to honor, I am ready to throw up my hands and say, Enough, already!

Did you know, for example, that in January alone we not only honor pies, with National Pie Day, we also proclaim National Soup Month, Prune Breakfast Month (I guess you are encouraged to eat more prunes every day), National Egg Month, and National Oatmeal Month. Now, if all we ate for a month was lots of prunes, eggs, oatmeal, soup, and pie, we would probably end up with a National Bellyache.

But no sooner do you get used to all those prune Danishes than Congress is urging you to take the month of February to honor potatoes and cherries. If that's not enough, February is also National Canned Food Month. I guess they couldn't make up their mind exactly which canned food, so they included them all! And how about this one: February is also National Snack Food Month. I wonder which junk-food lobbyist waltzed that one through. The pancake lobby should find out—their folks only got a week.

Now along comes March, and guess what? Congress says that's a month in which we should honor nutrition. (I wonder if that's because of what they did with February and snack foods?) Also, in March we pause to honor peanuts and sauces. They didn't spell out which sauces, so I guess we could say that includes hot sauces, like Tabasco and—I read this right off the label—"Kick Me in the Ass and Call Me Margie" hot sauce. Also, March is National Pig Month and Johnny Appleseed Month, honoring apples, I guess.

Something happened in April. Either Congress went home, or the lobbyists took a vacation. There is only a hint of food on the national calendar for April—National Garden Month.

They made up for it in May. It's Asparagus Month, National Salad Month—and National Hamburger Month. So far it's almost a full meal. For dessert, Congress declared May National Strawberry Month, as well.

It's National Barbecue Month, too. Pickles must be important, because a whole week in May was set aside for International Pickle Week. Even herbs got on the calendar, with National Herb Week.

Now when June came along, I think Congress got a little confused and forgot that they had proclaimed May as National Salad Month, because now they say the month of June is National Fresh Fruit and Vegetables Month. Seems a little redundant to me. They also said June would be National Dairy Month, just to keep the rest of the farmers happy.

Okay, in July the lobbyists out in California must have been real convincing, because that was named California Salmon Month—nothing about those salmon they catch up in New York, Maine, or Minnesota, just California. And there's more redundancy. Just listen to this: Congress also said July was National Baked Bean Month, National Hot Dog Month, and National Ice Cream Month. Then they said it's also National Picnic Month. What else would you do with hot dogs, baked beans, and ice cream?

They must have been on vacation again in August: there is no special day, week, or month observed then.

But September rebounds with National Chicken Month, and it has also been set aside by Congress to honor honey, rice, mushrooms, and breakfast—specifically something they call "The All American Breakfast," probably ham and eggs and flapjacks. If it is, then it makes some sense that they also declared September National Cholesterol Education and Awareness Month!

In October, Congress urges you to celebrate National Pasta Month, National Pork Month, National Seafood Month, and National Dessert Month. (I celebrate *that* one at every meal.)

Maybe they took a look back at some of the things they invited us to honor when it came to November, because in that month the leadoff celebratory item is National Good Nutrition Month. It's also Peanut Butter Lover's Month. And the first week of November has been set aside as National Fig Week. I suspect all that leftover turkey from Thanksgiving suggested to Congress that the third week of November should be declared National Sandwich Day. (I haven't figured out how a week can be turned into a day.)

As I said before, I think Congress has too much time on its hands. But on the other hand, I always like an excuse to have a piece of pie. Let's see, when was National Pie Week?

For People on Special Diets— and Those Who Read the Labels

Because we seem more aware of health and nutrition today—or have to be careful for medical reasons—more and more of us are asking questions and reading the labels of the food we buy.

If you have ever been forced to restrict your intake of salt or sugar (or, in case of allergies, dairy products), you know how frustrating it is to go into a restaurant and ask some 17-year-old server what kind of sugar-free drinks they have. Some of the answers I have received: "I've tasted the Mountain Dew, and I didn't think it was very sweet" "We don't carry any sugar-free products because the owner doesn't like to be involved in political things" "Everything we have is sugar-free, I just wave a wand over it and the sugar disappears!" "Sugar-free? Is that like you're an alcoholic?" and, my favorite, "I don't think our water has any sugar in it, but I better check."

It gets even worse if you are on a salt-restricted diet and try to question the servers about the ingredients in the food. Let's face it: in most cases the servers don't have the foggiest idea what's in the food—they didn't cook it. In some cases they probably don't even know how to cook, and they have already worked eight hours and don't feel like walking back to the kitchen to ask some sweaty cook, who is already short tempered with the help, a silly question like "Did you put any salt in the soup?" So you get answers like "We don't use salt in our cooking here," said with a straight face and fingers crossed on both hands; "I'll be happy to go back and ask the cook to take out all the salt in your dish"; or, "Oh, they use some, but I'm sure it's not very much."

To be fair, we shouldn't expect kitchens to cater to all of our needs. The majority of people can drink vast amounts of sugar-laced drinks with no side effects, or down glasses of milk or dishes of ice cream with nary a symptom. And almost all kitchens use salt in their cooking, because the majority of their customers expect it and would complain if the salt were left out. (I remember how bland everything tasted when I first stopped using salt, before I discovered herbs and salt substitutes.)

The problem is that most of us on restricted diets, after a few forays into the world of uncaring restaurants, give up and do one of two things: stay home, where we have control over what is and isn't in our food, or ignore our medical conditions and eat foods that are not good for us, sometimes paying a very high price for an evening that was supposed to be enjoyable. There are some things you can do about all of this. Be persistent. Remember, it's your health that you are talking about. Ask to speak to the manager of the restaurant. Explain that you often eat out and that you have dietary restrictions and need to ask questions of the cook. Let them know that you enjoy this restaurant, would like to come back again, and would tell all your friends about it, especially if they are accommodating about preparing special dishes or offer a variety of sugar-free or lactose-free beverages and food. Take the time to educate them about the sheer numbers of people who suffer the same ailments that you do and are potential customers. Lobby a little bit, suggest to the manager that if they carried, say, Crystal Light beverages you would be willing to pay a premium price just to have something more than diet cola and iced tea as your choice of diet drinks in the establishment.

Offer to send their kitchen some salt-free recipes that are tasty and could be enjoyed by everyone. Suggest products that are low in sodium or sugar. If enough of us do it, you can be sure that the restaurants will listen. After all, they are in this business to make money.

ONE TANK TRIPS
TRIPS
Road Food

85 Diners

The first diner I recall eating in was in Birmingham, Ohio, in Erie County, just across the county line from the small farming community where I grew up in Henrietta, in Lorain County. It was called the White Diner and operated by a young news photographer by the name of Walt Glendenning. (I didn't know it at the time, but he was to become a dear friend and have a direct influence on my getting into television—but that's another story.)

When I was a sophomore at Henrietta High School, the diner was our favorite hangout. It was an old trolley car that had rolled across northern Ohio in the 1920s. An earlier owner had purchased the car when the trolley lines stopped running and permanently parked it at the corner of State Route 113 and Route 60. You entered in the middle of the car, which was painted all white. To the right were four or five booths; to the left was an L-shaped counter that took up the rest of the car. The food was typical diner fare: hamburgs, milk shakes, fountain drinks, and a few blue-plate specials like meatloaf and spaghetti.

I was particularly fond of their milk shakes, because they used Esmond Ice Cream out of Sandusky and chocolate ice cream in the chocolate milk shakes.

Beyond that, I don't remember much about the food, because I was thrown out of the place on my third visit and never allowed back in while Walter was the manager. It happened this way:

One night after basketball practice, one of the older members of the team, who had a driver's license, suggested we all go to the White Diner for a snack. We filled a couple of booths. Like most teenagers, we were a noisy, disruptive group. When someone at the next booth asked me to pass the catsup, I tossed it up in the air instead. It arced through the diner, barely missing the hanging lights, and landed safely in the hands of its intended receiver. Problem is, Walt Glendenning was watching and gave me a stern warning that if I ever did that again, he would throw me out and not allow me back in.

Now Walt, at about six-foot-one, towered over me, and I believed him. But, of my friends, Joe Cucco, didn't hear the warning, and when somebody at another booth yelled for the catsup, Joe launched it like a football. The receiver, I think it was Jack Dodd, wasn't ready. He missed the bottle, which shattered against the back of the booth, splattering catsup all over the booth and nearby counter. Walt, who at that moment had his back turned toward us and did not see the incident, wheeled around at the noise of the shattering bottle, put down his grease-covered spatula, and walked directly to me. He grabbed me by the back of my neck and, to the amusement of my classmates, propelled me out the door into the parking lot, informing me I was no longer welcome in his restaurant!

I tried unsuccessfully to tell him I was not the guilty party, but he wasn't listening. So I sat on the fender of a car watching my classmates through the window, laughing and pointing at me as they finished their food. Even weeks later when I went to the White Diner, Walt ordered me out of the place as soon as I walked in. It was months before he ended my expulsion and allowed me to come in again. I never did convince him, until years later when both of us were working in television, that I was not the person who had thrown the catsup.

Walter became a very dear friend and mentor. He went on to become a pioneer news photographer in Cleveland television and covered many major stories, including an exclusive shot of Cleveland newspaperman Robert Manry in his history-making one-man sailing trip across the Atlantic Ocean. Walter and Bill Jorgenson, a reporter for WEWS in Cleveland, found Manry in the middle of the ocean and scooped the world that was waiting for him to arrive in Europe.

The White Diner went through a series of owners in the '50s and '60s and, sadly, eventually was carted away to an uncertain end.

THE DINER INSIDE THE HARLEY-DAVIDSON GARAGE

If you like unusual settings, this one has to rank right up there with the best of them. This 1950s stainless-steel diner, still operating, is located inside the service department of South East Harley-Davidson Sales in Bedford Heights, Ohio. It ended up there for a rather practical reason.

Debbie Myers, the daughter of the dealership's owner, aware that many folks were asking for a place to get a sandwich while waiting for their motorcycles to be repaired, decided to buy a diner that had been abandoned in Massachusetts. Problem was, when she got it back to Bedford Heights, local zoning officials told her she couldn't put it just outside the dealership because the area wasn't zoned for restaurants.

Debbie finally solved the problem by moving the diner inside the dealership's service department. By locating it in an existing business, she circumvented the zoning requirements.

The diner was duly restored and started serving steakburgers made from freshly ground beef, thick milk shakes, and some of the best hand-cut French fries around. The food and the ambiance became so popular that they had to add on to the diner.

The new addition, which includes an ice-cream parlor, is called the Road Tales Café. That alone should make this place worth a stop. But wait, there's more. Debbie was also a big fan of Elvis Presley, long before Cleveland was the home of the Rock and Roll Hall of Fame. She went to several auctions, where she purchased Elvis's Harley-Davidson motorcycle, his white jumpsuit, his gold sunglasses, and a host of other Elvis-related items and opened her own museum in the Harley dealership's showroom.

When the service manager complained that Debbie had taken up his office space with her diner, she bought a 1929 gasoline station, had it moved into the service department, restored it, and made it into the service manager's office.

Her next major project began when she heard an area amusement park was selling some of its rides. She traveled out to Conneaut Lake, Pennsylvania, and came back with the children's carousel from their kiddieland. She promptly moved it into the service department, where it still gives kids rides. Today it is the centerpiece in a children's clothing store located—where else—inside the service department.

Debbie no longer works there, but she created perhaps America's most unusual motorcycle dealership, and given birth to an idea that has been copied to a lesser degree in dealerships across the country. Take time to visit the original. Open seven days a week.

(For nearby attractions, see Trips 5, 15, and 16 in Book 1.)

South East Harley-Davidson Sales ☎ 440-439-5300
23105 Aurora Road • Bedford Heights , Ohio
Region: Northeast Ohio (Cuyahoga County)
Handicapped access: Steps into diner.

ONE OF THE COUNTRY'S BEST

This diner, a part of downtown Cleveland since the 1930s, was abandoned and sat empty for some time before Ruthie and Moe Hellman took it over in 1989, renovated it, and reopened it.

The original 1938 Jerry O'Mahoney diner was merged with a 1956 Kuhlman diner to create what is now known as Ruthie & Moe's Diner. The popular Internet site, "Roadside," which specializes in diners across America, has declared Ruthie & Moe's one of the country's best.

They offer all the standard diner fare, like meatloaf and macaroni and cheese. The burgers are homemade, and the fries are fresh, not frozen. What is unusual are the other things that occasionally show up on the menu, like Creole chicken and even Hungarian paprikash.

However, you can only enjoy this diner for breakfast and lunch, Monday through Friday, between the hours of 6 a.m. and 3 p.m.

(For nearby attractions, see Trips 5, 15, 16 in Book 1.)

Ruthie & Moe's Diner   ☎ 216-431-8063
4002 Prospect Avenue • Cleveland, Ohio
Region: Northeast Ohio (Cuyahoga County)
Handicapped access: Yes.

BACK IN TIME

If you want to really experience what a diner in the 1950s was like, head on down to Lisbon, Ohio. You not only get to drive on a legendary highway (the Lincoln Highway, America's first coast-to-coast roadway), but on the corner of Lincoln Way and Jefferson Street you will find a grand old O'Mahoney diner that has been restored to the "Happy Days" of the 1950s.

The owner, Earle Hersman, used to go to this diner when he was a kid back in the '50s. In 1992, when longtime owner Shirley Davis decided to sell, Earle and his wife, Jacki, stepped in. What they did was take the place back in time. They brought back real mashed potatoes and hand-cut French fries. Earle brought in his mother and a friend to make the pies fresh every day. (Their oatmeal pie is so good that it has been written up in national diner magazines.) He tossed out the cigarette machine and installed a jukebox that plays songs of the '50s. He also dressed up the outside of the diner with neon that makes it glow at night like a giant caterpillar.

It's diner food, pure and simple—breakfast, lunch, and dinner done right. The food is fresh, well prepared, and served hot. You can't ask for much more. Oh, did I mention that they make their milk shakes with ice cream, so thick that the straw stands up in the middle?

Open 24 hours a day most of the time—may shut down after midnight for a couple of hours on slow nights.

(For nearby attractions, see Trip 56 in Book 2.)

Earle and Jacki's Steel Trolley Diner   ☎ 330-424-FOOD
140 East Lincoln Way • Lisbon, Ohio
Region: Northeast Ohio (Columbiana County)
Handicapped access: Yes.

INSPIRATION FOR "MEL'S DINER"

Remember the title character in the TV series *Alice*, and "Mel's Diner" where she worked? Well, it has been said that Lester's Diner, a fixture since the 1960s in Bryan, Ohio, was the model that the producers of the TV show used for "Mel's."

While the show has become TV history, the diner is still doing just fine. Two things have not changed through the years: the size of their coffee cup—a staggering 14-ounce size, a caffeine lover's dream—and their "stacked to the ceiling" club sandwiches. Both are signature items. But there is more: baked chicken, Swiss steak, barbecued pork ribs.

They use locally produced syrups on their pancakes and even make the coleslaw fresh each day. Very few things here come in tubs and cans. You can usually tell how good a place is by the crowd at lunchtime, and people are usually standing in line for a seat here. It could be because the prices are reasonable, but the food is fresh and good, too.

(For nearby attractions, see Trip 23 in Book 1.)

Lester's Diner   ☎ 419-636-1818
233 South Main Street · Bryan, Ohio
Region: Northwest Ohio (Williams County)
Handicapped access: Steps into diner

A DIFFERENT KIND OF DINER

If you like rare and unusual diners, this place fills the bill several ways.

First it's a tourist attraction, because it's in a large antique mall located on an interstate highway in the southwest area of the state. It was the brainchild of Don Miller of Cridersville, Ohio. He loved antiques, classic automobiles from the '50s, '60s, and '70s, and fine food in diners. What he built combines all three of his interests.

The building, located on I-75, just south of Wapakoneta (Neil Armstrong's hometown), contains 64,000 square feet of space—that's bigger than four football fields. It consists of four wings running off a center hall.

Two of the wings contain a huge antique mall with more than 100 dealers. Everything for sale must be at least 25 years old, and authentic. He also tries to keep down the number of dealers selling the same items, or with the same specialty, for the sake of variety.

Another wing houses Miller's unique collection of cars. He likes "muscle cars," but has many standard cars as well. What truly sets his collection apart is that most of his cars have never been restored; they are simply stock cars with low mileage that give you a real idea of what the vehicles actually looked like when they were nearly new. For instance, a 1961 Chevy he owns has fewer than 21,000 original miles on it. He only has a portion of his collection on display and is always wheeling and dealing for new cars. He also allows other collectors to place their cars on display. As a result, the museum is constantly changing, and always interesting.

Finally, there is the food. Now understand, looks can be deceiving. In the center court of the mall stands a square white building that resembles local diners of the 1950s. Inside, the same image is created with red-and-black vinyl tables and counter, and Coca-Cola memorabilia abounds. You almost expect to see a smiling "soda jerk," wearing a paper hat and a black bow tie, ready to serve you a hamburg and milk shake.

Well, you can get the milk shake, but if you want the hamburger, you may have to travel down the road to one of those chain places with the yellow arches. What they serve here is fine food. For instance, the luncheon menu offers six specialty sandwiches, and not one of them contains hamburger. For example, they have a Vermont Cristo. That's sliced honey-baked ham and smoked Vermont cheddar cheese grilled inside battered raisin walnut bread. The sandwich is accompanied by deep-fried vegetable chips—not potato chips—here you get chips of beets, parsley, sweet potato, and so on. For dinner they put out white tablecloths, and the chef really goes to work. They feature dishes that include Black Angus beef, as well as chicken and lamb chops. They offer pan-roasted salmon made with porcini mushrooms and spinach risotto with sun-dried tomato vinaigrette. By the way, prices are very reasonable for this quality of food. On our last visit, in mid-1999, prices ranged from $8.75 for chicken to $15.75 for Black Angus steak.

For dessert they offer homemade ice cream in a variety of flavors, and the chef's creations are wonderful to look at—the maple-raspberry bread pudding with vanilla sauce was a treat for the eyes as well as the stomach.

Open Monday through Saturday, closed on Sundays.

(For nearby attractions, see Trips 9 and 24 in Book 1.)

Endless Endeavors   ☎ 419-645-6050
501 South Dixie Highway • Cridersville, Ohio
Region: Northwest Ohio (Auglaize County)
Handicapped access: Yes

86 Cafeterias

I must confess: I am not wild over buffets, salad bars, or anyplace that puts food out where the public can touch it. I admit that buffets can offer good bargains, especially if you are a big eater and like to really load your plate up. Also, buffets are perhaps the quickest places to get lunch or dinner when time is short. But they are a great place to spread germs. The next time you eat in one of these places, spend a few minutes just watching people help themselves at the buffet. I have seen people pick up food with their fingers, sample it, and then put the uneaten portion back in the dish! Unwatched by his parents, a small youngster with a runny nose, obviously sick with a cold, grasps the edge of the counter near a large salad bowl and sneezes all over the unprotected food. A man with hands that look as though they had not seen soap or water in weeks digs through a basket of buns looking for his favorite. The same man, apparently confused by the lack of labels for the salad dressings, takes the serving spoons and tastes each one. I have also seen soup ladles used the same way.

I long for the good old days of the Automat in New York, where each food item was individually placed in a locked box, and your deposit of nickels or dimes allowed you to open the door. Only you and the person who had placed the food in there ever came in contact with it. I also favor the fast-disappearing cafeterias, where the food was behind glass windows, and an attendant with a serving spoon and disposable gloves stood waiting to put the portion you pointed to onto a plate to be slid down the counter on a tray. There are only a few such places still around.

CAFETERIA ON A HILLTOP

Mehlman's is a fixture that sprawls across a hilltop along the Ohio River in southeast Ohio on the edge of St. Clairsville, the county seat of Belmont County, on the old National Highway, U.S. Route 40. It started out as a small truck stop and lunch place and has grown into a tourist attraction that draws visitors from three states. Located inside are two cafeteria lines, both placed into service when customers stream out the front door and around the side of the building.

The reason for the long lines is the food. Everything here is made from scratch each day in the sparkling-clean kitchens. Salads are prepared, pies and cakes are baked, beef roasts and hams are popped into ovens. The smell of baking bread and rolls fills the air in the morning.

Baked steak, a variation on Swiss steak, is a longtime favorite of many customers. Each food item is individually priced, and you pay for what you order. A light eater can have a meal for a couple of dollars, while someone who wants a heavy meal will usually be served more than enough food for five to seven dollars. Two of my favorites here are the banana cream pie and the pot roast.

For those on sugar-free diets, they do offer some pies and cakes with no sugar added. By the way, don't let the long lines discourage you. They have learned to keep them moving very rapidly. I can't remember ever standing in line more than 20 minutes before reaching the serving lines, even on their busiest days. Obviously the best times to visit here are weekdays, and try to visit before or after lunchtime for the shortest lines.

(For nearby attractions, see Trip 35 in Book 1.)

Mehlman's Cafeteria　☎ 740-695-1000
15800 National Road · St. Clairsville, Ohio
Region: Southeast Ohio (Belmont County)
Handicapped access: Yes.

A CAFETERIA IN A GROCERY STORE

A lot of local folks swear by this place. Over the years I have eaten here a couple of times when in town to speak to a local organization. Hawkins Food Stores in Wooster have been around a long time, and they were one of the pioneers in giving their customers a place to eat while shopping. The cafeteria has grown through the years and has its own separate rooms where banquets and awards dinners are held. Everything they serve is made on the premises, including a wonderful assortment of pies. Their fried chicken and roast beef are above average. Portions are ample, so you won't go away hungry.

(For nearby attractions, see Trip 28 in Book 1.)

Hawkins Cafeteria　☎ 330-264-8908
2305 Portage Road · Wooster, Ohio
Region: Northeast Ohio (Wayne County)
Handicapped access: Yes.

87 Drive-In Restaurants

Back in the early 1950s, Ed Tuttle of Conneaut, Ohio, was raising turkeys long before turkey was discovered by the "health-conscious." Back then, turkey was usually served only on holidays and special occasions. Ed wanted to find a way to increase the demand for his turkeys, especially during the summer months when business was really flat.

When he and his wife, Marge, would prepare a turkey, say at Christmas, they would freeze the leftovers for sandwiches later in the year. They developed a special recipe for ground-up turkey meat that, served on a hamburger bun, made a rather tasty sandwich. One day Ed had a thought: why not open a drive-in restaurant on busy U.S. Route 20 during the summer months and serve his turkey sandwiches? That would give him an additional outlet for his turkeys and provide some extra income in the summertime.

At that time the Richardson Root Beer Company was offering franchises across the country for a simple root beer and sandwich stand. The stand could be opened on three sides by just raising the large wooden shutters. About six or seven stools surrounded the stand on all three sides.

So Ed bought a franchise, and in 1952 the White Turkey Drive-In opened at 388 East Main Road. At the time it was just one of perhaps hundreds or even thousands of similar drive-in restaurants open only during warm weather because they were exposed to the weather on three sides and did not even have screens. The front of the stand was dominated by a large Richardson Root Beer barrel. The menu was simple: root beer, turkey sandwiches, hamburgers, French fries, coleslaw, "red hots" (hot dogs), and "black cows" (root beer and ice cream mixed together like a shake). People would drive up and either take their food to their car or sit on a stool at the counter, which ringed the edge of the building. The rock 'n' roll era was just beginning, so Ed added a jukebox to the tiny restaurant.

It's been nearly half a century since Ed Tuttle started the White Turkey Drive-In. Ed is gone now. His son, Gary, and Gary's wife, Peggy, own the restaurant today, but little else has changed. Today the White Turkey Drive-In may be the last such drive-in restaurant in America still operating.

The big root-beer barrel still takes up most of the front counter. The tall stools still line three sides of the building. There are still no screens, and Gary says when it rains and starts to blow, he just lowers the shutters on that side of the stand and his customers move to the opposite side. And, yes, they still serve the turkey sandwich (though today the turkeys are provided by a South Carolina turkey farm). Gary and Peggy still spend nearly a month in the wintertime cooking, preparing, and freezing the turkey meat for the summer.

Three generations of customers have visited the drive-in, and about the only changes in all those years have been some additions to the menu, like cheeseburgers, a super-hamburg named the "Big Ed" for Gary's dad, and a super–turkey sandwich called "Large Marge" for Gary's mother. They also have added fish, chili cheese dogs, onion rings, and a host of soft drinks, but they also still sell the original Richardson Root Beer. They make their own ice cream now, and you can get a wonderful root beer float served in a tall, frosted root beer glass.

They open each season on Mother's Day and close on Labor Day. They are open every day from 11 in the morning until 10 at night.

If you are old enough to remember the rock 'n' roll era, or want to know what it was like, this is the place to capture its essence, especially on a nice summer's night. You can sit at the counter and enjoy trucks and cars whizzing by on U.S. Route 20 while the jukebox blares a song by Elvis. The frosty mugs sweat as the foam of the root beer pours over the edge. The smell of fries, hamburgs, and hot dogs blends together in a kind of nostalgic perfume.

(For nearby attractions, see Trip 9 in Book 1.)

White Turkey Drive-In   ☎ 440-593-2209
388 East Main Road · Conneaut, Ohio
Region: Northeast Ohio (Ashtabula County)
Handicapped access: No

SUMMIT COUNTY DRIVE-IN RESTAURANTS

When the 1950s left us, it seemed that the icon of that age, the drive-in restaurant, left us, too. But a smattering of drive-ins survived. In fact, they did more than survive—they have prospered.

There is a school of thought that when Ray Kroc bought out the McDonald Brothers and launched a new concept—people getting out of their cars and walking up to the window to get their food—he not only saved restaurants money by doing away with carhops, he homogenized America by creating just one standard menu. The day of the hand-sliced potato fries and eclectic menus slowly faded away, and national chains of burger restaurants arrived. But those well-run local drive-ins that offered good food and good service were able to compete, and some did survive.

First off, for those that have never experienced a drive-in restaurant, there is no restaurant per se—it's just a carryout place, where if you want to eat there you do it in your car. Clerks run out to your car to take your order, bring the food to your car, and, when you are done, come and take away the tray and the garbage. And they do it efficiently. Like at Swenson's in Akron, which over the years has grown to four locations. Swenson's built their business on good food and fast service that continues today. In fact, part of the entertainment is watching the carhops (they call them "curb-servers") literally run to take your order and then run the order into the kitchen. These guys, and a few girls, have to be in great physical condition for all of the running they do here.

Incidentally, some very prominent local and nationally known folks have worked as "curb-servers" at Swenson's, including probably their best-known alumnus, Dick Jacobs, owner of the Cleveland Indians, who apparently helped put himself through school back in the 1940s by hustling to wait on people at Swenson's. The folks at Swenson's won't say whether he ever drops in these days for a hamburger, but some of the present curb-servers swore to me that they have occasionally seen him eating there in his car.

The big seller here is the cheeseburger, recently proclaimed by a writer for *Forbes* magazine as "America's best cheeseburger." They buy their rolls from a private baker, and the sauces and the meat here are prepared, Swenson's employees say, with a "secret recipe" hammered out by the founder, "Pop" Swenson. That same recipe is still in use 65 years later.

(For nearby attractions, see Trip 14 in Book 1.)

Swenson's Drive-In Restaurant   ☎ 330-665-1858
40 Brookmont Road • Montrose, Ohio
Region: Northeast Ohio (Summit County)
Handicapped access: Yes

Swenson's Drive-In Restaurant   ☎ 330-864-8416
18 South Hawkins Avenue • Akron, Ohio
Region: Northeast Ohio (Summit County)
Handicapped access: Yes

Swenson's Drive-In Restaurant   ☎ 330-928-8815
658 East Cuyahoga Falls Avenue • Akron, Ohio
Region: Northeast Ohio (Summit County)
Handicapped access: Yes

Swenson's Drive-In Restaurant ☎ 330-678-7775
4466 Kent Road · Stow, Ohio
Region: Northeast Ohio (Summit County)
Handicapped access: Yes

Swenson's Drive-In Restaurant

A LAKE COUNTY DRIVE-IN

Annabelle's Diner in Lake County has become an institution, especially on weekends in the summertime for folks who preserve cars of the '50s, '60s, and '70s. It's an authentic diner that once served folks in Euclid. In its new home in Mentor, it has indoor seating in the diner, carhop service, and some outdoor picnic tables. On Friday and Saturday nights when they hold "cruise-ins," hundreds of old hotrods and classic cars turn out to be shown off, while the car owners dance to a live band that plays music from the '50s. I heard one young person, who wasn't old enough to remember the drive-ins and carhops, say he felt like he was in the movie *American Graffiti*. Full meals at affordable prices make this a great place for the whole family.

(For nearby attractions, see Trip 13 in Book 1.)

Annabelle's Diner ☎ 440-255-6924
8637 Twinbrook Road • Mentor, Ohio
Region: Northeast Ohio (Lake County)
Handicapped access: Yes.

MORE DRIVE-INS

It seems like central Ohio has most of the drive-in restaurants that still believe in carhop service. One of these is Porky's, which has been a fixture on Route 42 since back in 1949. That was the year Paul Blasberg opened Porky's Drive-In on Ashland Road. The menu was fairly simple: hamburgers, foot-long hot dogs, fries, milk shakes, and—a novelty even then—freshly made root beer.

It's been 50 years, and Porky's is still going strong. They still offer all of the above, and they still have year-round carhop service. So you can eat in your car or squeeze into the tiny restaurant that offers just six booths and a counter. It's still owned by Paul's family, Dan Blasberg and his wife, Alice, who now continue the tradition started by Dan's dad. There have been some changes: where Paul used to grind his own beef each day for the burgers, Dan has a local butcher prepare the meat for them. They still make the root beer, but today, like the ice cream, it comes from a commercial mix. Those fries are still made from real potatoes, and they leave on the skins for that distinctive taste.

Oh yes, they also still have a jukebox that plays songs from the 1950s.

(For nearby attractions, see Trip 59 in Book 2.)

Porky's Drive-In ☎ 419-589-9933
811 Ashland Road • Mansfield, Ohio
Region: Northeast Ohio (Richland County)
Handicapped access: Yes.

4 Restaurants with a Past

I admire the owners of longtime, established restaurants. I know from experience just how difficult it can be to work the long hours needed to be successful in the restaurant business, to make the difficult decisions that must be made from day to day about menu planning, to suffer that helpless feeling when all the help calls in sick at the last minute just before the busiest weekend of the year.

How do I know all this? In 1990 my wife, Bonnie, and I decided to explore the world of self-employment as a trial run, so to speak, of something we might like to do when I retired. We had long thought about operating "The Stand," a 60-year-old soda fountain and restaurant at Linwood Park in Vermilion, where I grew up. When the operator did not renew his lease, we suddenly had the opportunity to take over the business. Little did we know what we were getting ourselves into.

Our first lesson arrived in April when we surveyed the stand after signing the lease. It was a 60-year-old building, all of the equipment that came with it was old, worn out, and, for the most part, didn't work. I frantically started calling companies that lease industrial refrigerators, coolers, and restaurant equipment. My first lesson: most companies would lease to us only by the year. Since we were only planning to be open June, July, and August, they weren't interested.

My second lesson: new or even used equipment like coolers and commercial refrigerators can cost thousands of dollars—thousands more than we projected we would even make that summer. Since we weren't sure we would want to run it for more than one year, we were reluctant to invest in the new equipment. The park, which owned "The Stand," was sympathetic to us and did offer to pay for a new cooking stove, on which my wife hoped to duplicate recipes from a long-gone hotel that had once graced the park's lakefront. But they balked at replacing or buying new coolers and refrigerators; that was the responsibility of the lessee (us).

I finally solved that dilemma through a friend, Kevin Ruic, who had just closed down a racetrack he operated and had put several coolers and refrigerators in storage. Toft Dairy in Sandusky, whose ice cream we planned to carry, felt sorry for us and finally rented us a used ice-cream dipping cooler for the summer. We were finally ready to open.

That was when we discovered the wonderful world of teenage help. We could only afford to pay minimum wage, (but the local burger chains were paying a dollar to a dollar and a half above the minimum wage.) When we did find teenagers willing to work for us, we learned about band camp, cheerleader camp, football practice, and a host of other school activities that go on during the summer months and that teenagers are expected to attend. It left less than a month during the summer when we were not frantically trying to find someone to fill a shift left vacant by a teenager who had to go off to cheerleader camp.

By pressing my sister-in-law, Susan Nager, into double duty as book-keeper and soda fountain clerk and hiring a young woman just out of high school, we staggered through the summer. You may remember the summer of 1990—it rained on 11 of the 14 weekends that summer.

Did I say staggered? We lurched from one problem to another. There was the night before the Fourth of July—the biggest single weekend of the summer. That was the night someone forgot to close the upright freezer door in the back room where all our spare ice cream and meat products were stored. Did I mention the building was not air-conditioned? In the morning we had gallons and gallons of ice-cream soup, and pounds and pounds of rotting hamburgers and hot dogs.

Then there was the evening the park board of directors held an ice-cream social just across the lawn from our store, effectively killing off our ice-cream business for that night. To add insult to injury, they bought their ice cream from another store outside the park.

To make this story mercifully short, the whole summer was like that. I vividly remember working alone in the store late one night after having spent the entire day on the road doing a "One Tank Trip." The temperature was still in the upper 80s at 11 that night when I closed the stand and started to mop the floors. When I went to count the day's receipts, I discovered that for an 11-hour day, we had made exactly $14.25. I decided at that point that perhaps I wasn't meant to be successful in the restaurant business.

So believe me when I say that I have great admiration for those restaurateurs who survive through the long years, who hand tradition down from one owner to the next.

A TAVERN WITH A REAL HISTORY

A perfect example of what I am talking about would be Gary Haskins of Unionville, Ohio. Gary is, I believe, the fourteenth owner of the historic business, the Old Tavern.

Believe it or not, the Old Tavern has stood on this spot since 1798—it is the oldest operating tavern in the entire state of Ohio, providing food and drink to travelers for more than two hundred years! For years it was a tavern, stagecoach stop, and restaurant.

Back in 1798 one of the first crops planted in the area was corn. Since it was in ample supply, the tavernkeeper ground some up, mixed it with flour, and cooked it up in boiling lard.

The "corn fritter" became a signature dish at the tavern, and now, two hundred years later, they are using the same recipe, with a few modern refinements like low-cholesterol oil and modern refined flour, to make the same dish. They did make one change in the 1920s—they started serving it with local maple syrup. That is still the way they serve it, and it brings customers back again and again.

Today the Old Tavern's food and surroundings are a far cry from when it was a beacon in the frontier forest. The formal gardens of the tavern are a highlight every spring and summer for customers who drive hundreds of miles to dine here. While the tavern no longer rents rooms to sleep in, many weddings are still held here, as they have been for over two hundred years. The gazebo in the garden has become the most popular place for the ceremony, and the ballroom on the third floor resounds with wedding receptions and anniversary parties.

As for the food, chicken has long been a specialty here. Chicken salad and chicken and biscuits are usually found on the menu. However, there are specialties on the menu nearly every weekday.

On one of our visits the special of the day was barbecued chicken wings, scalloped potatoes, and fresh corn. The famous corn fritters are always available and can be ordered with any entrée. Another tavern favorite is their own tomato jam.

They don't do breakfast here, but they are open every day for lunch and dinner. On Sundays they do open at 9 a.m. for brunch and then switch to dinner at noon. They do suggest reservations to be sure you'll get a seat—the tavern, now on the National Register of Historic Places, attracts customers from all over northern Ohio and western Pennsylvania.

The Old Tavern is located on the county line between Lake and Ashtabula counties, and is very close to many of the covered bridges, wineries, and garden nurseries that have made this part of the state so popular.

(For nearby attractions, see Trip 9 in Book 1.)

The Old Tavern   ☎ 440-428-2091 or 800-7-TAVERN
Route 84 at County Line Road   • Unionville, Ohio
Region: Central Ohio (Union County)
Handicapped access: Yes.

ROOKWOOD POTTERY: A CINCINNATI TRADITION

Some of America's most famous pottery was made in Cincinnati at Rookwood Pottery, located at the top of Mount Adams in downtown Cincinnati. From 1892 until the 1960s, the Tudor-style building here used to house the giant kilns that fired the artists' work. When the pottery closed, the value of their work increased as collectors from around the world searched for items bearing the now-extinct label.

You'll find Rookwood pottery in many famous museums around the country. What we are interested in, though, is what happened to the pottery building: It became a restaurant.

The Tudor-style building appears little changed from the outside. Inside you will still find the giant kilns, but today they are used as small private dining rooms for customers of the Rookwood Pottery Restaurant. There is even a small display case full of the pottery once made here. I'm somewhat disappointed that the management put the display case in the smoking section of the restaurant. If you want to look at it, you also have to inhale second-hand smoke from diners in that room.

The restaurant's decor is a mix of pottery, gallery, sports bar, and cafe. It has an eclectic feel that fits right in with the moderate prices and predictable menu. The food is good, not spectacular, and is designed to appeal to families.

They are heavy on the hamburgers, named after local Cincinnati bigwigs like Barney Kroger, who started the Kroger chain of grocery stores. The Kroger Burger has peppers, mushrooms, and onions. My favorite thing on the menu is the almost unpronounceable Erkenbrecherburger, which turned out to be a burger with cheddar and bacon on it.

They have daily specials of pasta, fish, and meat. The night we visited I had a New York sirloin that was tender and cooked just right.

While it's nice to have a historic old building put to good use, especially one in such a scenic spot (from their parking lot you can see all of downtown Cincinnati and northern Kentucky, as well as traffic on the Ohio River), I think their menu seems to be stuck someplace back in the late '70s or early '80s. It would be nice to find some more imaginative entrées to keep their customers coming back.

But if you enjoy history and want to impress your friends with a beautiful view of downtown Cincinnati, this is a good place to eat that won't break the bank.

(For nearby attractions, see Trip 39 in Book 1.)

Rookwood Pottery Restaurant   ☎ 513-721-5456
1077 Celestial Street, Mount Adams • Cincinnati, Ohio
Region: Southwest Ohio (Hamilton County)
Handicapped access: Yes, to bar level.

Rookwood Pottery

THE SPREAD EAGLE TAVERN

Canal boats prompted the building of the Spread Eagle Tavern in Hanoverton, east of Canton, Ohio. This three-story Federal-style building, constructed as an inn, was built in the 1830s, when the Sandy and Beaver Creek Canal went through here,

The current owner, Pete Johnson, is a successful businessman active in state and national Republican politics. Johnson owns a tile company and has supplied tile to many of the McDonald's Restaurants around the world. When he restored the Spread Eagle Tavern, it was his political clout that brought both former vice-president Dan Quayle and GOP presidential candidate Robert Dole to Hanoverton, adding to the list of famous guests who already have stayed there.

The inn has five bedrooms with private baths and two rooms that share a bath. There are seven dining rooms. Diners can choose to eat in front of a fireplace or outside in a pleasant courtyard with a fountain. There is also a rathskeller with 12-foot-high brick vaulted walls and ceilings. The Tavern has its own smokehouse and specializes in smoked meat dishes, like pheasant, lamb, and beef. I have eaten here three times and never been disappointed by the extensive choices of food or the wonderful quality and preparation. It's easy to tell that the people in the kitchen care about how their food is presented.

Something to look for: In the rathskeller, mounted in a glass case, is one of the original death masks of the 1930s FBI most-wanted criminal "Pretty Boy" Floyd. Floyd was shot to death by the FBI and local authorities not far from here, near East Liverpool, in 1934.

Hanoverton is a bit off the beaten path, but it's well worth the effort to find this historic tavern and spend a day, or more.

(For nearby attractions, see Trip 56 in Book 2.)

The Spread Eagle Tavern and Inn   ☎ 330-223-1583
10150 Historic Plymouth Street · Hanoverton, Ohio
Region: Northeast Ohio (Columbiana County)
Handicapped access: Yes, but restrooms are tight.

EAT IN THE COUNTY JAIL

You can literally do just that in downtown Wooster, Ohio. The 130-year-old county jail, which was replaced a few years ago by a new justice center across the street, has been through a couple of metamorphoses. The one that seems to have stuck is a fine dining establishment and microbrewery.

Now, I never spent a day in the old jail, but I would guess that the food today is far better than any prisoner ever had. They specialize in prime beef for their dinnertime-only crowd. Where once the hardest of the hard cases served time in the basement of the old jail, today there is a dining room.

There are still traces of the building's former incarnation: a cell door here, some brick walls there, and pictures, just in case you didn't catch the drift of what this building used to be. Out back, where the police cars used to be stored, there's now a tavern with casual dining.

(For nearby attractions, see Trip 28 in Book 1.)

The Olde Jaol Brewing Company and Restaurant   ☎ 330-262-3333
215 North Walnut Street · Wooster, Ohio
Region: Northeast Ohio (Wayne County)
Handicapped access: Yes.

88 Dinner and a Play

"Dinner theater" is a term that is sometimes abused. I have been to several theaters whose idea of dinner is cold fried chicken and long lines. You gobble the food down only because there is no place else to go, or that's the way the tickets were sold—dinner and a play. I wish they would be truthful and say, "bad food, but we're going to entertain you."

I have even gone so far as to stop at a fast-food place on the way to one of these "dinner theaters" and scarf down a quick hamburger because I know that 1) I may not eat until much later, 2) the food will be so picked over that when I get to it I will lose my appetite, or 3) they will run out of everything that has protein in it, and I will be left munching on curled-up celery sticks, brown-shaded, limp carrot sticks, and some rusty-looking lettuce that I scraped from the bottom of the salad bowls.

Generally, when I go to a place like this, I am not going for the food. In fact, I usually forget the lousy food, as long as the play, or musical, or other entertainment is good. But it is very nice to know there are a few "dinner theaters" that do live up to their names.

"THEATER IN THE ROUND," AND DINNER, TOO

Prescott Griffith took over a "theater in the round" dinner theater in 1978, in an old abandoned supermarket in Ravenna, Ohio. The dinner was a buffet, but an unusual buffet in that they offered a variety of foods and entrées.

In 1988 Prescott bought the Breakaway Nightclub in Akron. He remodeled it into America's largest dinner theater offering professional productions. Today, the Carousel Dinner Theater can seat upwards of 1,100 customers and offer them fine dining and a play. It's perhaps one of the best entertainment bargains around.

Unlike his other theater, this one has a stage and tiers of dining tables and booths grouped around it in a half circle. There really isn't a bad seat in the whole house. Despite its large size, the theater's design makes every seat seem to be only a few feet from the stage.

It also allows him to offer fine dining to his customers, featuring white tablecloths, lots of well-trained servers, and an eclectic menu that often reflects the current stage production. They also offer a signature dish, prime rib of beef. There is ample time to have a leisurely dinner before the production starts.

As the lights go down, orders are quickly taken for dessert. At the intermission, as the lights come up, the servers hustle up and down the tiers of tables laden with trays of specialty desserts, coffee, and a complimentary chocolate. The cost: about what you might pay for just a theater ticket in other professional theaters.

Unlike other professional dinner theaters which often feature aging stage or movie stars in leading roles, the Carousel has gone another route, using young, relative unknowns just starting out in their careers. What they lack in experience they make up for in the energy that they put into their roles. I have enjoyed some of the performances I have seen here better than Broadway productions with big-name stars in the lead.

Closed on Mondays.

(For nearby attractions, see Trip 14 in Book 1.)

Carousel Dinner Theater   ☎ 330-724-9855 or 800-362-4100
1275 East Waterloo Road · Akron, Ohio
Region: Northeast Ohio (Summit County)
Handicapped access: Yes

Carousel Dinner Theater

MUCH MORE THAN MERE THEATER

Don Strong is the founder and chief executive officer of the Richards restaurant chain in Indiana. Many years ago he wanted to find a getaway for his family out in the country, away from the hustle and bustle of cities and crowded neighborhoods. Bearcreek Farms is what he discovered. It's tucked away on a country road near Bryant, Indiana, a couple of miles from the Ohio-Indiana border. The nearest community of any real size is Celina, Ohio. The peace and quiet for his family were fine for a couple of years, and then he decided to turn his barn into a restaurant and theater. That was the beginning.

Over the next few years Bearcreek Farms continued to grow. At first there was a private zoo, with lions and tigers to go with the barn, theater, and restaurant. Then he added a fort, like something out of the Old West. He started to allow groups such as the boy scouts to spend the night in the fort's barracks.

Then they added a campground and some Indian teepees. A miniature railroad was added another year, and the track wound over much of the 250 acres that make up the farm.

In the years since, the Strongs have built three theaters, the largest one holding more than 600 people. The zoo was dismantled for insurance reasons, and in its place a small amusement park was erected with a merry-go-round and a whole host of rides big enough for both kids and adults. A village of shops was also built where visitors can buy fresh bakery, candy, cheese, and crafts from the area.

A museum holds a dozen or more classic cars that the Strongs own.

For guests who wanted more modern accommodations for overnight stays, he built a series of cottages that resemble small farmhouses. The cottages are fully equipped motel rooms with TV, air conditioning, and private baths.

The building goes on and on. The Good Times Theater—the largest one—is the scene of a song and dance revue twice daily. On special occasions, it is also used for performances by visiting big-name entertainers.

Just recently completed was the hospitality center that houses the Farmhouse Restaurant and another of the three theaters. Former vaudevillian Buddy Graf, who once worked with Red Skelton, Mickey Rooney, and Sammy Davis, Jr., is the resident comedian here, headlining a daily musical comedy revue for diners.

In the theater the dining is market-style buffet, offering a wide variety of made-from-scratch foods, everything from salad, to pasta, to pot roast, to pizza.

An abundant serving staff works behind the counters to keep the food trays filled and to carve the featured ham or beef.

For those like me who don't like buffets, there is a fine dining room where servers will take your order from an extensive menu. The signature dish here is fried chicken.

The buffet-theater is capable of seating 400 guests, and the sit-down restaurant will hold 150. Prices are low, considering all there is to do here. For example, in 1999 a day trip to the farm with a buffet lunch, two shows, and an ice-cream cone cost as little as $17.95 per person. If you want to stay overnight, they have package deals from $69.95 per couple, which includes a room in the farm motel, dinner, a show, and breakfast before you leave the next day.

(For nearby attractions, see Trip 72 in Book 2.)

Bearcreek Farms   ☎ 800-288-7630 or 219-997-6822
8339 North 400 East • Bryant, Indiana
Region: A couple of miles from the Ohio-Indiana border.
Handicapped access: Yes

89 Bed-and-Breakfasts

Sometimes the food at a bed-and-breakfast surpasses the accommodations. However, I have not included those places here. The good people who operate the inns and bed-and-breakfasts below also offer wonderful, often luxurious, accommodations along with fine food. I would be hard pressed in every case to say which is better, the bed or the breakfast.

Taverns, inns, and bed-and-breakfasts (once called "tourist homes") have historically offered food with overnight accommodations. I recall traveling with my family in the 1930s. We would stay at "tourist homes," which were usually just a way for a family to make a few extra dollars during the Depression. They usually didn't remodel the house, and might make their kids sleep on the couch in the living room so they could rent out their bedroom. In those days most homes only had one bathroom, and everyone shared it.

As for breakfast the next morning, you just squeezed in at the table and shared the family's meal, whatever it was. (I vividly recall getting sick on my first bowl of grits on a trip to South Carolina—that was the only thing close to cereal that the family we were staying with had.) Since this is a book about food, I will not go into the joys of sharing a bathroom with a strange family and their two large dogs that insisted on drinking out of the toilet. Or the guessing game we would play about how clean the sheets on the bed were. Let it just be noted that "tourist homes" have come a long way in the last 40 years.

Today some of the taverns, inns, and bed-and-breakfast places I stay at are better than the finest hotels in the vicinity, and the food is often extraordinarily good. The only problem is that many of these places are off the beaten path and sometimes a bit hard to find, but in every case well worth the trouble.

WORTH THE WAIT

I have a few very favorite places that I like to go every year. The Inn at Cedar Falls, tucked away in the Hocking Hills of southeastern Ohio, is one of them. If you want a romantic spot for a dinner, or even a weekend getaway, Ellen Grinsfelder and her crew can make it happen. A cabin built in the early 1800s, hidden away on a curving hillside road, is the heart of this operation. This is the kitchen and dining room of the Inn at Cedar Falls.

I have spent several evenings at this wondrous place with my wife and good friends, two of whom happened to be the former governor and first lady of Ohio, George and Janet Voinovich. In fact, you never know who has heard of the quality of Ellen's kitchen and might be sharing a candlelit table with you in the tiny cabin.

The Inn at Cedar Falls

At breakfast, Ellen serves things like praline and raisin pancakes, smoked ham slices, or potato-and-scallion breakfast soufflés with sage sausage patties. But dinnertime is when the kitchen truly stars. A typical menu might include warm sautéed cabbage-and-onion salad, black-and-white swirled black bean soup, filet of pork tenderloin with dried apple chutney, and a side of wild rice and seasonal vegetables direct from the cabin's garden out back. On one of my visits, Ellen served fennel and pumpkin soup with caramelized apples, sautéed shrimp with fresh basil and asparagus, a side of spinach linguini with homemade herb butter, and a shredded carrot Caesar salad. For desserts they often offer the likes of warm fruit strudel with raspberry cream, and raspberry-almond truffle torte.

I haven't even mentioned the appetizers: Wisconsin trio cheese ball, crackers, homemade breads, coffee, herbal teas, and hot cocoa. We have sometimes had these while sitting on the old wooden porch swing on the side porch of the cabin, watching the moon come up over Hocking Forest.

I always feel welcome when I walk into the tiny cabin or spend the night in one of the guest cabins or the barn that has been converted into a modern inn. Ellen and her staff are true ambassadors of hospitality for Ohio. Reservations are a must because of the small size of the cabin. It is well worth any wait.

(For nearby attractions, see Trip 25 in Book 1.)

The Inn at Cedar Falls   ☎ 614-385-7489 or 800-65-FALLS
21190 State Route 374 · Logan, Ohio
Region: Southeast Ohio (Hocking County)
Handicapped access: Yes

A HIDEAWAY INN

Probably one of the best-known hideaway inns in northern Ohio, the Inn at Honey Run has hosted senators, governors, and other prominent people looking for a quiet, secluded place to think or relax.

Located on 60 acres of woods and pastures, the inn features several different kinds of accommodations. The 25 guest rooms in the main building, hidden away in a grove of trees, offer quiet elegance. Then there's the honeycombs, an unusual set of 12 guest rooms dug into the side of a hill, each with a patio and commanding view of the small stream that gives this place its name. Finally, secluded on a hilltop are the guest houses, or cottages, each with a fireplace, lots of privacy, and lots of room. If you spend a night here, you'll know why they have won many awards.

But, even if you can't spend the night, be sure to make time to sample their food. The restaurant in the main inn is open to the public. The Inn at Honey Run is in Amish country, and many of the items on the menu reflect that locale. Other types of hearty country fare are also offered. One of their signature dishes is broiled Amish farm-raised trout. The pastries, all made from scratch, range from pies to specialty desserts to cake and ice cream. This is a very popular place for lunch, not only for local folks but for people from nearby cities like Akron and Canton. It's always a good idea to call for reservations, so as not to be disappointed after making the long drive.

(For nearby attractions, see Trip 29 in Book 1.)

The Inn at Honey Run   ☎ 330-674-0011 or 800-468-6639
6920 County Road 203 · Millersburg, Ohio
Region: Northeast Ohio (Holmes County)
Handicapped access: Yes.

The Inn at Honey Run

A MOST ELEGANT INN

Perhaps the most elegant inn I have stayed at in all my travels is in western New York state, about 45 miles from Buffalo. The Hillside Inn dates back to 1851. It is a gorgeous, white-columned mansion standing tall on a 48-acre hilltop overlooking the small town of Wyoming, New York. Over the years it has played host to such famous Americans as Franklin and Eleanor Roosevelt, Susan B. Anthony, and John Muir. Today it is known for its beautiful bedrooms—all with private baths, some with whirlpools, some with fireplaces and balconies—and its fine dining.

Even if you can't spend the night, you can still enjoy the wonderful food. The dining room is open to the public. A recent menu for dinner offered grilled chicken ragout—sage-rubbed grilled chicken with wild mushrooms and oven-dried tomatoes. Several steak and beef dishes were also on the menu, like veal chops and a filet grilled and served with a baked rock lobster tail, as was roast duckling with orange sauce. For those who prefer not to eat meat, the inn offered an entrée made of portobello mushroom stuffed with a blend of spinach and artichoke hearts, accompanied by garden rice.

Like all inns this one is small and intimate, and you can strike up some great discussions with the interesting people you meet there. Innkeepers Nancy and Bill Squier have done a great job, keeping the warmth and charm in every part of this grand old home.

(For nearby attractions, see Trip 44 in Book 1, and Trips 77 and 78 in Book 2.)

Hillside Inn   ☎ 800-544-2249 or 716-495-6800
890 Bethany Road • Wyoming, New York
Region: New York, between Buffalo and Rochester
Handicapped access: Yes to lower-floor rooms.

RUSTIC ELEGANCE

This one is so close to home, it often gets overlooked by people searching for a rustic but elegant getaway and a nice place to eat. The Bass Lake Inn has 12 large guest rooms, each with a gas fireplace, private bath, whirlpool tub, and patio or deck. The inn overlooks its namesake, Bass Lake.

Even if you're just hungry, not looking for a place to stay, this is also a good destination. The dining room, which is open to the public, is probably best appreciated in the autumn, winter, and spring, when the big fireplace is going full blast, creating a cozy spot for lunch or dinner.

This is the place for someone who enjoys wild game or an exotic meal. On the day I visited I had medallions of elk—it was delicious! I have also had Bass Lake's well-prepared ostrich and bison. They do offer standard fare, like pasta, fish, and chicken, for those who aren't so adventurous.

This can be a very busy place, especially around lunch and dinnertime. Be sure to call ahead for reservations.

(For nearby attractions, see Trip 9 in Book 1.)

Bass Lake Inn   ☎ 440-285-3100
400 South Street (Route 44) • Chardon, Ohio
Region: Northeast Ohio (Geauga County)
Handicapped access: Yes.

HAVE DINNER WITH A GHOST

Well, not really. But legend has it that the Buxton Inn in Granville, Ohio, is haunted. Many guests have reported strange sightings of a ghostly woman (believed to be a former owner of the inn) floating in and out of bedrooms on the second floor. True or not, it contributes to the charm of this beautiful inn that now stretches across a city block here in Granville, Ohio.

The Buxton Inn has been around since 1812 and has served as a place of rest and refreshment for the past 180 years. Neighboring homes have been purchased and are now part of the inn, giving owners Orville and

Audrey Orr a chance to expand the number of rooms while leaving the original inn intact. The rooms are beautifully decorated, and each room has a private bath. The gardens surrounding the inn are truly spectacular, especially in the spring and fall.

The Buxton Inn offers breakfast, lunch, and dinner in the public dining room. If you are going to spend a night or are just visiting for the day, it's worth making a layover to stay for dinner. The large menu offers everything from steak to seafood, including such entrées as Louisiana chicken (cubed boneless chicken rolled in seasoned cornmeal and sautéed, served on a bed of rice with mushroom pimento cream sauce and a vegetable) and garlic sesame swordfish (broiled swordfish steak topped with a garlic sesame crust). Vegetarians have several choices, from a wild mushroom stroganoff to a vegetable pasta casserole with three layers of cheese-filled pasta, fresh vegetables, marinara sauce, and more cheese.

Beautiful inn, wonderful gardens, good food, and who knows, maybe even ghost.

(For nearby attractions, see Trip 26 in Book 1, and Trip 62 in Book 2.)

The Buxton Inn   ☎ 740-587-0001
313 East Broadway • Granville, Ohio
Region: Central Ohio (Licking County)
Handicapped access: Yes, to lower floors.

STEEPED IN HISTORY

This is another charming old inn that looks like it just came to life from a Currier and Ives lithograph. Beginning in 1812, our ancestors traveling the stagecoach route from Buffalo to Cleveland, would stop to spend the night with Joseph Rider at his inn. Then, as now, travelers found a comfortable room and hearty American-style food and drink.

The present innkeeper, Elaine Craine, has modernized the rooms with private bathrooms, but the flavor and charm of the stagecoach days remain in the antiques and decor of the place. She offers historic tours of the old building and has some great getaway surprise packages for lovers looking for a romantic setting. (Contact Elaine and she can arrange a romantic dinner for two—just you and your significant other. At the end of the dinner, Elaine will offer both of you a tour. At the end of the tour, she presents the surprise for your significant other: she shows you the honeymoon suite and announces that the two of you are spending the night.)

Speaking of dinner. The inn's candlelit Colonial-style dining room offers early-American dishes, authentically prepared and served in traditional ways. Elaine and her staff use original 19th-century recipes for game and fish entrées, as well as beef, chicken, veal, and duck. On my last visit, I had an enormous slice of prime rib, accompanied by a baked potato and a garden salad of fresh greens and seasonal vegetables, plus freshly baked rolls and breads. The meal was well prepared, and the serving was more than enough, even for someone with a really hearty appetite.

(For nearby attractions, see Trip 13 in Book 1.)

Rider's Inn   ☎ 440-942-2742
792 Mentor Avenue • Painesville, Ohio
Region: Northeast Ohio (Lake County)
Handicapped access: Steps to second floor.

90 Amish Restaurants

Ohio is fortunate in having the largest concentration of people of the Anabaptist faith in the entire world. The largest settlement of Amish, or "plain people," is in the area of Holmes, Wayne, and Tuscarawas counties. Our second-largest Amish population is east of Cleveland in the Geauga-Trumbull vicinity. This means that those of us who love to eat can find a plentiful table at the many "Amish-style" restaurants that dot the countryside in these areas.

The Amish are renowned for their family-style dinners of chicken, beef, or pork with mountains of mashed potatoes and gravy, canned corn, peas, or beans, and baskets full of enormous dinner rolls just minutes out of the oven. For openers, there is usually a salad bar, and while I have expounded elsewhere on why I don't like salad bars (they allow too many people's hands to touch the food), I will admit that the Amish restaurants at least make a determined effort to keep the area cleaned up and wiped down from spills and fingerprints.

Salad bars in Amish country offer the usual condiments and fixings, but they also often offer a large assortment of things not commonly found in your neighborhood restaurant salad bar. For instance, pickled hard-boiled eggs, richly purple from the beet juice used in the pickling, fresh tapioca, or an Amish specialty: butterscotch pudding on a bed of graham-cracker crumbs with whipped topping. There are always several kinds of pickles and probably the best coleslaw ever made. I once pressured the folks who run the Amish Door Restaurant in Wilmot to let me have their secret coleslaw recipe. After months of my begging they finally agreed, somberly handing me a folded piece of paper. I opened it to see the first two ingredients: 200 heads of cabbage and five gallons of apple cider vinegar. Who says folks in Amish country don't have a sense of humor?

It has been my duty and pleasure over the last 20 years or so to eat at and report on many of the Amish-style restaurants in Ohio. On the whole, with few exceptions, they offer well-prepared meat-and-potatoes fare. You won't find anything too adventurous. They cater to families and don't serve too many spicy dishes. If you are watching your calories, this is probably not the best place to stop for dinner. While some Amish-style places have added lighter salads and dishes to their menus, by and large the main menu still contains lots of deep-fried, fatty, starchy, sugary dishes that were originally meant for farmers who needed this kind of fuel and would easily work off the calories on a normal day. Now these dishes have become the favorites of less-active tourists who flood this area each week. Also, with some minor exceptions, the menus at Amish-style restaurants are very similar. Here and there you will see some restaurants' efforts to cut away from the pack by introducing new specials and entrées. Acknowledging that many of their customers are faced with dietary restrictions, some restaurants are making an attempt to add sugar-free and "no-sugar-added" desserts and drinks to their menu. However, they are still doing little for customers with sodium or lactose restrictions.

Having said all this, how do I rate these restaurants? I think that all of them offer a great value in quality of food, quantity, and price. An added bonus: because of the huge crowds in the area (which is Ohio's fastest-growing tourist destination), the Amish have learned to build big restaurants and to serve people quickly. I have seen days at Der Dutchman in Walnut Creek when the line of people waiting for a seat might stretch four abreast out the front door, down the front of the building, and clear into the parking lot—yet, I can't remember ever waiting more than about 20 minutes for a seat.

One other thing to mention is the friendliness of the servers and owners at these restaurants. Considering the sheer numbers of tourists they have to deal with every day—complete with bad manners, loud voices, and sometimes nosy questions about the Amish—I have found them to be unfailingly kind and courteous. They remind me of the country folks I grew up among, with a way of life that is fast disappearing in our country.

ALPINE-ALPA: IN THE BEGINNING

Sixty-five years ago, not too many people paid attention to the Amish. At that time they didn't look much different from the rest of rural America. It was not unusual for people far out in the country to still use horses to work their farms, or use a buggy to go to town on Saturday night. What brought people to the Tuscarawas County area then was that it had such a large community of people from Switzerland (including the Amish, who came from Switzerland, Germany, and other countries).

The Swiss made cheese—good cheese. It seems like there was a small cheese factory on every rural road in this rich farming country. Today the Swiss cheese industry in Ohio owes a great deal to the promotional work done by a young married couple back in the 1930s. Hans and Alice Grossnicklaus were both born in Switzerland, and they met in this country.

Hans was working as a cheese maker in Wilmot, Ohio, and in the evenings he would pick up extra money by singing, yodeling, and playing his accordion over the radio at a station in Akron. Alice, who also played the accordion and could yodel, had been attending school in Cleveland, where she studied light opera. The radio station wanted Hans to sing some duets with a woman who could also yodel. He was introduced to Alice, and they started a professional partnership that eventually led to marriage in 1932. Some Amish farmers started a new cheese factory in Wilmot and hired Hans as the cheese maker. Over the next 18 years. Alice and Hans slowly bought out the farmers who had started the factory, and by 1950 they owned the controlling interest in the Alpine-Alpa cheese factory.

Swiss cheese was not a big seller in the 1930s, so Alice and Hans would take cheese with them to county fairs all over the state, and would sing and yodel to promote and sell their cheese. It paid off, and sales began to climb. They were finally able to import some Swiss entertainers to do the marketing, so they could devote more time to the cheese business. Alice's next idea was to open a real Swiss chalet that would sell their cheese, and offer the wonderful Swiss cooking she remembered from her childhood.

The Alpine-Alpa restaurant opened in 1962. To celebrate the event, Alice commissioned the creation of the world's largest working cuckoo clock, which still attracts tourists and has been featured in *Ripley's Believe It or Not* and in the *Guinness Book of World Records*. In 1983, Alice commissioned Amish artist Tom Miller to create his masterpiece on the ceiling and walls of her restaurant—a three-dimensional mural of Switzerland, complete with real waterfalls and a moving alpine train.

Because of their long involvement with the Amish of the community, Hans and Alice have mixed many Amish dishes with the Swiss cooking. The menu has always featured Alice's "Swissy Chicken," fish and ham dishes, and fresh baked goods, including pies. Of course they always feature Alpine-Alpa Swiss Cheese (their Baby Swiss cheese won an award as the fourth-best in the world in the early '90s).

Hans has been gone for more than 30 years, but Alice, now in her nineties, still develops new ways to attract customers to Alpine-Alpa. Many call Alice the "Grande Dame of Amish Country Tourism." This is one of the few restaurants in Amish Country that is open on Sundays.

(For nearby attractions, see Trip 61 in Book 2.)

Alpine-Alpa Heidi Restaurant   ☎ 330-359-5454
1504 U.S. Route 62 · Wilmot, Ohio
Region: Northeast Ohio (Stark County)
Handicapped access: Yes.

Alpine-Alpa Heidi Restaurant

THE FIRST REALLY BIG AMISH-STYLE RESTAURANT

Back in the 1960s tourism was just discovering the quaint area of Ohio called "Amish country" within the boundaries of Wayne, Holmes, and Tuscarawas counties. On weekends, non-Amish would take long drives through the countryside and gawk at the small, neat farms surrounded by flowers that Amish wives had planted. They would scan the side roads to get a glimpse of a horse-drawn Amish buggy heading to a neighbor's or sneak a peek into one of the small villages that dot this countryside. There wasn't much to see or do in those days and even fewer places to eat. The restaurants that did exist were usually small places that fit well into a country village, the owners eking out a modest living by catering to the breakfast and lunch needs of nearby farmers and townspeople.

Emanuel Mullet of Walnut Creek noticed the influx of curious tourists and realized that when people drove for hours across the rolling hills of Holmes County, they would also have to eat. And a restaurant offering the plain but filling foods that the Amish families ate might be very popular.

He purchased a small restaurant in Walnut Creek in 1969 and named it "Der Dutchman." At the time the restaurant could seat about 45 customers before it reached capacity. Mullet's prediction was correct: the restaurant was very popular with tourists, who filled it to capacity almost every day to eat family-style chicken, beef, and pork dinners and fresh, homemade pies and breads. It wasn't long before he had to increase the size of the dining room, beginning a seemingly endless job of making the restaurant bigger and bigger. Today it covers almost an entire city block with its parking lot and adjoining Carlisle Village Inn, which his company also owns. The seating capacity today is 900 in the restaurant and 500 next door in the Inn's banquet hall. On a busy day an estimated 5,000 people have been fed at Der Dutchman of Walnut Creek. They have also increased the number of restaurants to eight in Ohio and one in Florida. Emanuel Mullet died a few years ago, but his three daughters and their husbands continue to operate the parent firm, the Dutch Corporation, with an attention to detail and quality that reflects the Amish way of life.

(For nearby attractions, see Trip 30 in Book 1.)

Der Dutchman Restaurant ☎ 330-893-2981
4985 Walnut Street · Walnut Creek, Ohio
Region: Northeast Ohio (Holmes County)
Handicapped access: Yes

Other Dutch Corporation restaurants:

Der Dutchman Restaurant ☎ 330-874-1039
10911 SR 212, NE · Wilkshire Hills, Ohio
Region: Northeast Ohio (Tuscarawas County), near Bolivar and Zoar
Handicapped access: Yes

Dutch Valley Restaurant ☎ 330-852-4627
Old Route 39 · Sugarcreek, Ohio
Region: Northeast Ohio (Tuscarawas County), western edge of village of Sugarcreek
Handicapped access: Yes

Der Dutchman Restaurant ☎ 419-886-7070
720 SR 97 West · Belleville, Ohio
Region: Northeast Ohio (Richland County), just off exit for Belleville, on Interstate 71
Handicapped access: Yes

Der Dutchman Restaurant ☎ 614-873-3441
8690 Route 42 · Plain City, Ohio
Region: Central Ohio (Madison County)
Handicapped access: Yes

Der Dutchman Restaurant ☎ 513-897-4716
230 SR 42 • Waynesville, Ohio
Region: Southwest Ohio (Warren County), just outside the antique capital of the
Midwest
Handicapped access: Yes

Der Dutchman Restaurant ☎ 941-955-8007
3713 Bahia Vista • Sarasota, Florida
Handicapped access: Yes

Das Dutchman Essenhaus ☎ 219-825-9471
240 US 20 • Middlebury, Indiana
Handicapped access: Yes

A REAL MOM-AND-POP AMISH-STYLE RESTAURANT

There really is a "Mrs. Yoder" of "Mrs. Yoder's Kitchen" in the small Amish community of Mount Hope, Ohio. Gloria Yoder and her husband, Eli, also operate Yoder's Amish Home in Walnut Creek. Mrs. Yoder's Kitchen came about when Gloria noticed the large crowds on sale day at the Mount Hope Auction. The people who came to the small town had few options for eating except for getting fast food at the lunch counter in the auction house, or grabbing sandwich makings at a local general store. She guessed, and rightly so, that folks headed for the auction and tourists who come through town to stop at Lehman's nonelectric hardware store would appreciate a place where they could sit down at a table for a bountiful country meal.

There are no surprises here, just good, hearty country food, served in the large portions that people who work on surrounding farms have come to expect. Gloria does have a couple of specials: Amish Wedding Steak, a Swiss–steak-like dish traditionally served at Amish weddings, and one of my favorites, Amish date-nut pudding, best served with fresh homemade ice cream and topped with caramel sauce. Since Eli and Gloria both have strong ties with the Amish (Eli was raised in the Amish faith), you will find a lot of Amish families eating here, especially on Wednesday, when the auction across the street is going strong. The restaurant is very modern, but the food is still prepared as it might have been 20 years ago: one dish at a time, by country folks who know how to cook.

(For nearby attractions, see Trip 29 in Book 1.)

Mrs. Yoder's Kitchen   ☎ 330-674-0922
Route 241 • Mount Hope, Ohio
Region: Northeast Ohio (Holmes County)
Handicapped access: Yes.

AN AMISH-STYLE RESTAURANT WITH A TWIST

Dutch Harvest Restaurant is simply beautiful inside, from the roaring stone fireplace in the center of its dining room to the wall of glass that overlooks a pasture and creek where cows come to graze. It's a comfortable place that is big, but not too big. While it has its share of tourist buses, the restaurant is laid out so that each room seems very intimate and you don't notice the crowds. Another thing that sets this restaurant apart is their kitchen. They experiment frequently with dishes not normally found on the menus of other Amish restaurants, especially in the slower-paced wintertime when you may find salmon or barbecued ribs on the menu. They also do the usual chicken, beef, and ham dinners very well. In fact they offer a sampler plate for the hearty eater who wants to try a wide range of the different foods that ordinarily would only be found on the family-style menu. When it comes to desserts, they offer the obligatory fruit and cream pies and one very special dessert, called a "bag apple pie." A bag apple pie is literally baked inside a brown bag. It contains 12 to 13 huge golden-delicious apples and is topped not with a pastry crust, but a crust made of cookie dough. When the pie goes into the oven it is six to eight inches high. Needless to say it costs a bit more than the regular pies, but everyone who has ever enjoyed a piece of bag apple pie tells me it is worth every penny. If you ate too much for lunch, they do sell entire bag apple pies to take home with you to enjoy later.

The food is authentic to the Amish area. The Shrock family, which owns the Dutch Harvest, used to be Old Order Amish, and many family members still belong to the Amish faith.

(For nearby attractions, see Trip 28 in Book 1, and Trips 56 and 61 in Book 2.)

Dutch Harvest Restaurant   ☎ 330-893-3333
State Route 39 at Route 62 • Berlin, Ohio
Region: Northeast Ohio (Holmes County)
Handicapped access: Yes.

AN AMISH-STYLE RESTAURANT WITH TURKEYS

In Sugarcreek the Beachey family has long been associated with raising turkeys. So it was only natural that when they opened a beautiful new restaurant on the eastern edge of this quaint Swiss community, one of the main features on the menu would be turkey. Beachey's offers a delightful mixture of both Amish and Swiss cooking. (Some people claim there is little difference between the two, but with my own Swiss heritage, I think there is.) The exterior of the restaurant looks like a chalet. Inside you will find Amish quilts decorating the walls and an eager-to-please staff that works hard to seat you quickly and take your order. The items on the menu, with the exception of the turkey, are similar to those at the other Amish-style restaurants. The servings are usually large and reasonably priced. If you are still hungry when you finish, it's your own fault.

(For nearby attractions, see Trip 33 in Book 1.)

Beachey's Country Chalet   ☎ 330-852-4464
115 Andreas Drive • Sugarcreek, Ohio
Region: Northeast Ohio (Tuscarawas County)
Handicapped access: Yes.

THE DOORWAY TO AMISH COUNTRY: WILMOT, OHIO

The Amish Door Restaurant is part of a tourist stop here in Tuscarawas County on the edge of Amish country. It's been around for a long time, starting out as a restaurant in a replica of a small barn that just grew and grew. Today the complex consists of a huge new restaurant that resembles an old farmhouse and a new inn that from the lobby makes you think you are on board a riverboat. The inn offers a honeymoon suite complete with fireplace, whirlpool bath, and four-poster bed. There is also an exercise room and an indoor swimming pool. Shops now occupy the barn that once housed the restaurant, as well as an adjacent house, and there is a nearby farmhouse that serves as a bed-and-breakfast, and a barn filled with antiques for sale. They also have a furniture store featuring oak and cherry furniture made by local Amish craftsmen.

The new restaurant, like so many of the places in this part of the state, reflects the craftsmanship of local Amish talent. Lots of polished oak, winding stairways, and large chandeliers—everything modern and well appointed. They have the obligatory salad bar with what I already described as the best coleslaw in Ohio. The menu regularly offers family-style meals. A bakery not only supplies the restaurant but offers its surplus for sale to diners and visitors. This is another of those huge Amish-style restaurants that can handle several busloads of tourists quickly and efficiently. The line may be long, but the wait isn't.

(For nearby attractions, see Trip 61 in Book 2.)

The Amish Door Restaurant   ☎ 330-359-5464
U.S. Route 62 • Wilmot, Ohio
Region: Northeast Ohio (Stark County)
Handicapped access: Yes.

THIS IS THE WAY IT USED TO BE AND STILL IS

There is a small restaurant on the main street in downtown Berlin where all the local folks used to gather for breakfast and lunch. Boyd and Wurthmann's was just a bit more than a sandwich shop back in the 1970s, and it isn't much larger today. They have probably seen business triple in the last dozen years but have resisted the urge to move to larger quarters. If you have ever wondered what restaurants in Amish country used to look like before the tourists invaded, this is a pretty good example. They still feature home cooking with an Amish flavor, homemade pies, and friendly service.

(For nearby attractions, see Trip 28 in Book 1, and Trips 56 and 61 in Book 2.)

Boyd and Wurthmann Restaurant   ☎ 330-893-2353
U.S. Route 62 • Berlin, Ohio
Region: Northeast Ohio (Holmes County)
Handicapped access: Steps into restaurant.

HAVE LUNCH IN A BUGGY

This is a little out of the way of the usual Amish restaurants, but there are plenty of Mennonite and Amish folks who live in and around Shreve to give it authenticity. There is an Amish buggy in the restaurant set up as a table, so you can say you had lunch in a buggy. There is also a large fireplace where in the wintertime you often find ladies working on a large quilt. The name of the restaurant means "the Dutch eating house." The menu is pretty typical of Amish-style restaurants. Chicken, beef, and ham headline, with mashed potatoes, salad bar, homemade bread, rolls, and pies.

(For nearby attractions, see Trip 28 in Book 1, and Trip 56 and 61 in Book 2.)

Des Dutch Essenhaus   ☎ 330-567-2212
176 North Market Street • Shreve, Ohio
Region: Northeast Ohio (Wayne County)
Handicapped access: Yes.

RESTAURANT FINDS ITS IDENTITY

Along U.S. Route 30, the old Lincoln Highway, between Massillon and Wooster, is the town of Dalton (pronounced Daaal-ton), where a 20-year-old restaurant has finally found its identity. Originally opened in an old Victorian-style farmhouse, it was a tearoom and restaurant, serving dainty sandwiches and selling fresh-baked goods. Then it became a full-blown restaurant, and finally it has metamorphosed into an Amish-style eatery with family-style portions of fried chicken, ham, and beef—and crowds to match. The original restaurant has been dwarfed by a new addition that has probably quadrupled the size of the dining room. Like all Amish-style places, they have learned how to move large crowds along. Even on a busy Saturday night the wait is not very long. There is also a bakery, so you can take home a whole pie, loaf of bread, or some good sticky rolls.

(For nearby attractions, see Trip 28 in Book 1, and Trip 56 and 61 in Book 2.)

Das Dutch Kitchen Restaurant, Bakery and Gift Shop   ☎ 330-683-0530
U.S. Route 30 • Dalton, Ohio
Region: Northeast Ohio (Wayne County)
Handicapped access: Yes.

THE MOST ORNATE AMISH-STYLE RESTAURANT

The Hartville Kitchen Restaurant has come a long way, from its humble beginnings as a snack bar near an auction barn to a multimillion-dollar palace with sweeping stairways, huge chandeliers, artwork, and a series of shops. Oh, yes, there is a restaurant in there, too.

Most people expect an enormous restaurant when they see the new building—the building and parking lots take up nearly 45 acres along Edison Street in Hartville. But inside, the center is taken up by a candy store and bakery, and on the other end are a huge gift shop and a coin store. The restaurant, for all of the building's size, only seats about 400, with banquet facilities in the back for another 500. The Hartville Kitchen has been famous for years for their homemade salad dressings, which can be purchased in most northern Ohio grocery stores. You can sample the various dressings on your salads in the dining room here and stop at the bakery to buy it by the bottle, or even the case, to take home. Not surprisingly, there are lines at lunch and dinnertime, but they usually move quickly. The biggest lines are on Mondays and Thursdays, when the Hartville Flea Market is held across the street. They offer the usual Amish-style restaurant fare—fried chicken, ham, and beef, as well as some daily specials. Be sure to try their noodle dishes, and save room for the Hartville Kitchen homemade pies.

(For nearby attractions, see Trip 8 in Book 1, and Trip 58 in Book 2.)

The Hartville Kitchen Restaurant   ☎ 330-877-9353
1015 Edison Street • Hartville, Ohio
Region: Northeast Ohio (Stark County)
Handicapped access: Yes.

OHIO'S OTHER AMISH AREA

In Ohio's second-largest Amish settlement, Middlefield in Geauga County, there is an Amish-style restaurant that caters so thoroughly to the Amish folks that they have installed a drive-up window for horse-drawn buggies! Mary Yoder's restaurant started out in a storefront in downtown Middlefield a few years ago and finally moved to a brand new, larger facility on Route 608 north of the village, where they have a bakery, gift shop, and restaurant. I am particularly fond of their hot turkey sandwich here, a large serving of fresh-cooked turkey white meat, served with a mound of fresh mashed potatoes and swimming in a hot turkey gravy.

(For nearby attractions, see Trip 9 in Book 1.)

Mary Yoder's Amish Kitchen Restaurant   ☎ 440-632-1939
Route 608, North • Middlefield, Ohio
Region: Northeast Ohio (Geauga County)
Handicapped access: Yes

91 Vegetarian Restaurants: Good Food, and It's Good for You

When I was a youngster I thought vegetarians ate grass. I don't know why I thought that, but I suspect that a comic strip I read may have had something to do with it (I gained a lot of my knowledge in those days from comic books). Then one night, I was having dinner with my grandparents, and I realized I actually *was* eating grass! My grandmother casually mentioned that what I thought was spinach was in reality dandelion greens she had picked out of our backyard that day. At first I pushed them to the farthest side of my plate. But with coaxing from my grandfather, I took a small mouthful. Understand, I loved spinach and this looked like spinach, but the idea of eating something that I usually mowed and fed to the cattle, or used to make beds for my rabbits, was a bit unsettling. I chewed, and I chewed, and finally I swallowed it. It tasted like sweet spinach. I liked it. After that I never thought of people who eat grass as being silly. They knew something I didn't: grass is good—at least the way my grandmother cooked it. Today, though I am not a vegetarian, I sometimes head for a vegetarian restaurant for a break from the monotony of beef and chicken and fish. I have found a few that make things as good as that "grass" I ate as a kid.

THYME FOR VEGETARIAN FOOD

I'm not sure why, but I find most good vegetarian restaurants near college campuses. Maybe college students are more willing to experiment with food or more cognizant of the value of nutrition. (Having just written that, I suddenly remember looking in my daughter Melissa's refrigerator when she was in college and seeing only Twinkies and some spoiling fruit. Maybe that last theory isn't as good as I thought it was.) One of these is Tabor's Thyme in Berea, not far from Baldwin-Wallace College. Just reading through their imaginative menu is enough to start me salivating: sweet potato quesadillas, cajun red beans and rice, barbecue tofu with onions, paprikash with un-chicken (I'm not sure what that is, but it sounds good), Greek spinach-rice balls, tempeh fajitas, garden goulash, and creamy polenta with tempeh bolognese sauce.

They also make a great low-fat scone and some wonderful pies and cakes. Often the bakery is the best part of a vegetarian restaurant, but in this case they do everything equally well.

Tabor's is closed on Sunday and Monday. There is outdoor seating in good weather.

(For nearby attractions, see Trips 5, 15, 16 in Book 1.)

Tabor's Thyme Fine Vegetarian Cafe   ☎ 440-243-1011
34 Park Street • Berea, Ohio
Region: Northeast Ohio (Cuyahoga County)
Handicapped access: Yes.

A CASUAL STYLE CAFE

They call this a "casual-style" cafe. It is that and more. If you wander in in the late morning, you are liable to find a college instructor going over his papers at one table, two people playing chess at another table, and a family of four waiting for breakfast at another. The fare here is all vegetarian, coupled with a bakery that produces some of the best bread I have ever had. The day we visited they had fresh blueberry bread that was as pretty to look at as it was delicious to eat. A popular spot not only for Kent students, but for vegetarians around the Portage County area and anyone who wants to try something different and healthy.

(For nearby attractions, see Trip 6 in Book 1.)

The Zephyr Cafe   ☎ 330-678-4848
106 West Main Street • Kent, Ohio
Region: Northeast Ohio (Portage County)
Handicapped access: Steps into building.

VEGETARIAN AND NON-VEGETARIAN

While the menu here has meat and fish dishes, there is a significant section devoted to vegetarian meals and items. It's obvious that the owner is making a real attempt to satisfy as many of her customers as she can. On my last visit to the restaurant they were offering a vegetarian pizza, a veggie burger, and vegetarian soups and salads. The food is well prepared, and it's a good place to take a non-vegetarian friend, where both of you can probably find something on the menu that you like. Open year round.

(For nearby attractions, see Trip 31 in Book 1.)

Zoar Tavern and Inn   ☎ 888-874-2170 or 330-874-2170
162 Main Street • Zoar, Ohio
Region: Northeast Ohio
Handicapped access: Yes to restaurant, steps to inn on second floor.

92 **Tearooms**

My Grandmother Currier loved her tea. She liked coffee, too, but tea was her special drink. No teabags for her; she used a little metal contraption one of her ancestors brought from England many years ago to put the loose tea in, and she would hang it from an attached silver chain into an old but elegant teapot, also owned by that long-ago ancestor. The resulting brew was potent.

Problem was, Grandma was a working farm wife, and she would put the tea on to brew and then forget about it for several hours, while she became preoccupied with canning fruit, making supper, or repairing a pair of overalls on her ancient sewing machine. It might be evening before she would pick up the pot of tea, pour it into a saucepan to reheat it, and then pour it into her cup, which she would take with her to the dining room table to sip at for the next hour or so as she worked into the late hours on the farm records she religiously kept every night.

I recall in my early teen years pouring a cup of her steeped-all-day-long tea for myself. I threw a couple of ice cubes in it and some sugar and took a long swig. What coursed through my mouth and throat felt like battery acid! Grandma just smiled sweetly and said, "Isn't your tea warm enough, dear?" as I raced to the kitchen to spew it into the sink.

My grandmother looked forward each year to the annual Parent Teacher Association tea at our little country school. Card tables would fill the gymnasium, a sprig of lilacs would be tucked in a vase on each table, and the ladies would all bring their finest tea cups and saucers and make their best pies, cakes, and rolls. That's about as close as I ever got to being at a real English tea.

Grandma would have loved His Majesty's Tea Room in Madison, Ohio. I suspect that owner Michael Loparo had ladies like my grandmother in mind when she took over an abandoned bank building on the main square of the historic little farm village and decided to open a real tearoom.

She offers premium loose-leaf teas in dozens of varieties. She also has freshly baked scones and muffins with preserves. In fact, everything here is made from scratch in the tearoom's kitchen. If you want lunch with your tea, she even offers the hearty "Ploughman's Lunch," which consists of chunks of cheddar cheese with crusty bread, Branston pickles, a cup of soup, and, of course, tea.

Michael also has a menu of other sandwiches, soups, and salads to satisfy any appetite. But it is the afternoon tea, a wonderful four-course affair, that her customers come from miles around to experience. It changes monthly but usually includes her homemade scones, a sweet dessert, some tiny finger-sandwiches, soup, and the tea of your choice. The food is good, and as some of her customers told me the day I visited, "It gives you a little quiet elegance." The bank building that houses the tearoom adds to the experience. The walls are covered with paintings and wall hangings, and soft harp music plays in the background. Even the old bank vault is used—as a coat closet!

Customers from as far as Dayton have driven to Madison to experience what Michael calls "a proper afternoon tea." Grandma would have loved it. I know I did.

(For nearby attractions, see Trip 13 in Book 1.)

His Majesty's Tea Room   ☎ 888-606-6036 or 440-417-0220
63 West Main Street • Madison, Ohio
Region: Northeast Ohio (Lake County)
Handicapped access: Steps into building.

His Majesty's Tea Room

TEA FOR THE KIDS

Poling's Village, a newly created shopping mall on U. S. Route 250 between Sandusky and Milan, grooms tea drinkers young.

They encourage little girls to accompany their mothers for the mother-daughter tea they offer each day. For birthdays, they go all out, with fancy hats, boas, and even long gloves for the little girls to wear while having their tea. Then they have a fashion parade up and down the aisles of the mall to show off their costumes.

It's a fun place, and the tearoom, in the back of the mall, is curtained off into small rooms that make each group of guests feel almost like they are the only ones there. The food served with their tea is also worth noting.

On the day I visited I had an overstuffed croissant made with fresh chicken salad and an accompanying dish of coleslaw that included cranberries and other fruit. It was delicious! The tearoom is rather small, so reservations are strongly suggested. Its reputation for good food and interesting surroundings has made this a very popular place.

While you are there you might also want to explore the unusual shops that are in the same building. They have a fine-jewelry store with unique and expensive gems, as well as a place that sells antique wedding dresses. There is also a teddy bear museum, and a shop that makes beautiful floral arrangements.

It was a very pleasant way to spend a cold spring day.

(For nearby attractions, see Trip 18 in Book 1, and Trips 48 and 66 in Book 2.)

Poling's Village   ☎ 419-627-0851
9406 Route 250   •   Milan, Ohio
Region: Northeast Ohio (Erie County)
Handicapped access: Yes.

A SPOT FOR TEA

Located in a 150-year-old home in Lorain County, this quaint tearoom offers a variety of salads, sandwiches, and freshly baked muffins and cookies. It offers a good assortment of teas from around the world. My wife, Bonnie, who checked this one out, said she enjoyed the raspberry iced tea (it was a hot day).

Bonnie was there twice and sampled their roll-up sandwich that contained chicken and bacon in a tomato-flavored tortilla. It was accompanied by a small cluster of grapes, slices of orange, cantaloupe, watermelon, and banana. Bonnie's companion ordered the quiche of the day, and while it was tasty, the portion was rather small. Both commented that despite the building's age, everything was dusted, windows sparkled, and it was neat and clean.

There are three floors of antiques for sale, including furniture in the tearoom. The Tree House is open daily, 11 a.m. to 5 p.m. It's a small place, and they do take reservations, so it's a good idea to call before you go.

(For nearby attractions, see Trip 58 in Book 2.)

The Tree House Gallery and Tea Room ☎ 440-934-1636
36840 Detroit Road · Avon, Ohio
Region: Northeast Ohio (Lorain County)
Handicapped access: Old home with steps.

The Tree House Gallery and Tea Room

HAVING TEA AT THE CASTLE

You really can go to the castle to have a cuppa tea.

Ravenwood Castle Bed and Breakfast down in Hocking Hills (see One-of-a-Kind chapter), is a real castle, albeit a new one built just a few years ago. It was copied from real castles in Scotland. Be sure you take a tour of this interesting bed-and-breakfast.

Sue Maxwell, one of the owners, has added new buildings and shops to the castle grounds, one of them being the coach house, which is home to the tearoom. It is here that they offer lunches each day, as well as a "high tea,"—meaning you get food and tea. The castle offers just the right atmosphere for a tearoom.

They also have many special events during the year on the castle grounds. The castle is in a rather remote area of Ohio, so it is a good idea to call for reservations.

(For nearby attractions, see Trip 55 in Book 2.)

Ravenwood Castle ☎ 800-477-1541
65666 Bethel Road • New Plymouth, Ohio
Region: Southeast Ohio (Hocking County)
Handicapped access: Yes.

A TEAROOM IN OHIO'S ANTIQUE CAPITAL

There is a new tearoom in the center of Ohio's Antique Capital, Waynesville, Ohio. Angel of the Garden Tea Room is open to the public, but by reservation only. The popularity of the new tearoom has made the reservation-only rule necessary, as the daily teas have been selling out.

Angel of the Garden is located in a nearly century-old home on North Main Street. The home has been restored to its turn-of-the-century Victorian elegance and is filled with antiques of the period.

The unusual name of the tearoom is from the legend of Saint Dorothea, the patron saint of gardeners, brewers of tea, midwives, lovers, and young married couples.

In addition to serving a five-course afternoon tea Tuesday through Saturday, they also offer dinner at 6:30 on those days. Again, reservations are necessary. One of the reasons you need reservations is that they also cater special brunches and dinners. That means the small staff has to make use of every minute.

A special note: You can have "Tea with Dickens"—that's Charles Dickens—during the Christmas season. It's just one of the many special events they schedule throughout the year.

(For nearby attractions, see Trip 40 in Book 1.)

The Angel of the Garden Tea Room ☎ 513-897-7729
71 North Main Street • Waynesville, Ohio
Region: Northeast Ohio (Warren County)
Handicapped access: entrance at the side, call ahead for assistance.

93 One-of-a-Kind

Nancy's Restaurant on North High Street in Columbus has gained a citywide reputation. The 30-odd seats and stools have borne the weight of just about anybody who is somebody in the state capital, or celebrities who might be passing through. If you don't believe it just look at the hundreds of autographed photos that paper the wall behind the counter. She had one of Elvis and the Jordainaires that fell down behind the range backstop, and they haven't been able to reach it.

What makes Nancy's a place where people will line up out the door and down the street waiting for a seat? It might be the food. But it also might be the menu. You see, Nancy's Restaurant cooks only one item for lunch each day. There is no choice on the menu. In fact, there isn't a menu (the staff assumes you have visited enough to know the way she schedules her food). If it's Wednesday, for example, then the lunch is homemade meatloaf, mashed potatoes and gravy, and cooked green beans, with two small Parker House rolls. If it's Thursday, then it's chicken and homemade noodles with mashed potatoes, and so on.

Cindy King is the manager of this family-owned business. She decided to take some of the decision-making out of people's lives about 12 years ago. "I didn't want to end up like my parents," she said, "they were both young when they died." She went on to explain that Nancy's Restaurant, named after her mother, had been started by her parents 32 years ago, but when they ran it, it was open from 6 a.m. well into the evening.

"They were always worrying about how much food to order," she said. "They couldn't predict the weather or crowds, and if they guessed wrong, the profits for that day ended up in the garbage can." She feels strongly that those constant concerns and worries hastened the deaths of both of her parents.

"I decided when I took over about 12 years ago, that I was going to make everyone's life a little easier," Cindy said. "'We all have too many decisions to make each day, and when I discovered how many people would order my homemade meatloaf on a Wednesday, I suddenly had an idea—just serve one thing, make it simple, no choices."

Today, with shortened hours for lunch and dinner, and only one entrée to serve, Cindy daily proves she was right on target. On Thursdays when she serves her legendary homemade noodles and fresh chicken, the line can snake out the door and down the block to the corner. These are the days when Cindy strongly enforces some unusual rules she has made for people who want to eat in her restaurant. "Eat it and beat it!" one large sign proclaims over the few tables and booths crammed into the tiny restaurant. If people don't get the hint, then Cindy may announce in a loud voice, "There will be four seats in a minute, those four guys against the wall have had plenty of time to eat . . . haven't you, fellows?"

The regulars don't seem to mind. In fact they seem to love the family-style, good-natured haranguing that goes on throughout the place.

And don't be surprised if Cindy tells you to give up the seat you have just waited for and give it to an older customer. "If a young person has a seat and an older person doesn't, the younger person will be asked to move or give up his seat. That's a rule!" Cindy declares.

And you don't have to sit down to eat. Cindy says she does just about as many carryout lunches and dinners each day as she does of the sit-down kind. The price, by the way, is always the same, also. Four dollars, and that includes tax. It's the same for dinner as it is for lunch. Coffee and soft drinks are extra, and tips are always appreciated.

Don't offer a credit card to pay for your meal—Cindy doesn't accept cards of any kind, or checks either—just cash. She confesses that if she had a credit-card machine she probably couldn't run it right anyway.

The customers give the food high marks, especially the meatloaf and the chicken and noodles. But she also varies the menu with what she calls her "kick-ass" marzetti, salmon patties, and different kinds of fish dishes.

Cindy also serves breakfast, and is apparently more flexible in the early hours of the day. She takes orders then, for bacon and eggs, muffins, fruit—just don't ask for pancakes. Cindy says she doesn't like pancakes, so she just won't make them for anybody.

Some of the customers also confided to me that Cindy can't stand to see anyone go hungry. That's apparent in the large portions that she serves. Some older customers ask for half-portions when they aren't going right home and can't take a doggy bag with their leftovers. Cindy has also been known to spot hard-up college students who will come in with friends but not order. She just serves them anyway and tells them to pay her next time. It's no shame to be hungry, she says.

(For nearby attractions, see Trip 26 in Book 1, and Trip 62 in Book 2.)

Nancy's Restaurant   ☎ 614-265-9012
3133 North High Street   •   Columbus, Ohio
Region: Central Ohio (Franklin County)
Handicapped access: Narrow aisles

THREE-COURSE DINNER FOR 79 CENTS

Pechin's Cafeteria is the home of the three-course dinner for 79 cents. This is not a misprint. Dunbar, Pennsylvania, has received a lot of national media attention because of a rather scruffy restaurant.

Seventy-nine cents. That is the full price if you want, say, a piece of homemade meatloaf, a generous spoonful of mashed potatoes and gravy, and a side dish of canned string beans.

Of course that doesn't include your coffee. If you would like a steaming cup of Sanka coffee, that will be another nickel! That's right, a cup of coffee in this restaurant still costs just five cents. If you want a large cup, that costs a dime.

It doesn't end there. They also have the cheapest hamburgers in America. Just 19 cents each. How about an order of French fries? Just 29 cents. A hot dog with all the trimmings costs 35 cents. People literally buy them by the bagful here.

This is not a promotional, once-a-year deal. These are the prices every day, and they have pretty much stayed the same for at least the last dozen years. Pechin's Cafeteria was sort of an offshoot of a larger shopping complex called Pechin's Shopper's Village, which consists of several stores, mainly a large grocery and meat store that offers equally good prices for bargain hunters.

Some of the customers we talked with had driven well over a hundred miles, packing coolers in the trunks of their cars to be filled with bargain cuts of meat and fish from the shopping complex.

It started out as the cafeteria for shopping-center employees. However, this is a small town and the folks all know what's going on, so when locals heard that workers at Pechin's could buy a three-course dinner for 79 cents, they started dropping in at the cafeteria too.

When the owner, Sullivan D'Amico, realized what was going on, instead of stopping the run on his employees' cafeteria, he ordered it opened up to anyone who wanted to stop in there. This is an area that has had some serious economic problems over the last few years, and this entrepreneur is a compassionate person. D'Amico has been recognized by the Catholic Church for his charitable work in Dunbar. He employs over 400 people in the complex.

(For nearby attractions, see Trip 75 in Book 2.)

Pechin's Cafeteria   ☎ 724-277-4251
1 Pechin Road • Dunbar, Pennsylvania
Region: Out of state
Handicapped access: Yes, but steps in restrooms.

OHIO'S BEST

What can you say about Maisonette? It is simply, in many people's minds, the finest restaurant in Ohio.

It has earned Mobil's prestigious five-star-restaurant award for 34 straight years! Probably the longest run of excellence in America. Pricey? Yes. Elegant? Yes. Maisonette's French cuisine served in an impeccable way.

I have eaten there only one time, and I am not sure it was representative of their normal service. My wife, Bonnie, and I were guests of then-governor of Ohio George Voinovich and his wife, Janet. It was Bonnie's birthday. The service was outstanding, the food magnificent.

Let's face it, you just are bound to remember an occasion like that the rest of your life. I know that Maisonette is not a place that most of us will visit every Friday night. In fact, for many of us, it's the kind of place you reserve for those special times in life, a place to celebrate landmarks in time. They do it well. It's been said that the president of the United States couldn't drop in on a Saturday night without reservations. The same is true for the rest of us. It's that kind of place.

Just for fun we looked through a recent menu. Here are some items and prices: For an appetizer you can have a French black truffle, warm Yukon gold and purple potato salad in a golden crust, and radicchio salad for $18.50, or perhaps venison and duck terrine, prune and winter lentil salad, and barley, balsamic, and hazelnut dressing with pommery mustard at $12.50. For a main course, how about roasted Mediterranean dorade lobster béarnaise, vierge sauce, fondue of julienne vegetables, black trumpet mushrooms, and rice flan for $30?

You could have endive salad with warm goat cheese or escoffier salad (bib lettuce, artichokes, hearts of palm, and mustard vinaigrette dressing) for $8.95. As for vegetables, you could have asparagus with hollandaise or butter for $8.25.

That's just a small sample of the many things on the menu and doesn't take into consideration the extensive wine and dessert menus.

(For nearby attractions, see Trip 39 in Book 1.)

Maisonette　☎ 513-721-2260
114 East 6th Street　•　Cincinnati, Ohio
Region: Southwest Ohio (Hamilton County)
Handicapped access: Steps into building. Call ahead for ramp installation.

Maisonette

A CANTON CLASSIC

It was the smell of slowly cooking hams that led us to Kennedy's Barbecue in Canton. Located in a tiny building almost across the street from the magnificent William McKinley Memorial, Kennedy's is a freeze-frame of the late-1930s small "Mom-and-Pop" type of restaurant that once dotted the country. There is a short lunch counter and a few booths. Total seating capacity is just 33 persons. In truth little has changed since it first opened 77 years ago.

Charles "Jack" Kennedy first came here as a teenager in high school. The year was 1940. It was called the V and N Diner then, a favorite stop after an evening at nearby Meyer's Lake Amusement Park. Twenty years later, "Jack" Kennedy had an opportunity to buy the small restaurant that for the last 39 years has borne his name.

Kennedy believes in the theory, "if it ain't broken, don't fix it." That's why he has changed very little at this Canton landmark. The barbecue pit is still outside in the parking lot next to the restaurant. Passersby used to be able to look through the glass windows and see the succulent hams and sides of beef and fresh turkeys slowly turning over the coals. However, he had to brick up the windows a couple of years ago when local young people continually broke them out each night.

Meyer's Lake is now a memory, and this area of Canton is no longer the part of town the night owls come to, so Kennedy's is only open a few hours each day—from 10:30 in the morning until 2:30 in the afternoon, and only Monday through Friday.

It has a small menu, just fresh-cooked ham, pork, beef, or turkey sandwiches with Kennedy's special relish, made from mustard, cabbage, and some other things. Kennedy won't say exactly what, but he'll gladly sell you a pint or quart of the relish to take home with you. He also cooks homemade soup and chili and offers chips and freshly made fruit pies from nearby Amish country.

He does almost as much carryout business as he does sit-down trade. It's not uncommon to find people lined up out the door. You'll find factory workers sitting next to salesmen, and next to them may be executives from a nearby plant. You might even find a football great who is in town visiting the National Football Hall of Fame. They all want some of Jack Kennedy's famous barbecue and relish, and, perhaps, a few moments in a place from another time.

(For nearby attractions, see Trip 11 in Book 1.)

Kennedy's Barbecue   ☎ 330-454-0193
1420 7th Street • Canton, Ohio
Region: Northeast Ohio (Stark County)
Handicapped access: Steps into restaurant.

BEEF-ON-WECK

Beef-on-Weck is a Western New York delicacy that can be found in one or two chain restaurants in Ohio. But I say there is only one true Beef-on-Weck, and it is made by Charlie the Butcher in Buffalo, New York.

Charlie has been officially designated "Western New York Food Ambassador for New York State." He is the fourth generation of his family to work as a meat butcher in Buffalo, New York. He took the trade another step when he opened his first restaurant and started carving "Beef-on-Weck."

Okay, what is "Weck"? The original German recipe was for a bun called a "Kummelweck" roll. "Kummel" is German for caraway, and "Weck" is the German word for roll. "Weck" today is a roll made with caraway seeds and sea salt. Several slices of slow-cooked beef are piled on, and it's topped with a little au jus and a dollop of freshly ground horseradish. Charlie then dips the top of the roll in the au jus and places it atop the beef and horseradish. There it is. A taste experience that just shouts "Western New York." It's a wonderful sandwich, and the very best ones are made by Charlie the Butcher. Charlie has three locations in and around Buffalo, New York, serving lunch and dinner, and open seven days.

(For nearby attractions, see Trip 44 in Book 1, and Trips 77 and 78 in Book 2.)

Charlie the Butcher's Kitchen ☎ 716-633-8330
1065 Wehrle Drive and Cayuga • Williamsville, New York
Region: near Buffalo, New York
Handicapped access: Yes.

Charlie the Butcher's Sausagefest ☎ 716-893-4920
Broadway Market, 999 Broadway • Buffalo, New York
Region: Buffalo, New York
Handicapped access: Yes.

Charlie the Butcher's Express ☎ 716-855-8646 or 855-TOGO
Ellicott Square Lobby, 295 Main Street • Buffalo, New York
Region: Buffalo, New York
Handicapped access: Yes.

FOR THOSE WHO CAN'T DECIDE

Have you ever had the argument where one person says, "I want Mexican Food," and another member of the family pipes up with "No, I want German Food"? I think I have found the answer. If you are anywhere close to Northwest Ohio, drop by Fritz and Alfredo's, a wondrous mixture of both German and Mexican food. You can mix your wienerschnitzel with a grande burrito or have a bratwurst with a taco, you decide. The kitchen has cooks that can do either ethnic specialty. They have a bar here, and guess what? They serve both Bavarian and Mexican beer.

(For nearby attractions, see Trip 23 in Book 1.)

Fritz and Alfredo's ☎ 419-729-9775
3025 North Summit Street • Toledo, Ohio
Region: Northwest Ohio (Lucas County)
Handicapped access: Steps into building.

BREAKFAST IN A GRISTMILL

I know there are other restaurants located in gristmills in the country, but the breakfast that sets this place apart.

I've told the story of the Clifton Mill, one of the largest water-powered mills still operating. Their incredible display of Christmas lights was featured in my first book, *Neil Zurcher's Favorite One Tank Trips and Tales from the Road.* But I only touched lightly on the incredible breakfasts they serve here year round.

I first became aware of the place when my son-in-law, Ernest McCallister, of nearby Beaver Creek, was working part-time as the University of Dayton wrestling coach. For a workout he would have the team run from John Bryan Park to Clifton Mills, about two miles, and then stop for breakfast at the mill. He said even really hungry wrestlers couldn't eat all the food put before them at the Clifton Mill.

The extensive breakfast menu features products produced by the mill. They make whole wheat, buckwheat, buttermilk, cornmeal, and oat bran pancakes. You can also have blueberries, chocolate chips, and/or raisins added to your pancakes. These are not your everyday itty-bitty pancakes, this is a "Millrace Country Breakfast." The pancakes are as big as a dinner plate and are stacked three or four high, which presents an interesting problem: because the pancakes hang over the edge of the plate, there is no place to pour the warm homemade syrup that comes with them, or to let the mound of butter melt on top of the hotcakes. No matter how fast an eater you are, nature takes its course, and the syrup and melting butter ooze over the edge of the plate onto the table. Plus, on top of all this you might also have a rasher of bacon or some fresh sausage sitting uneasily atop your stack of pancakes. So, as the syrup begins to cascade off the plate onto the table, no matter how careful you are, you end up wearing it on your hands, wrists, and even elbows. Mill owner Tony Satariano told me that rarely does even the hungriest diner finish the entire plate of pancakes.

If dinner-plate-size pancakes are not for you, the mill also offers mush, homemade gravy, and sausage with fresh biscuits, and a huge three-egg omelet with cheese, tomato, or onion, along with thick-cut white, whole wheat, or cracked wheat toast. They also make their own oatmeal here, served with brown sugar and walnuts. Also, see if there is any of their oatmeal and maple pie left. It's a specialty of the house and is made fresh every day.

They not only offer food for the stomach, but food for the eyes—the view of the Little Miami River gorge just outside the dining room is beautiful every season of the year.

(For nearby attractions, see Trip 41 in Book 1.)

Clifton Mill ☎ 937-767-5501
75 Water Street • Clifton, Ohio
Region: Southwest Ohio (Greene County)
Handicapped access: Steps into mill.

A RESTAURANT WITH BIG BEEF AND NO ROOF

Owner John Shaheen Jr. says the name of his restaurant once was Rumour's Cafe, but they dropped the "cafe" when they added more room, and, well, it doesn't really matter just as long as you remember the "Rumours" part.

The place is as unusual as the name. For openers, if John has his way with the contractors, this may become the only cafe or restaurant in northern Ohio with a retractable dome roof over its patio. Then they can use it year round and open the room to moonlight or sunlight in nice weather. Right now he has space heaters all over the upper level of his patio to keep patrons warm and cozy, even when the temperature dips below the freezing mark.

But it's the food that really makes this place one of a kind. John runs a prime-rib special twice a week, offering "king- and queen-sized cuts." This is what brought us to this Canton restaurant. John's idea of "king-sized" is a cut that runs to almost a full pound and a half of meat.

The cut measures almost four to five inches thick! We watched first-time patrons order the prime rib and saw their reaction when the server plunked down a piece of meat that looked like it might have come from a Brontosaurus that wandered into the kitchen. One petite woman exclaimed that she would have enough left over to feed her son—and his two sons—at home for the next two days! The real surprise came when they cut into the meat and discovered it was tender enough to slice with a table knife.

Along with the meat comes a wonderful homemade rice pilaf or your choice of potato. As for salads, I would choose an optional Greek salad made with feta cheese. They offer a full-service bar and a coffee bar that can prepare every kind of coffee drink.

You may have to search to find this place tucked away in a strip shopping mall, but it will be worth it, especially if you are really hungry.

(For nearby attractions, see Trip 11 in Book 1.)

Rumours Restaurant ☎ 330-452-0442
725 30th Street, NE • Canton, Ohio
Region: Northeast Ohio (Stark County)
Handicapped access: Yes.

GOOD FOOD AND A TUBA MUSEUM

Where else in the world would you find a tuba museum in a restaurant? Or, for that matter, a restaurant inside a tuba museum? Here in Okenos, a suburb of Lansing, Michigan, you have both.

First, let's talk about the restaurant. It began in 1982 when Jennifer Brooke and William White—two people who had traveled the world and love to cook, especially ethnic foods—formed a partnership and bought a former ice-cream parlor. They decided to call their new restaurant the Travelers Club International and to serve the foods of countries from nearly every continent.

Their success is reflected in their menu. For breakfast you can order huevos rancheros, French toast, eggs fromage, or even vegetarian sausage patties. When lunch and dinner roll around, you can skip from country to country. They offer souvlaki, humus, and falafel. Or, if you don't feel like eating in the Middle East, how about the Mediterranean with some pasta served Corsican-, Romano- or Genoa-style? They also have stir-fry that reflects the many countries of Asia, billed as Indonesian peanut, teriyaki, or garlic black bean. Or try a vegetarian dish of fresh-mixed greens and vegetables, sautéed with sesame oil over brown rice. Let's not forget the quesadilla, wet burrito, and nachos grande on the menu.

They also offer "grazing platters" that combine the food of various countries. They may include sourdough batards broiled with basil-pesto garlic, sun-dried tomatoes, and red wine. There is a Middle Eastern platter that contains feta cheese, falafel, babaganouj, humus, tahini, and pita bread. For vegetarians, they offer a platter of fresh tomatoes, green pepper, sliced onions, Greek olives, pepperoncini, pickled turnips, feta cheese, and pita bread.

By the way, they have the original soda fountain, and they also offer beer and wine. The day I was visiting, it took me a full five minutes just to read all the pages of their menu and try to decide what combinations of food I wanted to have.

The kitchen seems to know what it is doing. The taste is authentic, and the portions are large. This is a college town, and the clientele is eclectic. You will find lots of students, some studying, and business people who come here when they want something different to eat. New recipes are constantly being added to the menu. Many of the herbs used in the cooking and the flowers on the tables come from the gardens surrounding the restaurant.

Traveler's Club International Restaurant and Tuba Museum

Now, about the tuba museum. That started with William White. He has played the tuba since he was a youngster, and in the early days of the restaurant, since they were working long hours, he would bring his tuba to work and practice when business was slow. He often would leave it in the restaurant to be available should a visiting tuba player drop by and want to play some duets. Workers in the restaurant would hang William's tuba on the wall when he wasn't playing it. Customers thought it was on display and one by one started bringing in old tubas to add to the wall.

William has also added to the collection himself. All of the dozens of huge horns on the walls of the restaurant are in playing condition. Some are quite rare, like the only known example of a double E-flat Helicon tuba, inscribed "the Majestic Monster." It originated in Austria.

According to William, the tuba dates back to ancient Roman times, when the Romans used a military signal trumpet made of bronze and about four feet long, with a detachable mouthpiece made from a bone. They called the instrument a tuba. Through time the horn was reshaped and renamed probably a thousand times before it assumed its present role in the brass section of the orchestra and band.

William says tuba players from all over the country drive hundreds of miles out of their way to stop at his restaurant and tuba museum for lunch.

Worldwide cuisine and an unusual museum all rolled into one, just next door in Michigan. Open seven days a week.

(For nearby attractions, see Trip 71 in Book 2.)

Travelers Club International Restaurant and Tuba Museum ☎517-349-1701
2138 Hamilton Road • Okenos, Michigan
Region: greater Lansing, Michigan area
Handicapped access: Yes.

IF YOU ARE FOND OF FONDUE

If you are older than 35 you might remember the fondue craze of the 1960s. It just seemed like the most popular gift for a wedding was a fondue pot and a set of matching forks. Every party you went to in those days had the ubiquitous little pot bubbling over a lighted candle on the serving table, usually with an orange mixture of some kind of cheese and a stack of stale bread cubes sitting nearby to be speared and dipped in the cheese pot and then nibbled on while trying to balance a drink and an hors d'oeuvres plate, and attempting not to drip any of the hot melted cheese on your new dress or shirt. Sounds like fun, huh?

Well, as time went on and people became more concerned about things like cholesterol, the fondue pots started appearing in flea markets and secondhand stores; I know of one that was converted into a flowerpot.

So I was surprised one day to hear from the good folks at Potpourri Fondue Restaurant in Mentor, telling me that good fondue never went away and in fact had kept up with the times as they included low-fat items in their menu.

The Potpourri Fondue Restaurant is believed to be the only restaurant in northern Ohio, and one of only a handful in the United States, specializing in fondue. The first thing I learned is that fondue isn't exactly what it used to be.

Where cheese was the main ingredient used with the pot and stickers before, today the cooking pot may hold oil, or chicken broth for those concerned about fat intake. The bread cubes have been supplanted by cut-up pieces of shrimp, beef, pork, potatoes, turnips, beets, you name it, and you can cook them right at your table.

And that is the beauty of fondue cooking. You do the cooking at tableside, and you determine just how done you want your meat or vegetables. No more cool bites of beef roast left sitting too long while the cook waited for your dining partner's food to be done. You are the chef here.

And where you would only use one pot before, now you might use two or three different pots filled with different things to cook, or to coat your food with—like chocolate melted to a liquid consistency so you can dip bits of marshmallow, apple, strawberries, or even cake into the pot for a sweet dessert. And guess what, they still offer a pot filled with premium cheeses for those who want to remember the '60s. It's a fun way to eat out. You do the cooking; you decide what you will cook and when the food is cooked to your satisfaction. My only complaint is that they are open only for dinner, no lunches or breakfast.

(For nearby attractions, see Trip 13 in Book 1.)

Potpourri Fondue Restaurant   ☎ 440-255-4334
8885 Mentor Avenue • Mentor, Ohio
Region: Northeast Ohio (Cuyahoga County)
Handicapped access: Yes.

THE FLYING TURTLE

Lahm Airport in Mansfield, Ohio, has found a good use for its old, unwanted air terminal. It has become a full-service restaurant with the intriguing name "The Flying Turtle." What makes it special, beyond the name, is the location—right on the edge of one of the longest runways in Ohio, where, if you wait long enough, you will see some of the biggest airplanes in the world landing and taking off.

Already this year, a Russian transport plane said to be the second-largest in the world landed here to deliver a package to the John Glenn NASA Space Center in Cleveland. The next-door neighbor here is the Ohio Air National Guard; the C-130 Hercules in their fleet are usually coming or going. Combine this with an active general-aviation fleet, and there is always some activity to watch while having your breakfast, lunch, or dinner. You get to rub elbows with many of the pilots, some of whom fly out of their way to stop here and eat.

The Flying Turtle has an eclectic menu, everything from sandwich roll-ups, to soups and salads, to meatloaf. They also offer full dinner specials every day. It's all prepared from scratch in the restaurant kitchen, and the quality and quantity of the food keep customers coming back.

By the way, for those on sugar-free diets they offer more than the obligatory diet cola and iced tea. They also have a good assortment of flavors in Crystal Light available.

This is a great place to bring the kids, or anyone who loves to watch airplanes.

(For nearby attractions, see Trip 59 in Book 2.)

The Flying Turtle Restaurant ☎ 419-524-2404
2100 Harrington Memorial Road • Mansfield, Ohio
Region: Northeast Ohio (Richland County)
Handicapped access: Yes.

OHIO'S ONLY TRUE CASTLE

We have touched on this place in another chapter (see Tearoom chapter), but certainly Ravenwood Castle deserves to be listed again in this section. The owners, Sue and Jim Maxwell, used to own a large bed-and-breakfast in Circleville. When they sold that they built a real castle. They traveled to Scotland and looked at several castles, borrowing ideas from the best of them, then came back and sat down with an architect to design Ravenwood Castle.

The result of several years of work and planning today dominates a forested hilltop in Ohio's beautiful Hocking Hills area. The castle and its outbuildings, which include medieval-looking cottages, sit amidst 50 acres of forested hills. The rooms in the castle and cottages all have private baths and antique furnishings and make you feel as though you really are staying in a castle. The great room will take you back to the days of King Arthur, with its oversized fruitier, stained-glass windows, and gigantic fireplace at one end of the room. There's a suit of armor standing guard in the hall—and even a mock drawbridge to the front door!

Since they are a good distance from any towns or villages, they also offer dinners (even some special-occasion medieval dinners) by reservation to their guests and visitors. Here's a sample menu from a medieval dinner they served their friends on "New Year's Eve, 1066."

> Pease Porridge
> Hearty Brown Breads
> Fysshe Pye with Mushrooms
> Roast Boare
> Roasted Root Vegetables (spiced parsnips, rutabagas, and
>   carrots)
> Braised Caboches with Mace
> Gingerbread with Lemon Curd

On a more regular basis, this is what regular guests at the Castle could expect on a Saturday night:

> Leek and Potato Soup
> Homemade Butter Crescent Rolls
> Rock Cornish Game Hen with Fruit Stuffing and Mar-
>   malade Glaze
> Herb Roasted Potatoes

Fresh Seasonal Vegetables
Bread Pudding with Caramel Sauce
While dinners are extra, a full breakfast comes with your room when
you stay at the Ravenwood Castle.
(For nearby attractions, see Trip 55 in Book 2.)

Ravenwood Castle   ☎ 614-596-2606
65666 Bethel Road • New Plymouth, Ohio
Region: Southeast Ohio (Hocking County)
Handicapped access: Yes.

NOTHING BEATS PIE

If I had my way we would all have "birthday pies" instead of "birthday
cakes." I like pie, any kind of pie—be it fruit or cream. I have real affection
for banana cream pie, but I would be hard-pressed to choose between a
cool banana cream, and a hot peach pie, fresh from the oven. When it
comes to berry pies, I don't care what kind they are—elderberry, black-
berry, red raspberry—I love them all. I have even enjoyed mulberry pie.
My wife makes a pie called "better than sex pie." Now, I don't necessarily
agree with the name of the dish, but I must admit that there might be a
time in my life when I would not want to choose between sex and this pie.
It is that good. It consists of a chocolate cream pie filling, blended with
cream cheese, topped with whipped cream and shaved milk chocolate, in
a fresh, flaky crust, with chocolate syrup drizzled over the whole thing.
Ambrosia!

I digress. In my travels I have found several places that make pies so
good, I want to peek in the kitchen to see if my wife is secretly working
there. Mama Jo's pies, made in Amherst, Ohio, is such a place. The pies,
which are commercially made in huge ovens, still retain the flavor of the
family kitchen. Her deep dish apple pie always contains four to five
pounds of apples! When you pick up one of these pies, you know you have
a real treat coming. While Mama Jo's pies are sold in many stores in northern Ohio, I still think you can't beat one fresh from the oven at their bakery in Amherst.

(For nearby attractions, see Trip 58 in Book 2.)

Mama Jo's Pies   ☎ 440-960-PIES
1969 Cooper-Foster-Park Road • Amherst, Ohio
Region: Northeast Ohio (Lorain County)
Handicapped access: Yes.

94 Barberton Chicken and More

I like local dishes. I especially like the stories behind them. Take Barberton Chicken, for example. There's no secret recipe. It's just large hunks of fresh chicken, been deep-fried in pure oil until golden brown. Usually no special spices are added—just some salt and pepper, and very little of that. The real secret to Barberton Chicken is not in the chicken, but in the hot rice that accompanies it.

Barberton Chicken, most folks in Barberton agree, got its start back in the 1930s at a restaurant called the Belgrade Gardens. Dale Milich says his mother was working for a Serbian family by the name of Topalsky in 1935 when they bought the first small tavern that would become the Belgrade Gardens Restaurant. They introduced their customers to a chicken-and-rice dish that was Serbian in origin, with a few new ingredients.

Dale says the reason this chicken stands out is that real Barberton Chicken is always made with fresh—never frozen—chicken, and all the ingredients for the dishes that go with it are made as much as possible from scratch. For example, fresh—not frozen—potatoes are used in the French fries, and the sauce, well, that's still a closely held secret at each restaurant that has developed its own variation on the meal. But it's essentially the dish we all ate in public school called Spanish rice. At least, that's what it looks like. It's a tomato sauce base with herbs and other ingredients poured over white rice. Some make it spicier than others, but it doesn't rival real Spanish rice for heat. "The secret," according to Dale Milich, "is the taste. It just tastes like chicken should taste. There are no other spices or other ingredients to take away from the true chicken flavor." Dale should know: his family has been associated with just about every restaurant in the Barberton area that sells true Barberton Chicken. He speaks highly of his competition. "We all use the same fresh chicken and ingredients," he says. "That's why there isn't too much difference in the taste between restaurants." But what about the sauce? Ah, well there is a difference there.

Each restaurant has its own combination of spices and condiments used to flavor the rice. Today there are at least half a dozen restaurants in the Barberton-Norton-Cuyahoga Falls area that serve "authentic" Barberton Chicken. Some people tell me they have tried all of them, just to compare the different hot sauces. Now that sounds like a real fun project for a family.

Barberton Chicken is served at these locations:
(For nearby attractions, see Trip 14 in Book 1.)

Belgrade Gardens   ☎ 330-745-0113
401 East State Street • Barberton, Ohio
Region: Northeast Ohio (Summit County)
Handicapped access: Yes.

Belgrade Gardens (additional location)   ☎ 330-896-3396
3476 Massillon Road • Uniontown, Ohio
Region: Northeast Ohio (Stark County)
Handicapped access: Yes.

Whitehouse Chicken   ☎ (330) 745-0449
180 Wooster Road, North • Barberton, Ohio
Region: Northeast Ohio (Summit County)
Handicapped access: Yes.

Hopocan Gardens   ☎ (330)825-9923
4396 Hopocan Avenue, Ext. • Barberton, Ohio
Region: Northeast Ohio (Summit County)
Handicapped access: Yes.

Hoppy's   ☎ (330) 945-6555
1948 Portage Trail • Cuyahoga Falls, Ohio
Region: Northeast Ohio (Summit County)
Handicapped access: Yes.

Milich Village Inn   ☎ (330) 825-4553
4444 South Cleveland-Massillon Road • Barberton, Ohio 44203
Region: Northeast Ohio (Summit County)
Handicapped access: Yes.

WAYNE COUNTY CHICKEN

While we're on the subject of chicken, there's this place in Wayne County called Smithville that deserves mentioning. To begin with, the Smithville Inn is not some "Johnny-come-lately" when it comes to the chicken business. The Inn stood on State Route 585 before the road had a name. Back in 1818 it was a stagecoach stop between Old Portage (Akron) and Wooster. Passengers would often stop for a chicken dinner and sometimes spend the night. They say that President William McKinley once stopped by for dinner.

It was in 1929 that the Smithville Inn really started building a reputation. Paul and Sevilla Reining bought the old inn and started a tradition of always featuring chicken on the menu. The noodles that Mrs. Reining made to serve with the chicken were hung to dry on the second level of the back dining room. Those handmade noodles were the beginning of a company that today produces "Inn Made Noodles," which are sold all over the country and are still on the menu at the Inn today. A lot of people, plain and famous, from jazz musician Louis Armstrong to former president Franklin Delano Roosevelt, have dined on chicken here at the Smithville Inn.

The current owners, Mr. and Mrs. Rick Hammond, continue the long tradition of chicken dinners made with fresh—never frozen—chicken and served with fresh-baked, hot rolls and homemade apple butter, along with rich mashed potatoes. It's an all-you-can-eat, family-style dinner. My favorite is their "hot or cold fruit plate," which features hot chicken, cold chicken, or chicken salad as the main item, along with a heaping portion of fresh, seasonal fruit. It's a meal and a half even for a big eater. It also comes with a dish of fresh orange or pineapple sherbet to help it all go down. Another favorite is creamed chicken over their homemade, fresh, hot biscuits. You get lots of big chunks of chicken, peas, and gravy over the biscuits and a heaping serving of mashed potatoes. They also have chicken and dumplings.

Their homemade pies are worthy of mention. Depending on season, they always have a good assortment with specialties like peach and sour cream cobbler pie. It's always something different. Open six days a week, they are closed on Mondays.

(For nearby attractions, see Trip 28 in Book 1.)

Smithville Inn   ☎ 330-669-2641
109 West Main Street • Smithville, Ohio
Region: Northeast Ohio (Wayne County)
Handicapped access: Yes.

Smithville Inn

95 Buffalo and Ostrich

Among the more exotic things we have found on the dinner table in recent years have been buffalo (American bison) meat and ostrich. If you haven't tried it, don't knock it. I have had several opportunities to try both and have grown to prefer bison over beef for taste, aside from its health benefits. As for ostrich, well, let's just say I'm still deciding. I have had it prepared several ways that were very tasty, but I have had a couple dishes with large chunks of ostrich that were pretty tough. I ate it, telling myself that is the price you pay for healthy foods. However, I have since been told that cooked properly, ostrich can be just as tender as beef or pork.

Both meats are really much more healthy for all of us than the traditional beef, pork, and chicken. For example: a 100-gram serving of ostrich will have 1.2 grams of fat and about 111 calories. Compare that to a similar serving of beef: 9.28 grams of fat and 211 calories. Pork weighs in at 9.66 grams of fat and 212 calories, and even chicken has 7.41 grams of fat and 190 calories. Buffalo also weighs in on the healthy side. A 100-gram serving contains 2.42 grams of fat and 143 calories. In this health-conscious time, as people try to eat more healthy meals, both meats are being found in more and more specialty and gourmet shops.

But while both meats are enjoying a modest boom, many restaurants still haven't started adding them to their menus. That means you have to go out and look for restaurants that do serve them, or buy the meat from a dealer and do the cooking yourself. Here are a couple I have found.

BUFFALO ON THE MENU

Canton has a good neighborhood restaurant that has been serving bison for years. The Hideaway Restaurant and Lounge not only offers buffalo burgers, they always have buffalo on the menu in buffalo chili, buffalo stew, or buffalo steak. *(For nearby attractions, see Trip 11, book 1.)*

Hideaway Restaurant and Lounge   ☎ 330-452-4278
4021 Mahoning Road • Canton, Ohio
Region: Northeast Ohio (Stark County)
Handicapped access: Yes.

ARE YOU GAME FOR EXOTIC MEAT?

If you want to sample exotic meats in a place that is a bit more upscale, try the Gamekeeper's restaurants, with several locations around Cleveland. Gamekeeper's often has bison on the menu, and they also feature ostrich and sometimes other exotic meats like elk and venison. I have eaten both meats here, and they are always prepared very well *(For nearby attractions, see Trip 9 in Book 1.).*

Bass Lake Inn and Taverne   ☎ 440-285-3100
400 South Street • Chardon, Ohio
Region: Northeast Ohio (Geauga County)
Handicapped access: Yes, rear entrance (restrooms not handicapped accessible)

Gamekeeper's Lodge   ☎ 440-333-8505
19300 Detroit Avenue • Rocky River, Ohio
Region: Northeast Ohio (Cuyahoga County)
Handicapped access: Yes.

Gamekeeper's Taverne   ☎ 440-247-7744
87 West Street • Chagrin Falls, Ohio
Region: Northeast Ohio (Cuyahoga County)
Handicapped access: Yes.

ON THE HOOF

Now, if you want to buy your ostrich meat "on the hoof," or one step removed from the hoof, here's a place where you can. I have sampled their products and enjoyed them. And I don't know too many people who would want to "process" a live, seven-foot-tall ostrich or a 2,000-pound buffalo, so it's best to leave that up to these professionals.

One of the larger ostrich farms is located in Sugarcreek, Ohio. They offer tours so you can see how the ostriches are raised, from eggs all the way up to seven-foot-tall adults that are sold for breeding and for their meat. There is a store here where they sell frozen ostrich meat, as well as products made from the hide and feathers. It is also home to a beautiful bed-and-breakfast, located above the ostrich product store.

(For nearby attractions, see Trip 33 in Book 1.)

Willow Springs Ostrich Farm   ☎ 330-897-1019
5453 Evans Creek Road, SW • Sugarcreek, Ohio
Region: Northeast Ohio (Tuscarawas County)
Handicapped access: Yes.

96 Chili

Chili con carne. It warms the heart and the stomach. And it heats up a few arguments.

To claim that you make the very best chili is to open a Pandora's box. Everyone has an opinion about just where and how the best chili is made. There is the argument about beans. Some "aficionados" say real chili does not have beans. Then there is the other camp that says chili just isn't chili unless it is positively swimming in two to three different kinds of beans. And let's not forget "Cincinnati Chili," a sort of hybrid between chili and spaghetti sauce with a little cinnamon powder mixed in, which is poured over spaghetti or noodles.

How did chili originate? There is a lot of arguing by historians. Most agree that it probably grew naturally from the original practice of stewing various cuts of meat with chili peppers for flavor and as a way to preserve the meat in the hot areas of Central America. It's also believed that tomatoes were later added to give it flavor and consistency, and seasoning was used to disguise the flavor of rancid meat when diners had been on the trail too long and had no fresh meat. Chili entered the United States via Mexico, Texas, and the southwestern states. Beans were added later as a way to stretch the protein when there was only a small amount of meat available.

My first lesson about this dish was taught to me by my father many years ago, when he operated a small country store that served as gasoline station, grocery store for the community, and all-night truck stop for hungry drivers. He always had a big pot of chili cooking on the back of the stove. In fact, I cannot ever remember the pot being empty; also, for the life of me, I cannot remember the recipe. All I recall is that he would toss in things like a cup of coffee grounds, apple cider, and onions fresh from the garden once in a while. When the contents dipped below a certain spot on the pot's chili-encrusted innards, we would also dump in tomato soup, kidney beans, and a couple of pounds of hamburger, and add pepper until someone sneezed—preferably not into the pot. I suspect some other things got into the chili unexpectedly. For one thing, my father's ever-present cigarette was known to occasionally drop its ashes into the chili. Also, being a teenager at the time, when I was called on to refill the chili pot, I might have just come in the door from changing the oil in a car, and didn't take time to wash my hands before I scooped up a couple of handfuls of fresh ground meat to throw into the chili. I am also sure that on extremely hot summer nights when we would stir the chili with a large spoon, the perspiration from our foreheads would drip into the kettle. But the chili was our number-one best seller. In fact my father called it "never-ending chili." It never won any awards, but we sold barrels of it during the years we operated the little country store/truck stop/restaurant.

In spite of this—or maybe because of it—I have never exactly been crazy about chili. Oh, I have eaten it when I have been cold, or very hungry, but it is still low on my list of favorite foods. I've sampled the stuff from the chain burger places, and I have even tried several versions of Cincinnati Chili, three-way, four-way, and even five-way. I just didn't like it. But all that changed one wintry day a year or two ago when we stopped at a small diner near Marblehead, Ohio, and met Ken Kostal.

Ken is a man who takes chili seriously. So seriously, in fact, that he has won awards for his chili—so many that the contests have asked him to become a judge instead of a contestant, to give other restaurants a chance at winning. Just for the record Ken has won, among many other awards, first place in a nationwide competition in West Virginia and top honors in a Cleveland chili cook-off. His restaurant, called "Big Boppers," is in Marblehead, Ohio, on Lake Erie. It is here that he practices his craft.

"Chili, real chili," Ken Kostal says, "should never have beans in it. It should be a wedding of ground meat and seasonings. No beans." However, he admits, he does offer his chili with beans as a concession to those who grew up on the "imitation chili" made with kidney beans. He makes his beanless chili fresh each day in a crowded kitchen in his small Marblehead restaurant. He starts early in the morning because it takes about two and a half hours of cooking to reach the peak of flavor that makes his chili a champion. "If you don't cook it long enough," Ken says, "the chili doesn't absorb all the seasoning, and it just isn't quite right." What's in Ken's chili? Well, he's not about to give away his secret recipe; he says you would have to buy his restaurant to get that. He does admit that it's in the seasoning. He says he has used ground turkey and ground beef, but it doesn't make much difference in the taste. He prefers to use just plain old hamburger, no special blend. He also divulged that it's best when cooked in small batches. Ken serves chili on just about everything: eggs, hot dogs, cheeseburgers— he's even considering serving it on pancakes! He cooks only about three gallons each day. When it's gone, it's gone.

(For nearby attractions, see Trip 21 in Book 1.)

Big Bopper's Restaurant ☎ 419-734-4458
7581 East Harbor Road • Marblehead, Ohio
Region: Northwest Ohio (Ottawa County)
Handicapped access: No, steps into restaurant, narrow doorways.

Big Bopper's Restaurant

THE BEST CHILI IN TWO COUNTIES

Holmes County, home of the largest Amish population in the nation, is not known for spicy food. Amish food is relatively bland meat-and-potatoes fare. So when there was a chili contest in Wayne and Holmes counties, some of the big-city chili makers sort of laughed up their sleeves, expecting little competition from those local restaurants that serve all that fried chicken and roast beef. Well, they had not met the folks from the Berlin Cafe. They are not newcomers—some of them can trace their Holmes County ancestry back four or five generations. And, yes, they have grown up on plain meat-and-potatoes kinds of food. But somewhere they picked up a recipe for chili that knocked the socks off the judges at a recent Wayne-Holmes County Chili Cook-off, and they walked away with the "Favorite" and "Most Unique" titles. They serve their chili every day in the Berlin Cafe. They make just a gallon or two a day. It's chili with a mild bite. Not too hot, not too mild. A just-right, peppery mix that has about as much meat as beans in the mixture. They won't say just what spices or combinations of sauces they use. It's a secret, of course, but they do admit that instead of beef they use ground-up turkey in the chili. After sampling some, at first I thought they were kidding when they said the meat was turkey, not beef. I couldn't tell the difference. Right now the chili is only available at lunch and dinnertime at the Cafe, but hopefully they will soon add it to their breakfast menu, too. It would go great over eggs, or in a breakfast burrito.

Now, I don't mean to imply that all they make at Berlin Cafe is chili. Though it is located in the absolute heart of Ohio's Amish country, they decided to follow a different path when it came to their menu. Instead of heavy meat-and-potato dishes, they have lots of quiche, light, healthy salads, and all kinds of wondrous coffee drinks. They are also renowned locally for their chicken and tuna salad sandwiches. One novelty: they offer two peanut butter and jelly sandwiches. There's one for kids that is strictly PB&J, but they also offer an "adult version" that has peanut butter, jelly, bean sprouts, and fresh bib lettuce on homemade wheat bread, and it's served with fresh fruit. It was surprisingly tasty. (I thought it could have used more alfalfa sprouts, but then I am not a PB&J connoisseur.) For dessert they have a lot of fresh-baked pastry that comes from local kitchens, and the day I visited, strawberries had just ripened in a local farmer's field, and they were serving fresh, homemade strawberry shortcake, with real fresh-whipped cream on top. They try to have local seasonal fruit on the menu whenever possible.

Local folks eat here, as well as some of the tourists who have grown tired of the meat-and-potatoes routine at the big restaurants around Holmes, Wayne, and Tuscarawas counties. But whatever you order, try the chili.

(For nearby attractions, see Trip 28 in Book 1, and Trips 56 and 61 in Book 2.)

Berlin Cafe   ☎ 330-893-3835
4860 Main Street • Berlin, Ohio
Region: Northeast Ohio (Holmes County)
Handicapped access: Yes.

ABOUT CINCINNATI CHILI

There are some chili lovers who insist that it's not really chili, only spaghetti sauce that isn't real sure about its parentage. But the folks from the Queen City love their chili. An entire restaurant industry in that city has been built around it. Skyline and Gold Star are the two biggest chains, but a handful of other restaurants also make their own version of the chili. Cincinnati Chili comes a whole bunch of different ways. There's two-way, three-way, four-way, and probably a couple of other ways that I have not heard about. It starts out with basic chili poured over spaghetti. To make it a two-way, three-way, or four-way, they add fresh-cut onions, shredded cheese, and even sour cream. If you're ever in Cincinnati, or the many other towns in Ohio where some of the chili chains hang out, try it. Perhaps you will like it better than I did. I think it's an acquired taste. Some of the best I tried was at a place in Blue Ash (someday I have to stop and find out how that town got that name!), a suburb of Cincinnati. They make it just about every way it can be made.

(For nearby attractions, see Trip 39 in Book 1.)

Blue Ash Chili   ☎ 513-984-6107
9565 Kenwood Road • Blue Ash, Ohio
Region: Southwest Ohio (Hamilton County)
Handicapped access: Yes.

KEVIN RUIC AND CHILI

I have been accused of having some really strange friends. I don't think they are strange, but other people say that some of my friends are, well, different.

Take Kevin Ruic, for example. I first wrote about him in my second book, *More One Tank Trips*. Kevin is a man who loves practical jokes. I honestly believe if he were offered a million dollars or the opportunity to participate in the biggest practical joke in the world, he would take the joke. At least until his wife, Cindy, found out about it.

For example, Kevin, like me, loves flea markets and garage sales. He is always looking for that "special thing" he cannot live without. Recently at a flea market, he spotted a long white cane with a red tip on it. Obviously it had once belonged to a blind person. Kevin bought the cane, not really sure what he was going to do with it.

That afternoon as he was driving through Lakewood, a suburb of Cleveland, he noticed his gasoline gauge was showing empty, so he began to look for a gas station. Then inspiration hit him. He reached into the glove compartment, took out a pair of sunglasses, and put them on. Pulling the cane into the front seat, he drove on until he saw a service station with several young people milling around outside.

He pulled into the service station, swerved widely, narrowly missing the gasoline pumps, and stopped. The rear end of his car was about six feet away from the pump. With dark glasses in place he opened the door and, by tapping the cane on the sidewalk, started to feel his way to the gas pump. Through his dark glasses he watched as one teenager whispered to another and pointed at him. He had been alone in the car, he was obviously blind, and he was pumping gas into his car.

When the pump stopped and the tank was full he walked, tapping his cane and feeling his way, to the door of the service station, where the teenagers were all watching.

"Is anybody here?" he shouted into the face of the teenage attendant.

The teenager reeled back, saying "Yes. Yes, I'm right here, right in front of you."

"Oh, sorry," Kevin said, "I thought I heard someone, but didn't realize you were so close."

As he handed over the money for the gasoline, he asked the attendant, "Can you tell me where 182nd and Detroit is?" knowing it was just two blocks away.

The youngster pointed to the left and said, "It's just two blocks that way."

"I assume you're pointing in some direction," Kevin said. "Remember, I'm blind, tell me which direction, right or left?"

"Oh, uhm . . . yeah," the teenager replied, "it's two blocks to your right."

"Okay," said Kevin. "Can you tell me, are there any cars parked on the left side of the street?"

The youngster looked over Kevin's shoulder toward the empty street.

"No, no," he replied, "there are no cars on the left-hand side of the street."

"Okay," Kevin said. "If I turn to the right and go in a straight line would that put me back on the street?"

The attendant, looking very serious, walked around the other side of Kevin, turned slowly to the right, and peered in a straight line.

"Yeah," he said, "I guess so."

"Thanks very much," Kevin said and turned, tapping his cane in front of him as he felt his way back to the car, and striking the car with the cane a couple of times as he tried to find the door.

As he started up the car, in the rearview mirror he could see the attendant run inside the gas station and call the mechanics out to witness a blind man who was about to drive off.

With a small crowd watching, Kevin put the car in gear and peeled the tires as he shot out into the street, making a wide curve from curb to curb. In the mirror he could see five or six people at the service station standing and pointing with their mouths hanging open.

Kevin told me later, "I would have loved to know how they tried to convince their parents what they had seen that afternoon."

Kevin heard that I was writing this book and wanted to know if I was going to have anything about chili. He said that besides writing up the guy who wins all the chili-making contests, I should also take a look at a restaurant that makes wonderful chili but just can't seem to win a contest. I responded that probably the reason the restaurant didn't win any awards is that the chili just wasn't good enough.

He insisted that me and my wife, Bonnie, join him and his wife, Cindy, for dinner at the restaurant he was talking about.

We sat down to heaping bowls of a fiery chili covered with fresh green onions and grated cheddar cheese and sour cream. As much as I hate to admit it, he was right. It was delicious. It had the right mix of beans and meat, with a dark, dark chili sauce that had just enough bite to make it interesting but was easily cooled by the sour cream and onions. The restaurant is Stamper's Grill Pub in Fairview Park. The owner told us that the chili is called "Lester's Chili." He didn't explain who Lester was, but he said the chili is a mix of Southwestern and Western chili recipes. And, yes, he did admit that he had entered one of those chili contests and lost, but he said it hasn't dampened his customers' enthusiasm. And chili made Lester's way is still on the menu. Having tasted it, I think they deserve a recount. It's that good.

(For nearby attractions, see Trips 5, 15, and 16 in Book 1.)

Stamper's Grill Pub   ☎ 440-333-7826
21750 Lorain Road   •   Fairview Park, Ohio
Region: Northeast Ohio (Cuyahoga County)
Handicapped access: Yes, but restrooms are tight.

97 Perch and Walleye Sandwiches and Dinners

A week doesn't go by that I don't get a call from some viewer complaining that there are no good places to get a real Lake Erie shore dinner. They usually start out about the last time they were on the East Coast, and all up and down the coastal highways there were these quaint little shacks that fishermen would run where they would fix you some fresh-caught crabs or lobsters, and you would sit at a picnic table, the salt spray from the ocean in your face, butter dribbling down your chin as you scarfed down a two-pound freshly caught lobster, or whatever. Oh, and it only cost two dollars.

Now, there may have once been places like that along the Lake Erie shore. But first, I don't think too many fishermen are going to sell their catch that cheap today, and second, I don't think the Ohio Department of Health would smile on such a setup—cooking up leftover catch and selling to passersby. Having said all that, I have to admit there are some places I have stopped over the years that come very close to that description, and they are still serving some of the best fresh-caught Lake Erie perch and walleye that you could hope for.

One of my personal favorites is directly across Lake Erie from Cleveland. The tiny fishing village of Erie Au, Ontario, Canada, has a wintertime population of probably fewer than 500 people. The main industry here is the fish-processing plant, the place at the end of the dock where all the big commercial fishing boats head at the end of the day. They only have to bring the fresh fish about a city block to the kitchen at Molly and OJ's. And that is what they do. The restaurant sits just about on the beach; it's a combination tavern and restaurant. They even have entertainment on the weekend. Molly and OJ's has been a fixture in this town for years, and Canadians and Americans flock here for some of the freshest perch and pickerel you will find on Lake Erie. They cook it a half-dozen different ways. The last time we were in for an evening dinner we had perch, one fixed with lemon pepper and another Cajun-style. Both were delicious. They sell the perch by itself, or in seafood platters where you get a little of everything. The best part about eating here, besides the fresh fish and nice people, is that it's in Canada, and that means U.S. citizens get a real price break. A Canadian price of $7.95 for a three-piece plate of perch works out in U.S. funds to around five dollars, depending on the exchange rate that day. If you have someone along who doesn't like Lake Erie perch, not to worry, they do decent steaks and ribs here also. What can I say? Drive around the lake, fly across it, or take your boat and head north for Erie Au, Canada, eh, and a great shore dinner.

(For nearby attractions, see Trip 84 in Book 2.)

Molly and OJ's   ☎ 519-676-8812
875 Mariners Road · Erie Au, Ontario, Canada
Region: Southern Ontario
Handicapped access: Yes

FISH FAST FOOD

There are a couple of places closer to home that I have enjoyed over the years. Both are like fast-food restaurants and specialize in fish. Both have connections with a local commercial fisherman and, at least in the summer, usually have fresh, not frozen, perch on the menu. Neither place is fancy, just a counter where you walk up and order your fish and then pick it up when your order is ready.

A recent discovery I made was the Jolly Roger Restaurant along Route 250 in Sandusky. This is a branch of the Jolly Roger that has been operating in Port Clinton for years and has long had a reputation for serving well-prepared fresh fish. The new place is bright and clean, and you can see right into the kitchen where they fillet the fish and bread them. Service is on paper and plastic plates. They also offer very good hand-battered onion rings that go well with the fish.

(For nearby attractions, see Trip 18 in Book 1, and Trips 48 and 66 in Book 2.)

Jolly Roger Restaurant   ☎ 419-625-4240
3307 Milan Road · Sandusky, Ohio
Region: Northeast Ohio (Erie County)
Handicapped access: Yes

Jolly Roger Seafood House   ☎ 419-732-3382
1737 East Perry Street · Port Clinton, Ohio
Region: Northeast Ohio (Ottawa County)
Handicapped access: Yes

MORE FISH FAST FOOD

The other place we like has become a Sandusky fixture. At noon, people line up outside in their cars at the drive-up window, while other customers are lined up at the counter inside. Again, it's fresh perch and walleye that are featured. Also they offer homemade turtle soup that I thought was wonderful. DeMore's Fish Den lives up to its name.

(For nearby attractions, see Trip 18 in Book 1, and Trips 48 and 66 in Book 2.)

DeMore's Fish Den   ☎ 419-626-8861
302 West Perkins Avenue • Sandusky, Ohio
Region: Northeast Ohio (Erie County)
Handicapped access: Yes.

OUT ON THE ISLANDS

I had a wonderful perch sandwich on Kelleys Island at the Village Pump. It's not very fancy, and it sometimes gets overlooked because of the neighboring, better-known restaurants. The perch was lightly breaded and very fresh. It was piled on a Kaiser roll with slices of fresh tomato and Bermuda onion (open-faced, so you can use it or not), and served with a large plate of French fries. It was actually more than I could eat. Chris Reece, Fox 8 photographer, had the walleye, and he proclaimed it to be excellent as well. The friendly staff (just about everyone on the island seems to be friendly) and quick service were a decided plus here. The Village Pump is open late in the season, but not year round.

(For nearby attractions, see Trip 19 in Book 1, and Trip 63 in Book 2.)

The Village Pump   ☎ 419-746-2281
117 W. Lake Shore • Kelleys Island, Ohio
Region: Northeast Ohio (Erie County)
Handicapped access: Yes.

PERCH DINNERS OUT EAST

Brennan's Fish House in Grand River has been around since 1974 and has gained a wide following of local folks and tourists who come to the Grand River area to go fishing. Many fishing enthusiasts who have returned to the dock without getting even a nibble head over to Brennan's to at least have a taste of what they missed.

Perch and walleye are always on the menu, but they do not list the price, they only say "market price." On my last visit I was served a heaping portion of fresh perch fillets, along with Brennan's famous "hand cut, greasy French fries." (They note on the menu that if you don't like greasy fries, they also offer mashed and baked potatoes.) It was more than I could eat at a lunchtime meal. "Market price" that day turned out to be $12.95.

On this and a previous visit, at the height of their noon rush, I found the fish to be a bit overcooked. Also, if you want separate checks, make sure the busy servers understand you. On two visits we have had delays while the server had to go back and refigure separate checks for our group, even though we had asked for them when we ordered. They apparently do not like to take the time to do separate checks; their menu notes that they will not write them for parties of six or more. (There were only two of us at our table.)

On the positive side, we marveled at the pace set by some of the servers. Even though they were very busy, our order was taken shortly after we sat down, and our food was in front of us in just a matter of minutes, fresh and hot. They also offer carryout for those fishermen and fisherwomen, who want to eat their fish back on the boat or in the car. If you're looking for a "shore dinner," Brennan's certainly fills the bill.

(For nearby attractions, see Trip 13 in Book 1.)

Brennan's Fish House　☎ 440-354-9785
102 River Street　·　Grand River, Ohio
Region: Northeast Ohio (Lake County)
Handicapped access: Yes.

Brennan's Fish House

98 Fried Bologna Sandwiches

I am frequently asked, "Where is that place that sells the fried bologna sandwiches?" The place people are asking about is in central Ohio, but through the years I have discovered other places that sell similar sandwiches.

There is something comforting about fried bologna. Perhaps it's from being served this delicacy when we were young and associating it with growing up. In any event, the vast majority of viewers who have bothered to call or write all agree that their favorite fried bologna sandwich is the one served at the G & R Tavern in Waldo, Ohio.

It started over a quarter of a century ago, when the operator of the tavern had a local meat market prepare some German-style bologna according to his recipe. The sandwiches are made by cutting the bologna into slices about 3/4 inch thick and browning it on the grill. While it's cooking, a fresh Kaiser roll is also placed on the grill. When he flips the bologna, he places a large, fresh slice of Bermuda onion and a slice of Monterey Jack cheese on the meat. The finished sandwich is shoveled onto a plate, garnished with a pickle, and served.

They've been going strong for years and have served thousands and thousands of bologna sandwiches. In fact, people have had the sandwiches shipped all over the country.

You can't miss the G & R Tavern. It's on the corner in downtown Waldo. And just in case you miss that, they painted a large billboard on the side of the building proclaiming them to be the home of the world's favorite fried bologna sandwich.

Waldo is in the middle of a farming area, so don't be surprised to find yourself sharing the counter with farmers, as well as business types in their suits and ties. The service is usually good, and you can get in and out in about a half hour during lunchtime.

(For nearby attractions, see Trip 24 in Book 1.)

G & R Tavern   ☎ 614-726-9685
103 North Marion Road (U.S. Route 23) • Waldo, Ohio
Region: Central Ohio (Marion County)
Handicapped access: Steps into building.

SURE TO BE FAMOUS

There's a place down in Marietta, Ohio, that is making fried bologna their signature dish, billing the sandwich as the "sure-to-be-famous fried bologna sandwich."

The tavern is in a resurrected old building that once housed a dim, dark neighborhood bar that allegedly used only Christmas lights to illuminate the interior year round. The new owners opened up the windows and redecorated the interior in bright colors. Today it is an attractive place to visit while shopping and exploring the newest tourist area in Marietta.

Getting back to the bologna sandwich. It's made with a thick slice of German-style bologna that is grilled, placed on a toasted sesame bun, topped with mayonnaise, a slice of sweet onion, a piece of Monterey Jack cheese, and some lettuce and tomatoes. They will also add hot mustard, on request.

(For nearby attractions, see Trip 32 in Book 1.)

Harmar Tavern   ☎ 740-373-8727
205 Maple Street · Marietta, Ohio
Region: Southeast Ohio (Washington County)
Handicapped access: Yes.

NEW ADDITION: JALAPENO PEPPERS

They have been serving a fried bologna sandwich for years at this neighborhood tavern in Hinckley. But they do serve it differently. Instead of German bologna, they use deli-style, and a thinner slice, measuring a quarter- to a half-inch thick.

Like other places, they grill it until it turns brown, then put the bologna on a grilled bun with a slice of cheese and a slice of onion. Now, here is where they part company with the other places: they also offer to put a fried egg on the sandwich, which, they say, has become very popular along with another addition—jalapeno peppers. Both toppings are finding fans. They sell the sandwich as a meal in itself by adding a plate full of home-made fries. They also get top dollar—$6.95.

(For nearby attractions, see Trip 14 in Book 1, and Trip 58 in Book 2.)

Foster's Hinckley Tavern   ☎ 330-278-2106
1382 Ridge Road · Hinckley, Ohio
Region: Northeast Ohio (Medina County)
Handicapped access: Steps into building.

AND ANOTHER ONE

Sal and Al's (see Hamburger chapter) has also had a fried bologna sandwich on their menu for a long time. It's three slices of beef bologna, weighing about a half-pound, fried to the degree of brownness you like, then popped onto a roll and served with mustard, mayonnaise, lettuce, tomato, and pickle with a side of French fries. It, too, is a meal by itself.

(For nearby attractions, see Trip 58 in Book 2.)

Sal and Al's Restaurant   ☎ 440-282-4367
2261 Cooper-Foster-Park Road • Amherst, Ohio
Region: Northeast Ohio (Lorain County)
Handicapped access: Yes.

99 Corned Beef

I almost left this category out. I had hoped that during my travels I would find corned-beef sandwiches in other counties or cities that would at least match some of the great corned-beef sandwiches I have had in Cleveland. Corned beef is kind of a "sleeper." Most people associate Cleveland with pierogies, or kielbasa and other ethnic sausage dishes, but where Cleveland really shines is in the presentation of corned-beef sandwiches.

In 20 years of traveling I have yet to find a restaurant in other parts of the state that can top the size and taste of Cleveland's corned-beef sandwiches. I have no doubts that after this book comes out I will hear from corned beef lovers all over the state, challenging my statement that the best corned beef is in Cleveland. Well, let the debate begin. But I challenge them to visit one of the restaurants I have listed and compare a corned-beef sandwich there to one they are championing. I suspect that when they bite into one of the giant, flavorful Cleveland corned-beef sandwiches, when they taste that brown mustard mixing with the salty beef and the fresh caraway-studded rye bread, even the memory of another corned-beef sandwich will be erased from their thoughts.

What makes the Cleveland version of a corned-beef sandwich so special? Well, first it's the size. In the places I have visited, there is no set rule dictating how much corned beef they put on the bread. But in a very unscientific survey, I have found the meat sometimes to be piled as high as my ballpoint pen, which measures out at 5 and 3/4 inches in length. The bread adds at least another inch to the sandwich. So when you prepare for that first bite, you are faced with the problem of opening your jaws an incredible 6 and 3/4 inches to chomp on that sandwich! Another thing: the quality of the meat. It is usually very lean, with very little fat or gristle, unlike that served in a certain central Ohio restaurant, supposedly famed for their corned beef. There I found the beef contained large amounts of fat, and thicker slices of bread were used in an attempt to make the sandwich look bigger than it was.

Having experienced Cleveland corned beef, it is difficult not to laugh at some of the sandwiches that other cities pass off as "Giant Corned Beef," "Colossal Corned Beef," or, the one I laughed out loud at, "a corned-beef sandwich as big as all Cincinnati." In all of these cases the sandwich, even counting the bread, barely came up to the pocket clip on my pen, a distance of only 3 and 7/8 inches. Give me a Cleveland corned-beef sandwich any day.

Okay, here are my favorites, the places where I have never been disappointed by either the size or the taste. The sandwiches are always hot and steamy, and it's a challenge to get one to go and be able to drive back to the station while smelling the aroma of that fresh corned beef wafting from the brown bag at my side. I usually make it only a block or so before I have to pull over, rip open the bag, and have a bite.

WORKING PERSON'S DELI

Danny's is a working person's deli. It's only open Monday through Friday for lunch, not dinner. It's small and it's crowded, and you are liable to find a company executive in his suit and tie sitting next to a foundry worker in his work clothes. The noon hour is fast and furious here with two slicers at work, cutting both corned beef and roast beef. Also try the potato salad, some of the richest I have ever had and a perfect accompaniment to either the corned beef or roast beef sandwich.

(For nearby attractions, see Trips 5, 15, and 16 in Book 1.)

Danny's Deli   ☎ 216-696-1761
1658 St. Clair Avenue • Cleveland, Ohio
Region: Northeast Ohio (Cuyahoga County)
Handicapped access: Yes.

GIANT CORNED-BEEF

Now, my friends at the TV station don't always agree with me on the best corned beef. While they admit they like Danny's Deli, there are those who often go to Slyman's, just up the street near 31st. It looks almost like a carbon copy of Danny's—it's in an industrial area and attracts both truck drivers and young executives for lunch. The claim to fame here is also giant corned-beef sandwiches, which some of my colleagues say are so big they are unable to get their mouths open wide enough to take a bite. They claim that they have to dismantle the sandwich first and eat it with a knife and fork! I have had Slyman's sandwiches occasionally, and I agree that they help make Cleveland proud when it comes to corned beef.

(For nearby attractions, see Trips 5, 15, and 16 in Book 1.)

Slyman's Deli   ☎ 216-621-3760
3106 St. Clair Avenue • Cleveland, Ohio
Region: Northeast Ohio (Cuyahoga County)
Handicapped access: Yes.

A CORNED-BEEF SANDWICH FOR TWO

Okay, so Rocky River isn't Cleveland, but it's a suburb. Joe's Deli has only been here a couple of years, but since opening day it's been packing in the customers. Part of the appeal is the sparkling interior and deli counter that replaced a fast-food restaurant. Part of it, I am sure, is Jeanette, Joe's wife, with her bubbly personality. But most of the attraction is good food and big corned-beef sandwiches. Now, you can dine here and have a corned-beef sandwich, but be prepared to wait up to 45 minutes or more during the dinner hour. They are really that busy. What I do is call ahead and order a corned beef for carryout. Even though the parking lot is jammed, they have a couple of parking spots always reserved for carryout customers. I get mine to go, and while others are still waiting to see a menu, I'm at home enjoying a sandwich so big it nearly unhinges your jaw to take a bite. I've often seen two people order a corned-beef sandwich at Joe's and then split it.

(For nearby attractions, see Trips 5, 15, and 16 in Book 1.)

Joe's Deli and Restaurant   ☎ 440-333-7890
19215 Hilliard Road • Rocky River, Ohio
Region: Northeast Ohio (Cuyahoga County)
Handicapped access: Yes.

FOOD FANTASYLAND

My first experience with a real corned-beef sandwich, Cleveland style, was years ago when I first started at WJW-TV back in the 1960s. We had a legendary police reporter, named Sanford Sobul, who had been a newspaper reporter and now was finishing out his journalistic career working behind the scenes in television as our police contact. "Sandy" Sobul deserves a book of his own. He was a friend of the top lawmen in town, as well as some of the top criminals. It was said if you told Sobul something and asked that it not be repeated, it was like telling a priest in confession. But I digress. Sandy was working on a story with me one day when he suggested we go to the East Side for lunch. He suggested Corky and Lenny's. I had never been in an authentic Jewish deli before. It was like entering a food fantasyland. The glass display cases were loaded with mouth-watering cheesecakes. The meat counter had long salamis and kosher briskets of beef. The deli men were making, no, make that *constructing*, corned-beef sandwiches. We took our towering sandwiches and found a seat. My next wonderful surprise awaited me. At each table were little bowls filled with huge slices of kosher dill pickles. Oh, the taste. I start salivating even 30 years later remembering the taste of my first corned-beef sandwich.

(For nearby attractions, see Trips 5, 15, and 16 in Book 1.)

Corky and Lenny's   ☎ 216-464-3838
27091 Chagrin Boulevard · Woodmere Village, Ohio
Region: Northeast Ohio (Cuyahoga County)
Handicapped access: Yes.

100 Hamburgers

Back in 1995 I started a firestorm of protest (all right, I got six letters and a few phone calls) from people who wanted to take issue with my story about how the hamburger originated (*Neil Zurcher's Favorite One Tank Trips*, page 36). It seems there are at least four areas of the country that claim to be the birthplace of the ground-meat sandwich.

First a little history. Hamburger, the ground-up remains of parts of the cow usually deemed not worthy of a separate cut of meat, or the trimmings from the better part, has been around a long, long time. Historians have traced its history all the way back to the Mongolian and Turkic tribes known as Tartars, who first cut up pieces of tough beef into small chunks to make it more tender. The practice spread through the Baltics and into Germany before the 14th century. Here, it is thought, the meat product gained its name when it allegedly became the meat of choice of the poorer classes in Hamburg, Germany, becoming known, derisively, as "Hamburger."

Historians also believe that it made the leap to the United States in the late 19th century with the heavy wave of German immigration to this country. However, there are reports that a meat called "Hamburg steak" was featured on the menu at a New York restaurant as early as 1834.

But for our purposes, the real question seems to be: who was the first to take this piece of meat called "hamburger" and place it between some bread? That brings us back full circle to my original story about the Menches brothers of Akron. In 1885, while working their sausage concession at the Hamburg, New York, fair, they ran out of sausage on a hot day and found that the local butcher also had none available. So they took some beef, ground it up, added a few ingredients—like coffee and brown sugar—grilled it over their gasoline-powered stove, slapped it between some bread, and a new taste sensation was born.

But wait a minute. Out in Athens, Texas, they have a plaque on the side of a building proclaiming that this was the site of Fletch Davis's Cafe. It is said that in the 1880s, Davis, a laid-off pottery worker, started a cafe and was selling a sandwich he invented consisting of ground beef between two pieces of bread.

Still another claim comes from New Haven, Connecticut. Danish immigrant Louis Lassen leased a lunch wagon in 1895. At first he specialized in a sandwich made of thin slices of steak grilled and placed on toast. At night he would take the trimmings from the meat home and grind them up to make meat patties to fry and serve to his family. It was only a matter of time before he started serving the leftovers, which became the best seller in his lunch wagon.

And then there is the story of Charlie Nagreen out in Seymour, Wisconsin, who was selling meatballs at the Seymour Fair in 1885. He decided to flatten the meatball, put it between two pieces of bread, and call it a "hamburger." By the way, local folks here take the story very seriously. They even hold an annual Hamburger Festival, where they once cooked the world's largest hamburger (over 5,000 pounds), which they served at the festival. Seymour is also home to the Hamburger Hall of Fame.

So who was first? The problem is that until this century, and the advent of the hamburger chains, the hamburger was just another sandwich, and there was little concern about its origin. Most of the information about how it all started came in interviews supplied by the people claiming to invent it, long after the event—sometimes as much as 50 or 60 years. Memories tend to dim with time, and facts get fuzzy. Local pride can also get in the way as a legend begins to grow. Also historians have not spent a great deal of time or energy researching this topic.

Most, however, do agree that the hamburger as we know it today was first served at the St. Louis World's Fair in 1904. And—surprise—attending that fair and serving their specialty were both Fletcher Davis of Athens, Texas, and Charles and Frank Menches from Ohio.

In fact, the Menches brothers seem to have the best claim to having originated the burger, since the dates they offer agree with the dates of the fair in Hamburg, New York. It's intriguing that they were also at the St. Louis World's Fair. As for the other folks, their claims were made much later and don't correlate with the time period when most historians say the hamburger was already being served. In the case of the Texas claim, Fletcher Davis was always vague about when he invented the hamburger, claiming it was sometime in the "late 1800s," which would imply the end of that century. The Menches claim is more specific: 1885. I'm going to stick with the Menches brothers as the developers of the hamburger. They also lay claim to having created the ice-cream cone, but here they seem to be on rather shaky historic ground. We'll have more about this controversy in another chapter.

By the way, if you would like to taste the original hamburger recipe, descendants of the Menches brothers operate a restaurant between Akron and Canton where they sell hamburgers made the same way their great-grandfathers made them—with a little coffee and brown sugar, and other "secret" ingredients. At the entrance to the restaurant there is a display of some of the equipment the brothers used for making their historic burgers. *(For nearby attractions, see Trip 6 in Book 1.)*

Menches Brothers Original Hamburger Restaurant   ☎ 330-896-2288
3700 Massillon Road, Suite 130 • Uniontown, Ohio
Region: Northeast Ohio (Stark County)
Handicapped access: Yes.

SOME OTHER NOTABLE HAMBURGERS

Another place you can learn what original hamburgers may have tasted like is in the small town of Miamisburg, south of Dayton, home to what may be the oldest continuously operated lunch wagon in Ohio's history. The Hamburg Wagon has been a fixture on Market Square in Miamisburg since 1913! It operates today much as it did more than three-quarters of a century ago. There is one electric hotplate and one large cast-iron skillet. The servers place the ball of hamburger in the skillet, smash it with a spatula, and cook it at a high temperature until it is done. It gets tossed onto an open bun, and you get your choice of condiments—onion, pickle, or both. No catsup, no mustard, no lettuce, no tomato. Just hamburg, bun, pickle, or onion.

They sell them by the bagful at lunch and dinnertime. The secret is in the ingredients. All the owner will admit is that there is a sausage product that provides a distinctive taste. He says the recipe is the original one and will only be divulged to whoever buys the Hamburg Wagon some day.

The little wagon is just large enough for two people to work inside; one cooks while the other takes orders. People start lining up at the side of the wagon just before noon, and it's not unusual for the line to snake down the street and around the corner.

Now bear in mind, the only thing the Hamburg Wagon sells are hamburgers. No soft drinks, no chips, no fries, no nothing but hamburgers. People buy the little hamburgers by the bagful. The Hamburg Wagon was been a lunch and dinnertime tradition for at least five generations!

It all started when the great 1913 flood hit the Miami Valley. A local buggy maker, Sherman Porter, wanted to help with the relief effort for the hundreds of people who had been made homeless by the flood. He noticed that the Red Cross, which was cooking for the homeless, kept running out of hamburgers. He told them he could make the meat go farther with a special additive he knew of, and so he suddenly found himself making hamburgers.

When the flood was over and things returned to normal, many of the local folks remembered the tasty hamburgers that Porter had cooked for them and urged him to open a hamburger stand. So many people asked that he converted an old buggy into a hamburger wagon and started selling his hamburgers on Market Square in downtown Miamisburg.

In the early days he would cook and sell the hamburgers until he ran out of meat, then hook his horse up to the buggy and go home. He usually sold hamburgers only on Saturdays, his day off. People soon learned that if they wanted one of the tasty burgers, they had to get there early. It was not unusual in the days before World War I to find a line halfway around the square on a Saturday morning, waiting for Porter to arrive with the Hamburg Wagon.

So why did Porter never add soft drinks or fries to his menu? Gary Jestice, who bought the Hamburg Wagon from Porter in 1970, explains it this way: "'Gramps' Porter tried once to add tamales to the menu, and they were a big hit. But it kept him so busy, he couldn't do the hamburgs right. He decided it was best to do just one thing and do it right." Jestice also points to the small space inside the wagon—just enough for the two workers. There is no room for a cooler or for storage. "I've thought about it a time or two," Jestice admits, "but by this time the way we serve hamburgers has become tradition here, and I don't like to monkey with tradition."

Gary Jestice, who as a young boy worked in the Hamburger Wagon for "Gramps" Porter, says that when he gets ready to sell the wagon the one stipulation he will make is that the wagon remain on Market Square and continue to sell the hamburgers, with just pickle or onion. No catsup, no mustard, no pop, and certainly no fries. That's the way it's done at the Hamburg Wagon.

(For nearby attractions, see Trip 64 in Book 2.)

The Hamburg Wagon   ☎ (no phone)
Market Square · Miamisburg, Ohio
Region: Southwest Ohio (Montgomery County)
Handicapped access: Wagon sits on street.

A HAMBURGER CHALLENGE

When it comes to hamburgers, there will always be someone out there with a huge appetite. You know, the guy or gal who can down a whole bag of hamburgers and then ask for dessert.

Well, we have a couple of suggestions for the perpetually hungry. One of them is the "King Kong Deluxe" burger available at Doug's Classic 57 Diner in Alliance. If you order this, here is what you get: two 1/3 pound patties of freshly ground real beef, a slice of ham, three strips of bacon, Swiss, American, or Mozzarella cheese, topped with lettuce, tomato, onion, mayonnaise, catsup, mustard, pickles, and anything else they can find lying around the kitchen. It costs just under six dollars, but it's probably enough to feed two people with ordinary appetites. For an additional $1.35 you can have it in a basket with French fries and coleslaw, applesauce, or cottage cheese.

But if you are really, really hungry you might want to try the "King Kong Deluxe Challenge." It consists of three King Kong Deluxe burgers as described above, a quart of root beer, a small French fry order, and a side dish of cottage cheese or coleslaw. If you can eat and drink the whole thing in less than 30 minutes, it's free. If you fail it will cost you $20. Believe it or not, they have a list of 19 people who have accepted the challenge and walked out of the restaurant for free.

(For nearby attractions, see Trip 8 in Book 1.)

Doug's Classic 57 Diner   ☎ 330-821-2887
2031 South Rockhill Avenue • Alliance, Ohio
Region: Northeast Ohio (Stark County)
Handicapped access: Yes.

BETCHA CAN'T

They offer a challenge at Sal and Al's in Amherst, Ohio, that only the very hungry might want to tackle.

They make a "Betcha Can't" Burger on a bun that was made in a cake pan. Then they place a one-pound hamburger patty on the bread and top it with catsup, mustard, pickles, tomatoes, and lettuce. Did I mention that the bun itself weighs in at 16 ounces? When they get this beast assembled you have 20 minutes to eat the whole thing. If you do—without getting up—you get it free. If you fail to eat the whole thing, it costs you $8.49.

I am not sure why they came up with such an odd amount, but most people end up paying. However, if such a sandwich appeals to your sense of humor for a party, they also make a carryout version of this that you can feed a bunch of people by cutting it up in sections. This version sells for $10.49.

Wait, we're not done yet. If you don't like hamburgers, Sal and Al's has another challenge for you: a "Betcha Can't" sundae. It consists of 12 large scoops of ice cream in a punch bowl, covered with six toppings, three bananas, whipped cream, and a cherry. You get an entire 30 minutes to eat it all—at one sitting, with no help—or it costs you $12. If you succeed in finishing either the burger or the sundae, you get your name inscribed on a "big eaters" list they have on display in the restaurant.

(For nearby attractions, see Trip 58 in Book 2.)

Sal and Al's Restaurant   ☎ 440-282-4367
2261 Cooper-Foster-Park Road · Amherst, Ohio
Region: Northeast Ohio (Lorain County)
Handicapped access: Yes.

WHAT IS A THURMAN BURGER?

Most places don't intentionally set out to make a sandwich so big that people can't finish it, but that's what happened here at Thurman's in trendy German Village, in downtown Columbus.

Founded in 1937, Thurman's was a part of German Village long before the area became the upscale mecca it is today. Mike Suclescy and other members of his family are the third generation to operate the restaurant started by their grandfather. It was in the 1980s that they discovered their signature sandwich, the Thurman Burger.

What is a Thurman Burger? Well, it starts out with a 3/4 pound patty of ground beef. While it's cooking on the grill, mushrooms, onions, and hot peppers are sautéed. The sauté is poured over the hamburger as it nears completion on the grill.

They're not done yet. Then they transfer the hamburger, covered with sautéed mushrooms, onions, and hot peppers, to a bun, add three slices of ham, three slices of cheese, lettuce, tomatoes, and mayonnaise. Now you have a Thurman Burger. The total sandwich weighs close to two pounds by the time it's completed. They serve it to you with a side of pickles and chips. The price in 1999 was $6.95.

Suclescy says many customers take one look and call for the doggy bag, others insist on a smaller sandwich. But having eaten a Thurman Burger, I can tell you that you want to be very hungry, otherwise you'll have enough left over for your next meal. Thurman's is open seven days a week. *(For nearby attractions, see Trip 26 in Book 1, and Trip 62 in Book 2.)*

Thurman Cafe   ☎ 614-443-1570
183 Thurman Avenue • Columbus, Ohio
Region: Central Ohio (Franklin County)
Handicapped access: Very crowded during dinner hours

101 Hot Dog!

Nothing is more American than the hot dog. It ranks right up there with mother, apple pie, and a certain make of car.

Where did it start? Some say it was developed more than 500 years ago when some European had scraps left over after butchering a hog and decided to shove them into the intestines and boil them. Disgusting as it sounds, that's the way the first sausage was made. (Come to think of it, that is still the way it is usually made.) But the hot dog as we know it today is usually credited to a German immigrant, Charles Feltman, who operated a Mom-and-Pop restaurant in Coney Island, New York.

On a visit back to Germany, he picked up some new pork sausages from Frankfurt. He brought these "Frankfurters" back to New York to test out on his customers. The new sausage didn't sell that well. Then he had an inspiration. Remembering another German custom of serving sausage with a piece of bread, he improvised and inserted the Frankfurter into a soft roll. The rest is history.

Well, almost. You see the old adage "success has a thousand fathers, and failure is an orphan" is very true here. Another legend is that at the 1904 St. Louis World's Fair, sausage-maker Arnold Feuchtwanger sold sausages and gave his customers white gloves to wear while they ate them. He ran out of gloves and had an inspiration. He asked his brother-in-law, a baker, to make some sausage-shaped buns to hold the wieners.

Some claim that was the beginning. But my favorite legend, and the one I put most credence in, is this one: On a chilly April day in 1901, *New York Journal* sports cartoonist Thomas "Tad" Dorgan was at the Polo Grounds baseball stadium in New York City. Harry Stevens, a concessionaire, was selling sausages to the fans. But the chilly outdoor air cooled the meat too much, so he grabbed some rolls, inserted the wieners, and had his men walk through the crowd shouting "hot dachshund sausages." Tad Dorgan drew a cartoon of the vendors, but he didn't know how to spell "dachshund." Learning "hund" was German for dog, he improvised, and the cartoon showed the men selling "hot dogs!" It caught on with readers of the paper, and when fans would go to the ball game and spot the wiener salesman they would call for a "hot dog."

By the way, we really do like hot dogs. The National Sausage Council estimates that Americans will eat a staggering 20 billion of them this year.

Most of them—more than 7 billion—will be consumed between Memorial Day and Labor Day.

Hot dogs are also regional. We have such things as a "Chicago dog," a wiener made of beef in a bun, slathered with yellow mustard, minced onion, and "piccadilly" (a diced relish made of pickled tomatoes). In West Virginia a real hot dog is always served with a good portion of homemade coleslaw on top of the wiener. Of course there is the Coney Island hot dog with its chili sauce. In some places hot dog restaurants even outsell the burger chains. Flint, Michigan, has long been known as a hot dog town, dating back to the 1920s and '30s when auto workers would dash out to the hot dog stand to buy a couple for lunch.

Though some nutritionists wring their hands over the amount of fat (and sometimes other, unknown, ingredients) that makes up some hot dogs, most of us find it hard to pass up a sizzling red hot, reclining in a warm toasted roll, slathered up with mustard and chili sauce. It's as American as, well, America.

People can be very loyal when it comes to hot dogs. It's very difficult to convince anyone that they will ever find a hot dog that tastes exactly the same as the ones they grew up with. With that in mind, I still offer a few of the places we have found hot dogs that seemed extraordinary in taste, size, or presentation.

HOT, HEAVENLY DOGS

Jack O'Flanagan of Amherst, Ohio, started out as a teacher of physical education. But after six years he yearned to be his own boss. A friend and he decided to open a hot dog stand near the local high school. That was 23 years ago, and today Jack is perhaps the undisputed hot dog king of Lorain County. He specializes in hundreds of varieties of toppings for the wieners as well as fresh-cut French fries. He invented a hot dog sauce so good that it has been bottled and sold for use in such places as Jacob's Field, home of the Cleveland Indians.

The hot dog stand remains in a structure that has been standing on the same corner for well over one hundred years. The specialty of the house includes quarter-pound hot dogs with the famous sauce, fresh-cut fries with cheese sauce, and homemade ice cream. I once quoted Jack as saying, "If you want a hamburger, go to the burger chains, but if you want a hot dog, come to me." He has since mellowed. While hot dogs are still the number-one item on his menu, he has recognized the new eating habits of the '90s and now offers chicken, salads, and other lighter fare.

Service: both sit-down and carryout.
(For nearby attractions, see Trip 58 in Book 2.)

Hot Dog Heaven   ☎ 440-988-7404
493 Cleveland Avenue • Amherst, Ohio
Region: Northeast Ohio (Lorain County)
Handicapped access: Steps into store.

Hot Dog Heaven

WARREN GOES TO THE DOGS

Two guys fresh out of the service after World War II started what is probably the best-known hot dog establishment in northern Ohio.

It all started as a little knickknack store on the west side of Warren. It soon became apparent that people were crazy about the hot dogs they served, and soon hot dogs were about the only thing on the menu. Now, 55 years later, they sell between four and five thousand hot dogs every day!

The secret, employees say, is the secret sauce developed by the two ex-GIs. They also offer a more diversified menu in keeping with present-day eating habits.

Warren residents were concerned a year or so ago when fire heavily damaged the Hot Dog Shoppe, but after a few months the old place was repaired and back in business. People can still stop in and take home hot dogs by the bagful. Service: sit-down and carryout.

(For nearby attractions, see Trip 7 in Book 1.)

The Hot Dog Shoppe   ☎ 330-395-7057
740 West Market Street • Warren, Ohio
Region: Northeast Ohio (Trumbull County)
Handicapped access: Yes.

A CONEY ISLAND DOG

It's like walking into a time warp, except for the prices. The Coney Island Diner in downtown Mansfield, Ohio, looks, and probably smells, much as it did when it opened its doors in 1936.

Jim and Cathy Smith, the third owners of the business, were responsible for taking the longtime restaurant back to the way it looked in the 1930s.

Of course, back then hot dogs came in one long tube and had to be cut every six inches. They cost a nickel apiece in 1936! The "secret" sauce, to which Jim and Cathy attribute the restaurant's longevity, has been handed down from owner to owner.

The neon sign over the diner has remained the same, and so have many of the customers, who are quick to tell you they came here for hot dogs as children and now bring their grandchildren.

While hot dogs are what it's all about here, they do offer some other items for those who don't eat hot dogs.

Another reason to stop in is that the restaurant is located right across the street from Mansfield's famous Richland Carousel Park, where the featured attraction is a carved-wood carousel that is open year round. Service: sit-down and carryout.

(For nearby attractions, see Trip 59 in Book 2.)

The Coney Island Diner   ☎ 415-525-1406
98 North Main Street • Mansfield, Ohio
Region: Northeast Ohio (Richland County)
Handicapped access: Yes.

A SUMMER HOT DOG

There are those who swear the greatest hot dogs are those that can only be obtained in the summer at Ohio's first resort, Geneva-on-the-Lake.

They are referring to the hot dogs at Eddie's Grill and Dairy Queen. A part of the strip for half a century, Eddie's has been making foot-long hot dogs the same way since first opened back in 1949.

He deep-fries the dog and puts it on a toasted bun. Summer residents of the resort say they have never had a hot dog that tastes as good.

I visited Eddie's in the summer of 1998, and we sampled his famous dogs. I think part of the mystique about Eddie's is its location. The counter, where you can sit, is actually the front of the building. When they are ready to open for the day, they just raise a large shutter, and you sit down partly on the busy strip of downtown Geneva-on-the-Lake. This way you can eat and people-watch at the same time.

There is no air conditioning, just gentle breezes from Lake Erie, mixed with the smell of hot grease, onions, and suntan lotion. It fairly screams "summer" at you. I thought the hot dogs were good, and the ambiance of Eddie's made them taste even better.

(For nearby attractions, see Trip 56 in Book 1.)

Eddie's Grill and Dairy Queen   ☎ 440-466-8720
5377 Lake Road   •   Geneva-on-the-Lake, Ohio
Region: Northeast Ohio (Ashtabula County)
Handicapped access: Sidewalk is part of front counter.

ON-THE-SQUARE HOT DOGS

Actually, Dan's Dogs in Medina is just off the square in a small restaurant that looks like a cross between *Happy Days* and a neighborhood bar from the 1950s. The atmosphere inside helps set the mood for food that brings back memories of the '50s.

The hot dogs are creations—no plain dog and bun here. Here you get things like jalapeno peppers, coleslaw, and hot mustard. Some of the dogs have fanciful names like "Junkyard Dog," which has just about everything but the kitchen sink on it.

Good milk shakes, homemade lemonade, and even root beer floats. A fun place to have a really fancy hot dog.

(For nearby attractions, see Trip 14 in Book 1, and Trip 58 in Book 2.)

Dan's Dogs   ☎ 330-723-3647
111 West Liberty   •   Medina, Ohio
Region: Northeast Ohio (Medina County)
Handicapped access: Steps into building.

Dan's Dogs

A MONUMENT TO HOT DOGS

Did you know that there is a place in Ohio that has a monument to a man who helped popularize hot dogs? In Niles, Ohio, they have dedicated a city park to the memory of Harry Stevens. Who was Harry Stevens? He was a Niles resident at the turn of the last century who had the foresight to sign with major ballparks across the country as their food supplier. He decided that hot dogs were perfect because you could hold them in your hand and they were an inexpensive sandwich. Stevens is the man generally credited with making hot dogs a part of the professional baseball experience.

(For nearby attractions, see Trip 7 in Book 1.)

Harry Stevens Park ☎ (no phone)
North Cranden Street Extension • Niles , Ohio
Region: Northeast Ohio (Trumbull County)
Handicapped access: Yes.

SOME CLEVELAND-MADE HOT DOGS

I think some of the very best hot dogs I have ever cooked myself were made in Cleveland. The Sausage Shoppe on Memphis Avenue has been in the sausage business since 1938. When Hans Kirchberger and his brother-in-law, Theo Johanni, arrived from Bavaria, Germany, they opened this little sausage shop that makes authentic German sausages.

Since 1974 Norm Heinle, a longtime employee, and his wife, Carol, continue the same attention to tradition that made the Sausage Shoppe a West Side Cleveland landmark. They make over 20 kinds of bratwurst.

They recently introduced a new hot dog they call the Expansion Dawg, to honor the new Cleveland Browns. It's a large German wiener without garlic, stuffed with three kinds of cheese to give the lean meat some moisture.

I don't know about the new Browns, but Norm Heinle has a winner here.

(For nearby attractions, see Trips 5, 15, and 16 in Book 1.)

The Sausage Shoppe   ☎ 216-351-5213
4501 Memphis Avenue • Cleveland, Ohio
Region: Northeast Ohio (Cuyahoga County)
Handicapped access: Yes.

HALF A DOG IS STILL A HOT DOG

Years ago, the original Tony Packo found a way to sell more hot dogs by slicing them in half lengthwise and selling two dogs for a dime, even though it was just one hot dog cut in half.

This is the official version put out by the restaurant that bears his name: It was the height of the Depression, and the Packos, like most American families, were trying to stretch their money as far as it would go. At the bar they ran, they served a cheap hot dog, covered with a spicy sauce that would make patrons thirsty so they could sell more drinks. Packo's half-a-dog hot dog was born and christened "Tony Packo's Hungarian Hot Dog." Two Hungarian Hot Dogs and a bowl of Rose Packo's great chili became a common Toledo meal during this era.

Tony Packo's place might have remained simply a local watering hole had it not been for Toledo native Jamie Farr, one of the stars of the hit 1970s TV series *M*A*S*H**. On one episode, Farr, playing Corporal Max Klinger, the cross-dressing medical corpsman—who, coincidentally, was from Toledo—made the remark, "If you're ever in Toledo, Ohio, on the Hungarian side of town, Tony Packo's got the greatest Hungarian hot dogs. Thirty-five cents . . ."

This plug, together with others made before the show ended in 1983, not only made Tony Packo's famous locally, but also brought people from all over the world to the little bar and restaurant seeking the half-a-hotdogs.

The second marketing coup scored by the little restaurant happened in the 1970s, when television and movie star Burt Reynolds was in town appearing in a summer theater production.

Nancy Packo, Tony's daughter, knew that Burt was going to go out to eat somewhere, so she wrote him a letter inviting him to her dad's place. Reynolds showed up a few nights later. When Nancy asked him to sign something to commemorate his visit, Reynolds good-naturedly signed a hot dog bun with a marking pen. (The bun, now mummified and framed, is still on display on a wall of the restaurant.)

This started a tradition of "bun signing" by famous visitors to the cafe, which by today include presidential candidate Walter Mondale, the cast of *M*A*S*H**, and scores of other celebrities.

Today the half-a-dog is still served, but the restaurant is run cafeteria style. Crowds line up at noon and dinnertime to order Hungarian hot dogs, Rose's chili, cabbage rolls, and a host of other items. The best seller is still Tony's half-a-dog.

(For nearby attractions, see Trip 23 in Book 1.)

Tony Packo's Cafe   ☎ 419-691-6054
1902 Front Street • Toledo, Ohio
Region: Northwest Ohio (Lucas County)
Handicapped access: Yes.

DOGS BY ANOTHER NAME

Local folks here head for the local beverage drive-through at lunchtime. In nice weather the grill is flaming right next to the driveway, and some of the best bratwurst in Bucyrus is slowly cooking. It's a quick way to grab lunch—a "brat" on a bun.

This is the outlet for the W.P.I. Company, which makes bratwurst. It has a carryout, a bakery, and a small restaurant where you can have bratwurst and a few other things. By far the best thing they serve is the freshly grilled brats, available on nice days every so often.

(For nearby attractions, see Trip 24 in Book 1.)

W.P.I. Drive-Thru Bakery and Restaurant   ☎ 419-562-3332
700 North Sandusky Street • Bucyrus, Ohio
Region: Northwest Ohio (Crawford County)
Handicapped access: Yes.

102 **Pizza**

THE PIE ALL AMERICA LOVES

Peasants in Italy have eaten pizza for many centuries. The modern version is credited to baker Raffaele Esposito of Napoli (Naples), which is in the Italian region of Campania. As the legend goes, it happened in 1899. Esposito, who worked as a baker for Pizzeria di Pietro, baked a special pizza for visiting Italian king Umberto I and Queen Margherita. One of the pizzas was topped with mozzarella cheese and basil. The green basil, the white mozzarella, and the red tomatoes reminded the royal couple of the Italian flag. They scarfed it down, commenting that it was a very patriotic dish.

Esposito named it Pizza Margherita, after the queen, and it became a favorite in their bakery, soon making Naples the pizza capital of Italy. It was served in the United States as early as the turn of the 20th century, but it wasn't until World War II and the influx of American GIs into Italy that the food really gained popularity with Americans.

There is no doubt in my mind that "Ma" Cucco made the finest Sicilian pizza I ever tasted. "Ma" was Lillian Cucco, the mother of my high school buddy, Joe Cucco. Their farm was just around the corner from my grandparents' farm in Henrietta, and Joe and I spent a lot of time together at each other's homes.

I was sitting in their kitchen talking with Joe one evening when I noticed the most wonderful smell coming from their oven. I asked "Ma" what it was. She replied, "Pizza." I had never tasted pizza, never even heard of it. She pulled a deep metal pan from the oven, filled with a golden crust and swimming in rich tomatoes and parmesan cheese that had turned lightly brown on top. The whole thing was dotted with bits and pieces of Italian sausage. She took a knife and cut a large square of the pie, placed it on a plate, handed it to me, and said, "Here, taste some real Italian food." I have had the opportunity to try many new foods from around the world in the years since, but I don't think I will ever forget the wonderful taste of "Ma" Cucco's pizza.

Through the years I have tried to no avail to find pizza parlors that could match that original pizza. The closest I have ever come to it was on a sunny afternoon in Cleveland's Murray Hill. I was sitting at a small table outside Mayfield Italian Imports. Videographer Ralph Tarsitano and I had just stopped to get a quick lunch. Tarsitano, who is fondly known as

"Tarts," had been talking all day about this place as having the best pizza in town. He was right. As I bit into a large slab of pizza, memories of "Ma" Cucco's creations came tumbling into my mind. It wasn't quite the same, but it was good, very good.

Many times since then, when I get a longing for real pizza, I travel up to Murray Hill. The store has changed, but the recipes are the same. The new owner, Dino Lauricella, is the son of the man who ran it for over a score of years. Dino has increased the lunchtime trade by adding a lot of new dishes to the menu, including pastas and sausage. He also offers a full line of Italian groceries. The sidewalk tables and chairs are still there, so is the great view of downtown Cleveland. And while you enjoy your pizza or pasta you are surrounded by the heavenly aromas that fill this part of Cleveland known as Little Italy.

(For nearby attractions, see Trips 5, 15, and 16 in Book 1.)

Dino's Italian Eatery and Market Place   ☎ 216-791-0700
12018 Mayfield Road • Cleveland, Ohio
Region: Northeast Ohio (Cuyahoga County)
Handicapped access: Yes.

THOMAS EDISON DIDN'T INVENT PIZZA

Now, while Thomas A. Edison invented a lot of things—from the electric lightbulb to the motion picture projector—to my knowledge he didn't invent pizza. He probably never even tasted it. That's his loss. If he had stuck around the place where he was born (Milan, Ohio) and lived long enough, he could have joined a lot of other Milan residents who enjoy pizza from Jim's Pizza Box on the square. The building doesn't look historic, like the other buildings that surround the town square. The decor inside has a distinct 1970s family-restaurant flair, but the pizza and the other pastas that come from the kitchen are right out of the 1990s. How good is the pizza? Well, on just about any weekday you will see office workers from surrounding towns dashing in at the noon hour to pick up their carryout pizza. They think it's good enough to drive 20 miles and give up most of their lunch hour.

As I said, they have the usual array of pizza choices—I haven't found one I don't like—and they also offer a good selection of pastas. I had a very good lasagna one day while visiting the restaurant with Milan police chief James Ward and WMJI radio personality John Lannigan.

(For nearby attractions, see Trip 18 in Book 1, and Trips 48 and 66 in Book 2.)

Jim's Pizza Box ☎ 419-499-4166
10 South Main Street • Milan, Ohio
Region: Northeast Ohio (Erie County)
Handicapped access: Yes.

DEAN MARTIN SLEPT HERE

That's the legend at DiCarlo's Original Pizza. Dean Martin, a Steubenville native, worked at DiCarlo's when he was young. Even afterwards he could be found, legend says, sleeping in the back room on top of the bags of flour when he couldn't make it home after a long night. Today the town honors Dean with a giant mural of his career in show business, and they honor DiCarlo's by still buying lots of their pizza. The boast here is that the pizza is always fresh and always hot. They bake them in large squares and don't keep the ones they don't sell once they cool off. As one of the employees told me, pizza is always best when it's fresh and hot from the oven. They don't skimp when it comes to putting on the sauce and cheese—their pizza seems to be swimming in both.

(For nearby attractions, see Trip 56 in Book 2.)

DiCarlo's Original Pizza ☎ 614-264-3634
45 Sunset Boulevard • Steubenville, Ohio
Region: Northeast Ohio (Jefferson County)
Handicapped access: Yes.

THE WRIGHT BROTHERS WOULD HAVE LOVED THIS PIZZA

It's too bad that Marion's Piazza (that's the way they spell it) wasn't around in Orville and Wilbur's time. They might have stayed in Dayton to do their early flight-testing instead of going off to North Carolina. It's only been 34 years since Marion's opened their first pizza—sorry, piazza—restaurant. There are seven of them scattered around Dayton today. My family likes the branch in Beavercreek, Ohio, a suburb of Dayton, where the toppings are put on so thick, you can't see the tomato sauce. They also cut the pizza, or piazza, into smaller square pieces, which makes it easier to eat for the little kids. Their crusts are also smaller, and the topping goes right to the edge of the pie.

(For nearby attractions, see Trip 41 in Book 1.)

Marion's Piazza ☎ 937-429-3393
1320 North Fairfield Road • Beavercreek, Ohio
Region: Southwest Ohio (Greene County)
Handicapped access: Yes.

YOU RASCAL, YOU

Lakewood is home to the latest location for this store, which sells the favorite pizza of students at Cleveland State University. The original Rascal House is located just across the street from the university on Euclid Avenue, and that's where a lot of greater Clevelanders got their first taste of Rascal House's decidedly different pizza.

They use fresh dough each day, and a smoky provolone cheese that gives their pizza a distinctive flavor. Real fans of Rascal House pizza say it's the amount of toppings they put on a pie that makes theirs a bit more expensive, but worth every penny. My personal favorite is their Hawaiian Luau pizza, which contains pineapple, bacon, ham, and cinnamon. West Siders can now enjoy the pizza without going all the way downtown.

(For nearby attractions, see Trips 5, 15, and 16 in Book 1.)

Rascal House Pizza   ☎ 440-228-4144
16815 Madison Avenue · Lakewood, Ohio
Region: Northeast Ohio (Cuyahoga County)
Handicapped access: Yes.

The original Rascal House   ☎ 216-781-0904
2064 Euclid Avenue · Cleveland, Ohio
Region: Northeast Ohio (Cuyahoga County)
Handicapped access: Yes.

PIZZA UNDER COVER

If you want to mix a little history with your pizza, there is a perfect place to do it in Ashtabula County. A pizza restaurant there is built inside half of an old covered bridge that once spanned a stream in Ashtabula County. When it was determined the bridge could no long carry traffic, the county put it up for sale. The pizza shop owner bought it and cut it in two halves. One of them is now a pizzeria in North Kingsville. The other half was also made into a restaurant, in Andover, Ohio, which is also in Ashtabula County. People who like to tour covered bridges will love this place because he has kept the interior of the bridge as it was, graffiti and all. Instead of cars, there are tables and chairs on the bridge today. You can eat a pizza and contemplate all the history that this old bridge has seen.

(For nearby attractions, see Trip 9 in Book 1.)

Covered Bridge Pizza Parlor   ☎ 440-224-2252
6541 South Main Street · North Kingsville, Ohio
Region: Northeast Ohio (Ashtabula County)
Handicapped access: Yes.

103 Buffalo Wings

It's perhaps one of the most popular dishes in restaurants today. Sometimes it's an appetizer, other times it's an entrée. It's Midwest soul food—hot, spicy, cholesterol-boosting, vein-clogging chicken wings.

Let's go back to the beginning—a Friday night in 1964 at the Anchor Bar on Main Street, near downtown Buffalo, New York. Dominic "the Rooster" Bellissimo, owner of the restaurant, was entertaining some friends at the bar late in the evening.

They had requested something to eat, even though the kitchen was closed for the night. Since they were Catholics, Dom suggested they wait until after midnight so he could serve meat. They agreed, and Dom went into the kitchen where his mother, Teressa, was making chicken soup for the next day. In those days chicken wings were considered "soup parts." In other words, parts of the chicken that were considered worthless but could be used in soup.

However, that particular evening she was working with some of the largest wings she had seen, and she had an idea. She popped the wings into a deep fryer, and while they cooked she whipped up a hot sauce. Then she sliced up some fresh celery and carrots, spread them around a plate, added a couple of saucers filled with blue cheese salad dressing, and poured the hot sauce over the freshly cooked chicken wings.

From that night on, a steadily growing clientele demanded "Buffalo wings," the name that Dom had given them. The fame of the wings spread cross-country, and the Anchor Bar became the place to stop when in Buffalo. Vice President Walter Mondale asked that Buffalo wings be delivered to his plane when he visited the city. The same thing happened during a visit by First Lady Hillary Clinton. Stage and screen stars like John Candy and country singer Kenny Rogers have dropped into the Anchor Bar to have the original wings. Usually when professional athletes visit the city they make time for a visit to the Anchor Bar.

The folks at the Anchor Bar will even tell you how to make the wings. Here is the official recipe, straight from Ivano Toscani, the present-day executive chef and manager of the Anchor Bar:

2 $\frac{1}{2}$ pounds fresh chicken wings (12–16 whole wings)

$\frac{1}{2}$ cup original Anchor Bar sauce

If preferred, split wings at joint; pat dry. Deep-fry at 350 degrees for

10–12 minutes, or bake at 425 degrees for 45 minutes until completely cooked and crispy; drain. Put in bowl, add sauce, and toss until wings are completely covered. Serve with blue cheese dressing and celery. For milder taste add additional margarine or butter.

Of course, they won't tell you what is in the "secret" original Anchor Bar Sauce, other than to reveal the basic ingredients in any hot sauce. And the hot sauce seems to make the difference between anyone else's wings and true Buffalo wings.

(For nearby attractions, see Trip 44 in Book 1, and Trip 77 in Book 2.)

Anchor Bar   ☎ 716-886-8920
1047 Main Street · Buffalo, NY
Region: New York, in Buffalo
Handicapped access: Yes.

OTHER WINGS, BUFFALO AND CHICKEN

Some Buffalonians I have talked with claim there was no secret, just plain restaurant-grade hot sauce, cut with a similar amount of butter or margarine, and laced with vinegar. I have tried one recipe and believe that it comes very close. It calls for 5 tablespoons of Tabasco sauce, 4 tablespoons of butter or margarine, and 1 tablespoon of vinegar.

Of course, like the gunfighters of the Old West, once you are the best, there is always someone trying to challenge you. That certainly has happened in the chicken-wing business. A few years ago an eclectic restaurant operation in Sharon, Pennsylvania, rose to the task.

The Quaker Steak and Lube Restaurant, conveniently located in an old Quaker State Oil Company service station, began turning out hot wings. In fact, they entered a competition in Cleveland for the title "Best wings in the U.S.A." and won first place.

Now you can argue that while the contest was open to the whole country, the fact is that not every restaurant that serves wings entered the contest. But the win gave Quaker Steak and Lube bragging rights to the title. And if that isn't enough, the gritty little Pennsylvania restaurant decided to take the battle for "best wings" to the doorstep of the Anchor Bar.

The Quaker Steak folks cooked up a batch of their hot wings, packed them in heated containers, and shuffled off for Buffalo. They purchased some wings from the Anchor Bar and then went out on the streets of Buffalo and asked Buffalonians to try both wings and tell them which was best. They claim Quaker Steak won the contest.

Now Quaker Steak and Lube, which is part of a restaurant complex called Three by the River in downtown Sharon, Pennsylvania, sells millions of wings each year and has picked up many other awards for the excellence of their wings. Today they make a wide variety of wings, ranging from "mild" to "atomic" with such flavors as "golden garlic," "Parmesan peppercorn," and many more.

(For nearby attractions, see Trip 74 in Book 2.)

Quaker Steak and Lube Restaurant ☎ 724-981-7221
101 Chestnut Avenue · Sharon, Pennsylvania
Region: Western Pennsylvania
Handicapped access: Yes.

CLEVELAND WINGS

Now, if you can't take the time to drive to Pennsylvania or New York, then think "Cleveland" for some excellent hot wings.

For 40 years there has been a little carryout restaurant in Lakewood. While it doesn't enter contests or spend money on advertising, it consistently turns out some of the best hot wings around.

Tom Kromer took over the restaurant back in 1986. For his wings, he says he took a routine recipe and tinkered with it a bit. He won't say just exactly what he did, but the result is a hot-sauce combination that ranks right up there with Quaker Steak and Anchor Bar.

Not only wings, but also ribs have received his magic touch. He won't discuss what he puts into the sauces, but one of the secrets he will admit to is using only fresh ingredients and top-of-the-line products.

I think he also has some of the best coleslaw in town. He makes it fresh every day. The equipment here is old, at least 40 years old, and the restaurant offers only carryout and local delivery. His customers are very loyal, driving in from as far east as Mentor for his wings and ribs.

During the summer, he caters for Lonz's Winery on Middle Bass Island on holiday weekends, creating new fans for his food. Tom is talking of selling the restaurant but promises that if he does, the recipes will go with it.

(For nearby attractions, see Trips 5, 15, and 16 in Book 1.)

Chicken and Ribs Galore ☎ 216-226-3141
13615 Detroit Avenue · Cleveland , Ohio
Region: Northeast Ohio (Cuyahoga County)
Handicapped access: Yes.

104 Hot Sauces

Let's talk about hot sauces. You know, those small bottles of liquid fire that some people sprinkle across soups, hamburgs, barbecue, fish, ice cream.

Well, maybe not ice cream, but a true hot sauce fan will try it on just about anything else. I am a latecomer to hot sauces. My Grandfather Currier, of English descent, always liked to start his meals with a tablespoon of horseradish. (He said it cleared his nasal passages and honed his taste buds. However, my Grandmother Currier was not renowned as a cook, and I often suspected he ate the horseradish to kill his taste buds, but that is another story.)

I think I was about five years old when I decided to emulate him once at dinnertime. Before my mother or grandparents could stop me, I dug a large soup spoon into the horseradish dish and then popped it in my mouth. To this day I have suspected that liquid Drano would probably have tasted milder. I remember spewing out the horseradish all over the evening dinner. That pretty much took care of everybody's appetite that evening.

Later, when I was in my early twenties, in the Marine Corps, and dating my first wife, Gay, we were visiting my best friend, Sergeant Joe Velasquez, and his wife, Alice. Joe cooked up some hamburgs on a grill, and we carried them into the kitchen. He pulled a jar of homemade jalapeno pepper relish from the refrigerator and told me it was a gift from his mother-in-law, Mrs. Murrillo. He put a generous portion on his hamburg and nodded at me, asking if I wanted to try it. Now, understand we were both marines and were supposed to be tough. Besides, he was like a big brother to me, and if he did something, I took it as a challenge that I had to do it, too. What I didn't take into consideration is that he had been eating jalapeno peppers all of his life. So to him it was like eating a hamburg with sweet pickle relish on it. By contrast, I felt like I had just been given the world's largest shot of Novocain in my tongue and lips. Everything in my mouth went numb as I took a big bite of the hamburg with jalapeno sauce. Then it felt as if I had just swallowed a hot coal, as it worked its way down my gullet, flaming all the way into my stomach. I dashed to the kitchen sink and turned on the faucet full force. I twisted my head so that the water would run into my mouth, where I was certain that flames were now shooting at least a foot in front of me. To say that I was in pain is an understatement. I whimpered and choked as the water failed to cool my mouth. Joe called me a "candy-ass" (a derogatory term of questionable endearment from one marine to another), walked to a nearby cupboard, broke out a piece of a chocolate candy bar, and handed it to me. "Here, eat this," he ordered, "water won't stop the heat, but chocolate will neutralize it." He was right, the pain started to subside.

Hours later, though, my lips still burned, and I kept running my tongue over my lips to cool them. When I kissed my wife-to-be good night, she complained that she could taste the jalapeno sauce on my lips.

It was a long time before I ever tried hot sauces and relishes again. By the 1980s my taste buds had aged, the hot sauce generation was beginning to take over the kitchens of America. I discovered that Tabasco sauce could add flavor to an undistinguished cut of meat and that just because something is spicy, it does not have to be spicy hot. Gradually I discovered hot wings and hot barbecue. As the years went by, my tolerance of hot sauces started to increase, and I woke one morning to discover that I was hooked on hot sauces like so many other people.

The words "hot" and "hot sauce" do not necessarily describe what is inside those little bottles. To be sure, some of the contents do qualify as liquid lava, but others have multiple warning labels that are more bark than bite. The hot sauce industry uses a method called "Scoville heat testing" to rate just how hot each sauce is.

The heat is measured in "Scoville units," named after Wilbur Scoville, who devised the method (known as the organoleptic method) and test in 1912. Human tasters were used to evaluate how many parts of sugar water it would take to neutralize the heat. Today instruments take the place of human tasters. This is known as HPLC, or High Performance Liquid Chromatography, and it determines the amount of capsaicinoids in parts per million. HPLC is said to be more accurate than the organoleptic method. However, there are drawbacks. In some sauces, the ingredients can alter how hot a sauce actually tastes versus how hot it is rated. And different batches of peppers can have differing degrees of heat. What I think this all boils down to is that to determine the actual heat of each batch of sauce you would need to test that batch. So what we are left with is an estimation of heat that tests have shown in similar batches.

The simplest way to test hot sauce is to put a drop on the end of a pretzel or piece of bread and touch your tongue to it. If it doesn't burn a hole in your tongue, and you are still able to talk, just nod your head and say, "Not bad, a little tangy perhaps, but not bad."

One hot sauce company rated many of the products on the market by name. Here are a few of their results, with the Scoville rating each sauce received: "Da Bomb" seemed the most lethal. It has a Scoville rating of an incredibly hot 119,700 units. In other words, if you sniffed this stuff it would take nearly 120,000 glasses of sugar water to cool your mouth. Compare that with the old standby, Tabasco Pepper Sauce, at 2,140 units.

The top five, according to the hot sauce company, were: "Da Bomb" at 119,700 Scoville units; "Mad Dog Inferno" at 89,560; "You Can't Handle This Sauce" (that's really the name, not my opinion) at 84,000; "Dave's Insanity Gourmet Hot Sauce" at 51,000; and "After Death Sauce" at 49,220.

Listen to some of the other names: "Endorphin Rush," "Satan's Revenge," "Crazy Jerry's Brain Damage," "Scorned Woman," "Pure Hell," "Last Rites," and my favorite for the most unusual name, "Kick Me in the Ass and Call Me Margie."

NOT YOUR USUAL DELI

There are lots of places to buy hot sauces, but one of my favorites is down in central Ohio at Unusual Junction.

This is the brainchild of former Clevelander Jerry McKenna and his family. They have converted an old railroad station and some permanently parked railway cars into a most unusual business. It's perhaps the world's only bridal salon and . . . delicatessen.

On one side of the building they sell gowns for the bride, the wedding party, and the rest of the family. On the other side Jerry has built a delicatessen, and on one wall he has gathered some of the hottest sauces in the world. He says it all makes sense. Young guys come in with their wife-to-be, and while she is trying on dresses, the guy usually wanders into other parts of the store and discovers the delicatessen. Jerry says they usually spend a lot of time just looking at the hot sauce labels, but after a while they pick out two or three and then buy a ham sandwich and maybe a soda pop to go with it.

Jerry says the delicatessen is unusual, but it's the hot sauces that make this store truly unique and keep the grooms coming back long after the wedding. Oh, by the way, Jerry recently was ordained and will now be able to perform wedding ceremonies at the store.

(For nearby attractions, see Trip 68 in Book 2.)

Unusual Junction, Inc. ☎ 740-545-6007
56310 US Route 36 • West Lafayette, Ohio
Region: Northeast Ohio (Coshocton County)
Handicapped access: Yes.

Unusual Junction, Inc.

ANOTHER BIG SELECTION

I don't usually do chain stores, but this one seemed at first to be out of place in Berlin, Ohio, the center of the world's Amish population. The Amish are wonderful people, but their food could hardly be described as "highly spiced." Yet, this store has been very successful. They carry more than 500 different hot sauces ranging from "wimpy" to what they call "meltdown!" They usually have samples of several different sauces available so you can decide just how hot you want to go.

(For nearby attractions, see Trip 28 in Book 1, and Trips 56 and 61 in Book 2.)

Calido Chile Traders ☎ 330-793-3536
4813A Main Street • Berlin, Ohio
Region: Northeast Ohio (Holmes County)
Handicapped access: Yes.

SALSA MADE IN OHIO

Who says that great salsa has to be made in the Southwest? Some of the very best in the country is made right here in the Buckeye State. You probably have seen Jose Madrid Salsa in the fine food section of better grocery stores across the state, but never given a thought to the labeling that says, "made in Zanesville, Ohio."

Who the heck was Jose Madrid, and why did he made his salsa in Ohio? First of all, he was a real person. Jose Madrid was the grandfather of Mike Zakany, and he was a real cowboy out in Lincoln County, New Mexico. He created the salsa recipe for his family and friends.

His daughter, Estelle, moved to the Zanesville area, and years later when her son, Mike, decided to open a Mexican restaurant in Zanesville, Estelle dusted off her father's recipe and made some up for use in the new restaurant.

During the next 17 years the restaurant, considered one of the best Mexican restaurants in the state, featured the Jose Madrid salsa. When people started pleading to take some of the salsa home, Estelle and crew began to make the salsa in a kitchen in the basement of the restaurant. They made small batches to be canned and bottled, and Mike started peddling them to grocers around the state. The demand for the salsa has continued to grow to the point that Mike got out of the restaurant business and now makes salsa full time in the restaurant's 1884 historic building. They now produce as much as two hundred gallons a day to keep up with the demand.

Mike claims that what sets his salsa apart from all others is the fact that they use only natural ingredients, and no vinegar. Though this gives it a much better taste, it does shorten the shelf life.

The salsa is low in calories, has no fat, is cholesterol free, and has very little sodium. It comes in nine heat levels—from original, to mild, all the way up to XXXXXhot and one level up, which Mike calls "stupid hot."

You can get Jose Madrid at many groceries and markets, but you can also order it fresh from the kitchen here.

(For nearby attractions, see Trip 68 in Book 2.)

Jose Madrid Salsa   ☎ 800-931-2810
32 North 3rd Street • Zanesville, Ohio
Region: Southeast Ohio (Muskingum County)
Handicapped access: Yes.

105 Candy Factories I Have Known and Loved

I don't think I have ever met a candy maker I didn't like. I had the misfortune to grow up during the years of World War II, when candy was in very short supply, sugar was rationed, and many cocoa plantations were either in a war zone or had been conquered by the Japanese in the early days of the war. The bottom line, if you had a sweet tooth, and I did, was that you were pretty much out of luck.

A childhood friend's older brother was in the merchant marine, and I think I looked forward to his infrequent homecomings as much as my friend did. The reason: each time he returned he would bring along a whole carton of Hershey chocolate bars! It seems that servicemen could have as much candy as they wanted, and a box of candy bars in "ships' stores" was about a dollar. In any event my friend and I would stuff ourselves with Hershey bars for a day or two, then they would be all gone and we were back to spending our pennies and nickels on the candy substitutes that our candy store was offering.

I remember one item that sold for a penny was a small package of pumpkin seeds that had been coated in salt. Another was dried fruit. Neither was much of a substitute for real, melt-in-your-mouth chocolate. I vividly remember the day that candy bars reappeared in the store after the war. I bought a whole box of Clark bars and ate them in one sitting. I had a stomachache for two days, but it was worth it!

The candy bars of my youth seemed so much bigger, sweeter, and more chocolaty than the ones you get out of a vending machine today. Part of the problem is a fading memory, but I do think that the size of the candy bars has shrunk over the years, while the price has increased.

I put that question to the good folks in the consumer relations department at the Hershey candy company, and after much searching they admitted that indeed the standard Hershey chocolate bar is smaller today than it was prior to World War II. The bar in 1940 weighed 1.58 ounces; today it only weighs 1.55 ounces!

The really big candy makers, like Hershey's, in Hershey, Pennsylvania, don't let you tour the factory anymore to see your favorite candy bars being made. What they do instead is send you to this "Disney-like" ride at their welcome center that at first appears to be a copy of the old carnival ride, "Laugh-in-the-dark." But when you enter the tunnel in your automated car, what you see is a series of pictures and scenes that are supposed to simulate cocoa bean harvesting and the chocolate-making process. There are even a few fake assembly lines where Hershey Kisses parade by. The ride, which takes 12 minutes (and is free!), dumps you out at the entrance to what else? The Hershey store, where you can buy all the different products that Hershey makes.

But even if you can't get into the factory, there is the smell in Hershey, Pennsylvania. It certainly is the sweetest-smelling town I have ever visited. No matter where you walk, your olfactory senses are overwhelmed by the odor of fresh-made chocolate. Even the smell of flowers in the beautiful Hershey Gardens on a hilltop overlooking the town is sometimes overpowered by the smell of freshly roasted cocoa beans from the factory. It's enough to make tears of joy come to a real chocolate lover's eyes.

(For nearby attractions, see Trips 73, 74, 75, and 76 in Book 2.)

Hershey Information Center   ☎ 1-800-HER-SHEY (437-7439)
400 West Hersheypark Drive • Hershey, Pennsylvania
Region: Pennsylvania, near Harrisburg
Handicapped access: Yes.

OHIO'S BIGGEST CANDY FACTORY

Now, my friend Cedric Waggoner and his crew at Harry London Quality Chocolates in North Canton may not have a factory as large as Hershey's, but it is certainly the biggest in our part of the state.

Their beautiful new 80,000-square-foot headquarters, candy factory, and candy store sits just off I-77 next to the Akron-Canton Airport. You can see it from the highway. When you go on a tour of the factory, someone offers you a piece of candy as soon as you walk through the door. Now this is my kind of factory tour. In fact, the free samples just keep on coming as you see a short movie about candy making and then start trooping the corridors to watch through windows and see how the candy is actually made.

They make over 500 varieties of chocolate and gourmet candies, including the official candy version of the Ohio State symbol—the Buckeye (peanut butter with chocolate wrapped around it). There is a small charge for the tour, but you will probably get that back in the number of free samples they give you. Tours are Monday through Saturday from 9 a.m. until 4 p.m. and Sunday from noon until 3:30. Their attractive store is also open, and you can buy just about any product they make.

(For nearby attractions, see Trip 11 in Book 1.)

Harry London Quality Chocolates   ☎ 330-494-0833
Lauby Road • North Canton, Ohio
Region: Northeast Ohio (Stark County)
Handicapped access: Yes.

Harry London Quality Chocolates

THE BIGGEST CANDY STORE

This 100-year-old firm in Sharon, Pennsylvania, got its start in Ohio. Daffin's Candies was started in Woodsfield, Ohio, at the turn of the twentieth century by George Daffin. After World War I, his son, Alec Daffin, moved the candy business to New Philadelphia, Ohio. In 1936 Alec Daffin's son, Paul, took over the business and moved it to Canton, Ohio. Paul, whose nickname is "Pete," decided after World War II to build a store in Sharon, Pennsylvania.

He started small in 1947 and just kept growing. Today with a candy showroom that covers 20,000 square feet, he claims to have the "world's largest candy store."

"Pete" passed away in 1998, and today the store is operated by his wife and their daughter, Diane, who is the fourth generation of the family to make candy.

The highlight of the Sharon store is the "Chocolate Kingdom," which includes a 400-pound solid-chocolate turtle, a 125-pound chocolate reindeer, 75-pound chocolate frogs, chocolate rabbits, a chocolate train, and even a chocolate Ferris wheel. Visitors are also offered free samples of the Daffin candies. *(For nearby attractions, see Trip 74 in Book 2.)*

Daffin's Candies ☎ 877-323-3465 or 724-342-2892
496 East State Street • Sharon, Pennsylvania
Region: Western Pennsylvania
Handicapped access: Yes

SOME PERSONAL FAVORITES

Aside from those mentioned above, I have several other favorites for various reasons—nostalgia, service, or just good candy. If you want something personalized in chocolate, the smaller candy makers are where you want to start. Also, it is here that you'll still find lots of hand-dipped and - decorated candies.

CHOCOLATE LEGS

Bob and Sandy Brummer literally run a "Mom-and-Pop" operation. They make the candy and sell it themselves. Bob is a third-generation candy maker, in a business started in New Jersey by his grandfather back in 1904. When Bob met and married Sandy, who hails from Vermilion, New Jersey's loss was Ohio's gain.

They have over 200 types of candy molds, including some used in the original New Jersey store at the turn of the last century. They even have a mold that can make a chocolate copy of a woman's leg! Brummer's also offers several other unusual creations, like a chess set made of solid chocolate and chocolate houses for the holidays. They carry an unusually large selection of homemade sugar-free candies. You can also watch them make the candy through a window into their candy kitchen. Nice people and wonderful candy.

(For nearby attractions, see Trip 20 in Book 1.)

Brummer's Homemade Chocolates ☎ 440-967-2329
672 Main street • Vermilion , Ohio
Region: Northeast Ohio (Erie County)
Handicapped access: Yes.

Brummer's Homemade Chocolates

CANDY MAKER

It isn't very often that a small town has two fine candy shops, but this is the case in Vermilion, Ohio. The Zahars name in Greek means "candy maker," and for eight generations they have lived up to their name. The present generation has even picked up some international awards for their candy. Their most popular seller—butter almond toffee wrapped in milk chocolate or dark chocolate.

(For nearby attractions, see Trip 20 in Book 1.)

Zahars Candy Shop   ☎ 440-967-6318
South Shore Shopping Center
4803 Liberty Avenue • Vermilion, Ohio 44089
Region: Northeast Ohio (Erie County)
Handicapped access: Yes.

PEANUT CLUSTERS!

A relative newcomer to the chocolate business, Jason Coblentz grew up in Ohio's Amish country. He decided to open a chocolate business using some of the recipes that family friends had been using for years. Only open since 1987, Coblentz's has become very successful. His operation is housed in a century-old home in Walnut Creek, heart of the Amish land. They hand-dip all of their chocolates using a special chocolate that they import from Pennsylvania. Their specialty—peanut clusters hand-dipped in chocolate. Open Monday through Saturday.

(For nearby attractions, see Trip 30 in Book 1.)

Coblentz Chocolate Company　☎ 800-338-9341 or 330-893-2995
2804R SR 39　•　Walnut Creek, Ohio
Region: Northeast Ohio (Holmes County)
Handicapped access: Step into store, crowded aisles.

MY HART BELONGS TO CHOCOLATE

This small factory at the edge of Ohio's Amish country not only makes some fine candy but also sells candy-making equipment, supplies, and molds. They specialize in personalized chocolates, such as you might use at a wedding. They also carry a good supply of sugar-free candies. Their candy maker once made candy for world-famous Godiva Chocolates.

(For nearby attractions, see Trip 8 in Book 1, and Trip 58 in Book 2.)

Hartville Chocolate Factory　☎ 330-877-1999
114 South Prospect Avenue　•　Hartville, Ohio
Region: Northeast Ohio (Stark County)
Handicapped access: Yes.

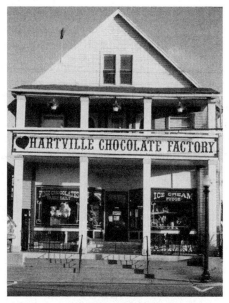

Hartville Chocolate Factory

FINE CANDY, INDEED

When I was growing up in Lorain County, a special occasion usually also meant getting a box of Faroh's chocolates in Lorain. Their French Chocolate Meltaways with rum, butter, creme de menthe, and peanut butter were particular favorites, then and now. Today they have stores all over the Cleveland area.

(For nearby attractions, see Trip 58 in Book 2.)

Faroh's Finest Candies   ☎ 440-288-8969 or 888-435-2550
1808 Henderson Drive • Lorain, Ohio
Region: Northeast Ohio (Lorain County)
Handicapped access: Yes.

ARE THE STRAWBERRIES READY YET?

It would be hard to put together a list of chocolate makers without including my longtime friends, Bill and Adele Malley. Bill's dad, Mike, started the business back in 1935 with a $500 loan. Three generations later it's a thriving business whose very name is synonymous with candy. Every year, people wait for Adele to announce that the chocolate-covered strawberries are ready to sell, or to make our mouths water with her descriptions of Bordeaux Chocolates, Billybobs (salted pecans, caramel, and milk chocolate), and chocolate-covered pretzels. Their ice-cream parlors are also well known for unusual sundaes. They now have 13 stores around the Greater Cleveland area and offer tours at the factory store on Brookpark Road.

(For nearby attractions, see Trips 5, 15, and 16 in Book 1.)

Malley's Chocolates   ☎ 800-275-6255 or 216-226-8300
13400 Brookpark Road • Brook Park, Ohio
Region: Northeast Ohio (Cuyahoga County)
Handicapped access: Yes.

106 Ice Cream

I don't know if anyone really cares who invented ice cream. I just know that I like it.

It's comfort food. When you are six years old and have just had your tonsils out, it's the first thing that you can eat. It's what you eat at a picnic, and on the Fourth of July. It's the one food synonymous with just about any celebration, holiday, or special event. Ice cream—some call it the true nectar of the gods.

There is some speculation that the Romans first created ice cream by mixing snow with fruit and juices. Another camp says that Alexander the Great used ice to make a chilled concoction using wines and juices. Still another says it was the Chinese who developed ice cream by mixing rice with snow and honey. Then there's the rumor that it was created in the court of Charles I of England, who reportedly told a chef who made ice cream that he was never to divulge the recipe, that ice cream was to be reserved only for royalty. But most historians say the Charles I story is just that, a story. It didn't happen. But ice cream did happen, and it spread across Europe sometime in the 17th or 18th century.

In 1700 Governor Bladen of Maryland is reported to have served "ice cream" to his guests. The first written records about ice cream are from 1774, when a caterer in New York by the name of Philip Lenzi, who had just moved from London, advertised that he had ice cream for sale. We also know that Dolly Madison, wife of President James Madison, served ice cream at the inaugural ball of 1813.

But up until 1851 the production of ice cream was pretty much a homemade operation. Jacob Fussell of Baltimore, Maryland, changed all that when he announced that he was opening a commercial ice-cream plant to wholesale the frozen confection.

However, people still had to sit down to eat ice cream, or carry it around in a paper cup. It was at the St. Louis World's Fair in 1904 that the world first discovered the ice-cream cone.

Two Ohio brothers, Frank and Charles Menches, were at the fair selling hamburgers (see Hamburger chapter) and ice cream. They ran out of dishes and suddenly had an inspiration. They were also selling waffles, so one of the brothers took a freshly baked waffle and wrapped it around a tent peg, making it into a cone. They filled the cone with ice cream. The new way to eat ice cream became very popular at the fair, and later in life the brothers claimed to have been the originators of the ice-cream cone as we know it today.

But the ice-cream cone, like the hamburger, seems to have had many parents. Syrian immigrant and pastry maker Ernest Hamwi was selling waferlike Zalabia pastry at that same fair. He claims that when a neighboring ice-cream stand ran out of dishes, he rolled some of his wafers into cones and sold them to the ice-cream maker so he could continue his busy sales. Thus Hamwi also claims the title of ice-cream cone originator.

Wait, it gets even better. The U. S. Patent Office says that though the claims by the Menches Brothers and Hamwi are interesting, the fact is that earlier that same year, 1904, Italian immigrant Italo Marchiony submitted the paperwork and a working model of an ice-cream cone mold. Marchiony claimed he had been selling cones made on his mold since 1896.

Now, it can be argued that even if Marchiony had a patent on making ice-cream cones, it still didn't make them the hit that they are today. Indeed, many influential people visited the fair at St. Louis that year, and there was much publicity for just about everything at the fair, including ice-cream cones. So who knows, the person or persons responsible for today's ice-cream cone could have been any one of the people who claim the honor.

Speaking of ice cream, did you know it was a woman who invented the hand-cranked ice-cream freezer? It was a vast improvement from the early system of stirring, and stirring, and stirring the ingredients. Nancy Johnson of Philadelphia, Pennsylvania, invented the hand-cranked freezer in 1846. Her ice-cream-making machine is still in use in some places today.

GREAT ICE CREAM AND BIG CONES

If I were tortured into confessing my favorite ice cream, it would truly be an agonizing decision.

In my memory I still salivate when I think of an ice-cream product called a "frosted malted" that was served from the 1930s until into the 1970s in the basement of Higbee's in downtown Cleveland.

The store is just a memory now, but as a youth I vividly remember watching the ladies mix milk, sugar, malt, and other ingredients, one batch at a time. From the stainless-steel ice-cream machines the light-colored chocolate-flavored ambrosia streamed into a tall glass. It originally cost a nickel. I often wore some of the malted on my nose and face as I tipped the glass higher and higher to get the last frozen remains from the glass into my mouth. When the store finally closed, the frosted malted stands closed, too.

When I heard that the Wendy's hamburger chain was going to offer a "frosted malted" as a regular item on their menu, I rejoiced. I couldn't wait to taste the first one. It was cold, it was creamy, it was chocolaty, but it wasn't like the frosteds of my youth. Something was missing. It didn't have the tangy malt taste, it was too stiff a mixture, it didn't pour out of the glass like the original. I tried to convince myself that the paper cup was the problem, but when I bought a frosted at Wendy's, brought it home, and poured it into a glass, it still didn't taste like those of my childhood. I finally decided that it was my childhood that was the problem—that things taste different when you are a child, before you grow older, and your taste buds lose their sensitivity.

I thought that way until one summer's evening in the early 1990s. My wife and I stopped in for a cone at a small family-run ice-cream stand in Fairview Park. It was called Weber's, and inside, at the counter, I saw an old machine that looked similar to the ones I had watched in the basement of the Higbee Company. It, too, was pumping a chocolaty mixture into cones. On the menu board I saw the words "Frosted Malted." I ordered one, and as it touched my lips and tongue, the years peeled back. I was six years old again in the basement of Higbee's. It was not quite the same: it was in a cone, not a glass, it was a bit more frozen in consistency, but the taste was there. I called the owner, David Ford, and talked with him. He said it probably is the same recipe that I loved as a youth. He was only the most recent owner of the recipe, but he related this story:

When Weber's first opened back in the 1930s, legend has it that the head of a downtown department store was a regular customer. He tried repeatedly to get the recipe for the frosted malted, but Weber would not sell it. The executive then tried another ploy. He hired one of Weber's employees to work at the department store. Problem was the employee did not know the recipe, he just knew what the ingredients were because he had watched Mr. Weber prepare it. The employee reconstructed what he thought was the right recipe, but when completed it wasn't quite thick enough for dipping into cones. So they poured the mix into glasses and offered the drink for a nickel instead of the dime that Weber's was charging. While the new drink became very popular, they never were able to match the original secret recipe, which David Ford says he still makes and sells. Same taste, just different consistency. Carryout only.

(For nearby attractions, see Trips 5, 15, and 16 in Book 1.)

Weber's Premium Custard and Ice Cream   ☎ 440-331-0004
20230 Lorain Road · Fairview Park, Ohio
Region: Northeast Ohio (Cuyahoga County)
Handicapped access: Yes.

A CANTON ORIGINAL: WHAT'S A "BITTNER"?

There seems to be a lot of argument over just who or what a "Bittner" was. But there is no argument that it's a Canton, Ohio, original.

The recipe is simple: press about three-quarters of a pound of home-made ice cream into a metal milk shake cup, pour in rich chocolate syrup, toss in handful after handful of buttered and salted pecans. Blend it all together, pour it into a large soda glass, top it with whipped cream, eat it with a spoon. That is a "Bittner."

They have been making them at Taggart's Ice Cream on Fulton Road since they opened back in 1926. Time has eroded the story of how the delicacy came to be named "Bittner," but it's generally believed it was named after an employee who created the concoction in the 1920s.

Pro football stars have been known to make Taggart's their first stop after visiting the Football Hall of Fame, to have a "Bittner." They also make a Turtle sundae that is a runner-up to the Bittner in popularity.

(For nearby attractions, see Trip 11 in Book 1.)

Taggart's Ice Cream   ☎ 330-452-6844
1481 Fulton Road · Canton, Ohio
Region: Northeast Ohio (Stark County)
Handicapped access: Yes.

THE LIST OF THE FAMOUS

Two Ohio ice-cream shops made national news in 1998 when *USA Today* selected them, along with a dozen other places in the country, as having the absolute best ice cream. I know, I know, it's just their opinion. But in this case I have to at least agree that they are certainly in the top 10 of my list of favorite Ohio ice-cream places.

Let's start with Handel's Ice Cream in Youngstown. I don't think I have ever had a creamier, richer ice cream. It's chock-full of nuts, berries, or whatever item belongs in each of the many flavors they make.

Back in 1945. Alice Handel wanted to make a little extra money and decided to set up an ice-cream stand in the corner of her husband's gasoline station.

She just had one ice-cream maker and some fruit from her garden. She made it one small batch at a time and made it the way she would make it for her family, only the richest cream, the freshest of fruit, and lots of it. More than the recipe called for. The result was a homemade ice cream that not only pleased the taste buds of returning soldiers, but also brought memories of the old hand-cranked-freezer ice cream of their youth. It soon became the busiest ice-cream stand in Youngstown.

That was over 50 years ago, and the stand is still there. Mrs. Handel is gone, but the present owner, Lenny Fisher, has kept her ice-cream recipes untouched.

They still make the ice cream in small batches and still put in much more fruit and/or nuts than the original recipe called for.

When I did a "One Tank Trip" there several years ago, Lenny invited my son, Craig, who was about eight years old at the time, to help make a batch of butter-pecan ice cream.

They used about a two-gallon pail full of ice-cream mix and then showed Craig where the large container of fresh pecans was. "Put in as many as you think it needs," they told Craig. He put handful after handful of pecans into the mixture. He kept doing it, while I began to wonder when they were going to stop him. Finally, after about 20 handfuls of the nuts had gone into the mix, Craig stopped and asked if that was sufficient. Lenny looked in the box, grabbed two more enormous handfuls, and said, "There, that ought to do it." Later I asked how they judged how much fruit and nuts to put in the ice cream, and he responded, "We put in whatever it needs. We never scrimp."

On top of all this, they usually have on hand about 60 different flavors of homemade ice cream. Ranging from their popular Chocolate Pecan, to such exotic flavors as Thin Mint Girl Scout Cookie, Grape, and Deep Dish Apple Pie.

(For nearby attractions, see Trip 56 in Book 2.)

Handel's Ice Cream ☎ 440-788-0656
3931 Handel Court • Youngstown, Ohio
Region: Northeast Ohio (Mahoning County)
Handicapped access: Yes.

THE RIGHT STUFF'S FAVORITE

You might say that Tom's Ice Cream Bowl in Zanesville has the "Right Stuff." It's a favorite spot for former U.S. senator and astronaut John Glenn and his wife, Annie. Tom's was also picked as one of the "Best in the US" by *USA Today*.

What all this is about is a tiny block building in an older section of Zanesville that hasn't changed very much since it first opened over 50 years ago. They have a simple policy that when you order a sundae it should have enough ice cream to fill a soup bowl and enough topping to run all over the sides and make a mess. They don't use any of those little two-dip tulip-shaped sundae glasses here. Instead they use those big, serviceable restaurant-quality, industrial-strength soup bowls that can hold four or five dips of ice cream.

They are only in their second generation of owners. Bill Sullivan, who started out working for the original owner, now owns the place, and he's never changed anything—especially the size of the sundaes.

The servers even wear those little white paper hats that soda jerks wore back in the '40s and '50s. The signature dish is a banana split, made in a soup bowl. It's a banana split you will never forget. But don't try to get one on Monday. Because that's the only day of the week that Tom's is closed.

(For nearby attractions, see Trip 68 in Book 1.)

Tom's Ice Cream Bowl   ☎ 740-452-5267
532 McIntire Avenue · Zanesville, Ohio
Region: Southeast Ohio (Muskingum County)
Handicapped access: Yes.

A REALLY BIG CONE

Like all of us, the Amish love ice cream. Back in 1996 we found our biggest ice-cream cone at a cheese house right in the middle of Ohio's Amish country.

For the most part, the Walnut Creek Cheese Company sells cheese, mostly brands made in Holmes County and its environs. But along with a lot of other goodies for the tourists, they also have a small ice-cream and snack bar.

Folks who have been here before love to take new visitors to the ice-cream counter and watch their faces when they order a "double-dipper."

The clerk starts to pile it on. First a large scoop of ice cream fills up the cone, and then they pile on the dips: one, two, three, sometimes four dips, until it looks like the whole creation is going to collapse. By this time, the customer usually is telling the clerk that all they ordered was a double-dipper. That's when they are informed that this is a Walnut Creek Cheese Company double-dip cone.

The cost, by the way, is less than two dollars. I have seen a family of four sit down and share one double-dip cone. They are closed on Sundays.

(For nearby attractions, see Trip 30 in Book 1.)

Walnut Creek Cheese   ☎ 330-852-2888
State Route 39 • Walnut Creek, Ohio
Region: Northeast Ohio (Holmes County)
Handicapped access: Yes.

Walnut Creek Cheese

A LAKE ERIE–SIZED CONE

Toft's Dairy has always been well known for the quality of their ice cream as well as the size of their ice-cream cones.

I don't know if they were the first to make really big cones, but they have certainly been consistent about it for nearly 30 years. For example, if you walk into the Dairy's ice-cream parlor and ask for a small cone, you end up with what most places call a double-dip.

But they really outdo themselves when someone who is really hungry for ice cream approaches the counter and says, "Gimme a large cone!" They really start piling the ice cream on. A "large" cone at Toft's consists of—count 'em—six large dips of your choice of ice cream. They usually will throw in a paper milk shake cup to help steady the tower of ice cream that they hand you.

The cost for all of this: under three dollars. Toft's Dairy is open every day.

(For nearby attractions, see Trip 18 in Book 1, and Trips 48 and 66 in Book 2.)

Toft's Dairy, Inc.   ☎ 419-625-5490
3717 Venice Road (U.S. Route 6) • Sandusky, Ohio
Region: Northeast Ohio (Erie County)
Handicapped access: Yes.

ICE CREAM BY THE POUND

Now if you really like ice cream and can scarf it down faster than they can dip it, you want to try the cones at the Grocery Bag convenience store in Millersburg, Ohio.

Here they sell their cones by the pound. For example: a "baby" cone consists of about a half-pound of ice cream. The regular cone is huge and holds about three-quarters of a pound of the cold stuff. But for the really big eater they have the "Large," and that has a full pound and a quarter of whichever of their 16 flavors you favor.

One other important fact here: they are open seven days a week. This is Amish country and you won't find too many businesses open on Sunday.

(For nearby attractions, see Trip 29 in Book 1.)

The Grocery Bag   ☎ 330-674-0833
106 North Clay Street • Millersburg, Ohio
Region: Northeast Ohio (Holmes County)
Handicapped access: Yes.

YOU BUY ONE DIP, THE STORE BUYS THE NEXT DIP

They have a novel approach to ice-cream cones in the tiny community of Olivesburg, Ohio, tucked away south of Ashland, on the Ashland-Richland county line.

The Olivesburg General Store is the oldest business in town. It's a real general store, just like in the movies, except this is real life. They carry a little bit of everything, from plumbing supplies to movies for the VCR. They also sell ice cream at an antique soda fountain.

What makes this one unique is that if you buy a dip of ice cream, the store buys you another.

For example, if you order a single-dip cone, they automatically dip two dips onto your cone. The second dip is on the house. They do this all the way up to triple-dippers. That means if you are a big ice-cream eater and you walk into the Olivesburg General Store and order a triple-dip cone, you end up with six dips of ice cream!

Owners Jim and Carol Coffey say they love to see the look on faces of tourists who stop in and ask for a big ice-cream cone. The Olivesburg General Store is open daily most of the year. They say they do close down on a couple of major holidays like Christmas and Thanksgiving, so if you plan to visit on a holiday, it would be a good idea to call them first.

(For nearby attractions, see Trip 59 in Book 2.)

The Olivesburg General Store   ☎ 419-289-7548
4778 State Road · Ashland, Ohio
Region: Northeast Ohio (Ashland County)
Handicapped access: Steps into store.

ICE CREAM FROM THE SOURCE

You can't buy your ice cream any closer to the source than at Young's Jersey Dairy in Yellow Springs, Ohio.

If you walk out the front door of the ice-cream parlor and look across the yard, you find the cows staring at you. This is the last dairy in Ohio that is not required to pasteurize their milk. They were operating before the laws concerning pasteurization went into effect and so are not required to put milk through the process.

The milk is safe to drink and meets other health and safety requirements, and is probably some of the richest milk on the market today. What all this leads up to is that in the making of their ice cream this family dairy uses only their herd's milk, which has upwards of 14 percent butterfat in it. It's just about the richest ice cream you can buy.

All the ice cream they sell here, in cones, sundaes, milk shakes, and sodas, started out in the barn across the yard.

Actually, Young's is a tourist attraction in this part of Ohio. Besides the ice-cream parlor, they have a bakery and a restaurant; they also have a petting zoo at the barn next door, where the kids can pet and feed baby goats, cows, and other farm animals. There are also retired farm tractors mired in permanent parking places that the kids can climb and play on, and there are hayrides around parts of the farm.

They also offer miniature golf, batting cages, a driving range, and a brand new restaurant, the Golden Jersey Inn, in a barn like log cabin, which offers fine dining at moderate prices.

My grandchildren, Allison and Bryan McCallister and Ryan Luttmann, consider this one of their favorite stops for seeing animals up close and for ice cream.

(For nearby attractions, see Trip 41 in Book 1.)

Young's Jersey Dairy   ☎ 937-325-0629
6880 Springfield-Xenia Road · Yellow Springs, Ohio
Region: Southwest Ohio (Greene County)
Handicapped access: Yes.

Young's Jersey Dairy

ICE CREAM WITH A BIT O' HONEY

Back in 1974 a Cleveland fireman, Frank Page, came up with a sweet idea: he mixed honey into his ice cream for additional sweetness. He started with a modest little ice-cream shop on State Road, and today he has four ice-cream stores stretching across the southern suburbs of Cleveland.

Just how popular is it? Just try to get up to the window on a warm day. The lines can sometimes be intimidating, but the taste is worth the wait.

Honey Pecan seems to be a favorite, although I favor Orange Blossom. All are made with natural ingredients and have no preservatives or artificial ingredients. They also offer a host of flavors, all with honey.

(For nearby attractions, see Trips 5, 15, and 16 in Book 1.)

Honey Hut Ice Cream Shoppe   ☎ 216-749-7077
4674 State Road • Cleveland , Ohio
Region: Northeast Ohio (Cuyahoga County)
Handicapped access: Yes.

Honey Hut Ice Cream Shoppe   ☎ 440-885-5055
6250 State Road • Parma, Ohio
Region: Northeast Ohio (Cuyahoga County)
Handicapped access: Yes.

Honey Hut Ice Cream Shoppe   ☎ 440-843-6677
6677 Pearl Road • Parma Heights, Ohio
Region: Northeast Ohio (Cuyahoga County)
Handicapped access: Yes.

Honey Hut Ice Cream Shoppe   ☎ 440-526-0606
7304 Chippewa Road • Brecksville, Ohio
Region: Northeast Ohio (Cuyahoga County)
Handicapped access: Yes.

ONE MILLION FLAVORS OF MILK SHAKES

Tom Kennedy runs a bakery with what he claims is the largest bakery display area in Ohio. He is always entering contests to get himself declared the best bread baker, and he's won several national awards for his breads. He also does lots of unusual cakes and cookies. He was one of the first to hire artists—all the way from Pittsburgh—to draw portraits of customers in the icing on his birthday cakes.

He also realizes that there are a lot of people out there on sugar-restricted diets, and he is constantly experimenting in his bakery kitchen to come up with sugar-free cookies, cakes, rolls, and other products.

But he really got carried away when he installed a machine to make homemade ice cream.

He started experimenting with flavored syrups in the kitchen and then started playing with a calculator. He makes the boast that to this day he has come up with—count 'em—more than one million different flavors for milk shakes. (He actually has about 40 of the flavors listed on a cardboard sign. He says he ran out of ink, so he stopped at 40. But he says if you can describe it, he can probably make it. So far, anyway, he hasn't been stumped.)

So, the next time you're in the mood for a chocolate-banana-grape-key-lime milk shake, just head south to Cambridge and Tom Kennedy's place.

(For nearby attractions, see Trip 36 in Book 1.)

Kennedy's Cakes and Donuts, Inc.   ☎ 614-439-2800
875 Southgate Parkway • Cambridge, Ohio
Region: Southeast Ohio (Guernsey County)
Handicapped access: Yes.

AN OLD-FASHIONED SODA FOUNTAIN

When you walk into Scooter's Soda Fountain, you get the feeling it has been there forever.

Well, at least since the 1920s. How else do you account for the old drugstore back bar, or the scattering of pictures of the old Euclid Beach amusement park on the walls? Or the old Dodgem car from the park that sits just inside the door, waiting to be ridden again. Well, it may not look that way, but Scooter's is only about five years old.

Katie and Don Arthur are the latest owners. They say they are trying to make the Soda Fountain fit into the town, just as though it had always been there. They have succeeded. But there is more here than just nostalgia. There is wonderful homemade ice cream, homemade fudge, even enormous hot apple pies, fresh from a local lady's oven. They serve a slab of the pie with two dips of ice cream in a large soup bowl.

And get this. They also make phosphates. What's a phosphate? It's what soft drinks were once called. "Soda-pop" drugstores (where ice-cream parlors were usually found) used to make their own seltzer water. In fact, seltzer was once believed to be medicinal and intoxicating and wasn't allowed to be sold on Sunday. To sell more of their seltzer water, druggists started adding some flavored syrups to it, and they called it a phosphate. If you added ice cream, you had a soda.

Katie and Don Arthur do all of their drinks in a first-class way that will transport you back to the soda fountains of your youth, or, if you're not that old, show you how they used to be. When it comes to ice-cream cones, they also make them big. A "single" contains almost two and a half dips of ice cream, while a "double" contains twice as much.

Scooter's, by the way, is named for the many children's scooters attached to the wall of the shop. The place is a little hard to spot while driving down Vine Street in Willoughby. They could use a bigger sign, but probably most people in Willoughby already know where it is.

(For nearby attractions, see Trip 13 in Book 1.)

Scooter's Soda Fountain   ☎ 440-946-7632
4127 Vine Street • Willoughby, Ohio
Region: Northeast Ohio (Lake County)
Handicapped access: Yes.

THE PRETTIEST ICE-CREAM PLANT IN THE STATE

I am not going to argue the merits of Velvet Ice Cream. For a commercially made ice cream, it is very good, one of my favorites. But when it comes to the place where they make Velvet Ice Cream, it wins the award, hands down, for the prettiest ice-cream plant in the state.

Located in Utica, Ohio, the plant is housed in a building designed to blend in with a reconstructed gristmill from the turn of the century. It sits on a parcel of land that resembles an old-fashioned city park with a duck pond, with paths to stroll and picnic tables and benches nearby.

Inside there is a small museum that traces the history of ice cream, including the way it was marketed and sold to the public, and a delicatessen with an ice-cream parlour.

Upstairs is where the ice cream is made in a modern, computerized factory. In fact, there is very little of the ice cream to be seen; it's more the packaging that you see through the frosty windows as pints and half-gallons go whizzing by on their way to the freezer.

Two brothers, Joe and Mike Dager, are the third generation of their family to make Velvet Ice Cream. Their grandfather, Joseph Dager, an immigrant from Lebanon, who came to America in 1903 and started making ice cream in the basement of a small candy store he operated in Utica. In the 1940s, his son, Charlie, decided that they made such a good product it should be sold statewide.

His marketing skills soon took the small ice-cream factory with hand-cranked ice-cream makers out of the basement and into a modern plant, where today grandsons Joe and Mike Dager oversee the third-largest ice-cream-producing operation in Ohio.

If you visit the headquarters you can tour the ice-cream museum and sample the ice cream at the ice-cream parlor in the mill. It is open annually from May 1 through October 31.

(For nearby attractions, see Trip 26 in Book 1, and Trip 62 in Book 2.)

Velvet Ice Cream Company   ☎ 800-589-5000
State Route 13 (1 mile South of Utica) • Utica, Ohio
Region: Central Ohio (Licking County)
Handicapped access: Yes.

A GREAT ICE CREAM

This company claims the affection of lots of Southwest Ohioans. It's been around longer than any other ice-cream factory in the state.

Louis Graeter founded Graeter's French Pot Ice Cream back in 1870, and, believe it or not, his family is still running the company, although today they ship their ice cream all over the country. The "French Pot" method is still used.

What is a French pot? It's a small freezer used by Graeter's to make ice cream the old-fashioned way one small batch of rich, creamy ice cream at a time. They claim the difference between the French pot freezers and today's modern methods of making ice cream is that no air is whipped into the mixture. The mix is swirled along the sides of the pot as it spins slowly in the refrigerant. As it chills and thickens, the pot operator scrapes the ice cream off the sides and into the middle with a paddle. When it's done, the ice-cream makers pack it into pints and also into tubs for commercial sales.

It takes about 20 minutes to make a batch of Graeter's, but as the folks in the Cincinnati area will attest, it's worth the wait. You can sample Graeter's ice cream all over Cincinnati, either at one of their many outlets or at grocery stores that carry their pints.

(For nearby attractions, see Trip 39 in Book 1.)

Graeter's Ice Cream   ☎ 513-721-6265
2145 Reading Road • Cincinnati, Ohio
Region: Southwest Ohio (Hamilton County)
Handicapped access: Yes.

ANOTHER BIG ICE-CREAM CONE

This one is in an out-of-the-way spot in Southeast Ohio, near Tappan Lake. Deersville is just a tiny little community, but everyone in the area knows the Deersville General Store.

That's the place of giant ice-cream cones. They make their own ice cream here. At present they make eight different flavors, some of which are only seasonal, like peach or fresh strawberry, because they require the availability of fresh fruit. The cones are an ice-cream eater's dream. For example, a single is actually about two and a half large dips of ice cream, and a double amounts to nearly five dips! In 1999 they were still selling their double for just $1.75.

Legend has it that famous Americans like Harvey Firestone and even Thomas A. Edison have stopped at the Deersville General Store, probably seeking out a really big ice-cream cone.

(For nearby attractions, see Trip 34 in Book 1, and Trip 60 in Book 2.)

Deersville General Store   ☎ 740-922-0831
212 W. Main Street • Deersville, Ohio
Region: Northeast Ohio (Harrison County)
Handicapped access: Yes.

Deersville General Store

107 **Popcorn**

Legend has it that when Columbus discovered America one of the first things the native Americans who met the boat tried to sell to Columbus and his crew was popcorn. It's estimated that Native American tribes in North and South America at that time were raising over seven hundred different kinds of popping corn! It is perhaps America's oldest indigenous food. Native Americans used it in many ways—for food, for decoration, they even made a primitive beer from popcorn.

Early French explorers who traveled the lower Great Lakes in the early 1600s reported that the Iroquois used a pottery vessel filled with heated sand to pop their popcorn. They would make soup out of the popped corn. There are even reports that when the Pilgrims sat down for the first Thanksgiving dinner at Plymouth, Massachusetts, one of the Native Americans brought a deerskin pouch filled with popped corn to the feast.

Housewives in the early days of the American colonies would pop corn in the morning and then serve it with sugar and cream for breakfast.

Ever wondered why popcorn pops? Here's the answer: each kernel of popcorn contains a small drop of water stored inside a circle of soft starch, covered by the kernel's hard outer shell. When it is heated, the water expands, causing pressure against the hard outer shell. Eventually the steam inside the kernel causes it to explode, turning the kernel inside out, exposing the soft starch inside, which has become inflated by the steam.

Did you know that popcorn is responsible for the invention of the microwave oven? Back in the 1940s inventor Percy Spencer discovered that he could pop kernels of corn by heating them with microwave energy. That experiment led to the many uses of microwaves for cooking and directly to the microwave oven.

If you like statistics, here's a couple: the Popcorn Institute in Chicago, Illinois, says that Americans consume a whopping 17.3 billion quarts of popped corn every year. That breaks down to about 68 quarts for every American man, woman, and child.

POPCORN MUSEUM

If there is anything that starts most people's mouths watering, it is the smell of freshly popped popcorn.

For years, movie theaters have arranged to make fresh popcorn just before a feature starts. They know the smell alone will account for most of their popcorn business. Let's face it, it's hard to resist purchasing a box when you walk into a theater.

When I was young many small towns still had popcorn wagons on the village square. They were usually big enough for only one person and had just enough room for a popcorn maker, supplies, and a man or woman to run it. A box of the freshly made popcorn usually cost a nickel or a dime. In my town we had a wagon that had had the wheels removed, and it sat on the southwest corner of College and Main streets in Oberlin. A little, white-haired lady ran the popcorn wagon. She was always there on Saturday nights when people would come to town to do their shopping and maybe see a movie at the Apollo Theater. As I recall, the Apollo also had a popcorn machine in their lobby, but in those days it was no big deal if you brought candy or popcorn from outside into the movie house.

We usually stopped at the popcorn wagon at the corner because it had this old porcelain coffee pot filled with melted butter that sat on a gas burner turned very low. When you bought a box of popcorn, the lady asked if you would like some fresh, melted butter on it.

There was no extra charge, and if you were a regular customer, she would shake the box and pour even more butter, until sometimes it would start leaking out the bottom of the box. I never knew the lady's name, or whether she owned the weather beaten old popcorn wagon. Sometime during my teens the wagon disappeared from the corner.

Occasionally you will still spot one. In Washington Park in downtown Sandusky, an old popcorn wagon still sits, its wheels flattened by time. It has not been operating on a regular basis for several years. At one time popcorn wagons were mounted on trucks and traveled from place to place, wherever the crowds were. These, too, have disappeared. If you would like to see what they looked like in their heyday, travel over to Marion, Ohio, to visit their popcorn museum in the old post office. There you will find dozens of popcorn makers and even some popcorn wagons from long ago. Each has been beautifully restored, and, yes, they still make popcorn in some of them.

(For nearby attractions, see Trip 24 in Book 1.)

The Wyandot Popcorn Museum   ☎ 617-387-HALL
Heritage Hall
169 East Church Street • Marion, Ohio
Region: Central Ohio (Marion County)
Handicapped access: Yes.

EUCLID BEACH POPCORN

One of the icons of the Cleveland entertainment scene for almost three-quarters of a century had its start with popcorn. The Humphrey family owned a farm in Wakeman, Ohio, and raised popcorn. They had several popcorn stands that did well, but Euclid Beach amusement park really made their name a part of Cleveland history.

Euclid Beach went into the history books when it closed forever in 1969, but the countless people who spent their youth at the park have refused to let its memory die. Books have been written about the park, and there is even a Euclid Beach Museum out in Kirtland, Ohio, that has one of the famous "Flying Turns" cars on display as well as a lot of memorabilia from the park. They also sell the famous Euclid Beach candy kisses, soft-serve ice cream, and, most importantly, the Euclid Beach popcorn balls. They had a special sweet, vinegary taste unlike any popcorn ball before or since. Maybe it was the home-grown popcorn, perhaps it was the Lake Erie climate. Who knows?

The good news is that my friend Dudley Humphrey, Jr., is still operating the Humphrey Company, and guess what? They still grow the popcorn out in Wakeman, and they still make the popcorn balls and the candy kisses. Instead of operating at the park, like in the early years, today the Humphrey Company is located in a plant in Warrensville Heights.

They still use the large hot-air popper to make the corn, and they still have the old copper kettles the candy coating is cooked in. They also offer souvenirs of the old amusement park in a catalogue. Humphrey also works with the Euclid Beach Nuts, a 600-member organization of amusement-park fans, to keep the memory of Euclid Beach alive.

The latest news is that the grand carousel that operated at Euclid Beach from 1910 until 1969 is returning to Cleveland. The carousel is being restored at the Carousel Magic Factory in Mansfield, Ohio. They hope that when it is complete funds can be raised for a building on East 9th Street, so another landmark can join the Rock and Roll Hall of Fame, the Science Center, the new Browns stadium, and the USS *Cod*.

As for the Euclid Beach popcorn balls, you can buy them in most area supermarkets and specialty stores, or order them direct from the Humphrey Company.

(For nearby attractions, see Trips 5, 15, and 16 in Book 1.)

The Humphrey Company   ☎ 216-662-6629 or 800-486-3739
20810 Miles Parkway • Warrensville Heights, Ohio
Region: Northeast Ohio (Cuyahoga County)
Handicapped access: Yes.

108 Potato Chips

I like mine burned. Well, at least a little dark-brown around the edge. However, the folks at Shearer Potato Chips tell me that those slightly brown chips that I lust for are not burned, they just look that way.

Really, what happens is some potatoes have more sugar than others, and when they get cooked in the hot oil, the sugar turns brown. It doesn't really change the taste either, they say, it just looks bad, so most potato chip companies throw out the dark-brown chips because they make the rest of the chips look burned. Seems like a waste to me.

If you were wondering where potato chips originated, most histories say that it all started with the French fry, which isn't French. The French fry was probably originated in America by Thomas Jefferson. (He was a busy guy, author of the Declaration of Independence, president of the United States, and inventor of many things, including the French fry.) It seems that Jefferson became addicted to the French way of cooking potatoes in hot oil. He referred to them in his writings as "Potatoes, fried in the French Manner," which eventually became known as "French fries." That was in the last part of the 1700s, but potato chips, as far as we know, didn't get invented for about 75 more years.

It was 1853, in Saratoga Springs, New York. An American Indian named George Crum worked as a chef at the Moon Lake Lodge. A customer who some reports insist was railroad magnate Cornelius Vanderbilt, ordered some potatoes cooked in the French way. Crum brought an order to the table, but they said the potatoes were too thick. He took them away and prepared another batch, same complaint. By this time the chef was starting to lose patience with his customers, but rather than insult them, he went back to the kitchen and took a sharp knife and a potato and started to shave very thin slices off the potato. He threw the "chips" into some boiling oil and let them brown. When they were nice and crispy, he scooped them out, piled them on a plate and sprinkled salt over them, and carried them back to his customers. It was meant to be a joke. But the joke was on George Crum.

When they tried to spear one of the chips with a fork, the chip broke. So they started eating them with their fingers. They finished the plateful and called for more. "Saratoga Chips" soon became the best seller at the Moon Lake Lodge. Soon other resorts were copying the chips, and even George Crum opened up his own restaurant that specialized in his potato chips.

Saratoga Springs prior to the Civil War was a very popular vacation spot for many influential people in America. It's believed they carried the news of this new snack food back to their home cities, and one of America's favorite snacks was born.

GET 'EM FRESH FROM THE COOKER

I like to recommend potato chips that are made right here in Ohio.

I especially like companies that have been around a long time. Like the Jones Potato Chip Company of Mansfield.

Jones's chips have been a fixture here since the 1940s, when Frederick W. Jones, a potato-chip distributor, decided to start his own potato-chip company, cooking the chips by hand in a kettle.

He was concerned about quality and freshness and serviced the stores that sold his chips often to make sure that the chips sold were always as fresh as possible.

He also noted when he started his company that there were no "wavy" potato chips, so he began selling the thicker, "marcelled" chips that work better for dips and dressings.

Today Jones Potato Chips are still a favorite in the Greater Mansfield area and are still made there. The company has grown, buying out another longtime Ohio favorite, Thomasson's Potato Chips of Elyria. They still sell chips under both names.

If you want a treat, go to the factory during the week when the chips are being made. You can buy fresh chips still hot from the cooker—they don't come any fresher than that.

(For nearby attractions, see Trip 59 in Book 2.)

Jones Potato Chip Company   ☎ 419-529-9424 or 800-466-9424
1125 National Parkway • Mansfield, Ohio
Region: Northeast Ohio (Richland County)
Handicapped access: Yes.

CHIPS FROM GRANDMA SHEARER

I like to buy chips from Ohio whenever I can, and I love a bargain anytime. That's what usually takes me over to Brewster, Ohio, to the Shearer Potato Chip factory. They operate a factory outlet store literally in the factory. When you are standing in the area where they sell the chips, if you stand on tiptoe and look to the rear you can see freshly made potato chips rolling off an assembly line into the packaging area where they are bagged up. The smell is heavenly!

Sorry, but they do not offer tours of the plant because of liability insurance costs. They do, however, sell just about every product they carry at the factory store, including their "seconds," chips that are brown around the edges or broken, that just didn't make it by the inspector on the production line. There is nothing wrong with these chips, other than their appearance. Usually they were made the same day they go on sale. The price in 1999 was $8 for three 3–4 pound bags. That's enough potato chips for just about any party.

Shearer's also will be glad to ship an order of fresh chips to you just about anywhere in the world. Shearer's is one of the largest private-label makers of chips in Ohio.

They cook about 30,000 pounds of potatoes every day. All their products are kosher, and for those who have allergies to certain oils, they label the types of oil they use on the side of their bags. They use soybean, peanut, and cottonseed oil in their cooking process.

A final note: Shearer's Potato Chips has won the award for "the Best Potato Chips in America" for two years running from the American Tasting Institute in San Francisco, California. The judges are a panel of 35 chefs from across the United States.

Everyone loves the chips, even the pigs at the Ohio State University agriculture college. Each week they receive up to 4,000 pounds of Shearer's Potato Chip scraps (the parts that are too brown or too broken to even sell as seconds). The ag school mixes the chips with regular grain and says the pigs really love it. In fact, the pigs grow just as fast with the potato-chip feed as they do when they are given 100 percent corn feed.

With chips that good, you might really think that Grandma Shearer was in the kitchen making them herself!

(For nearby attractions, see Trip 61 in Book 2.)

Shearer Potato Chips ☎ 330-767-3426
692 Wabash Avenue (State Route 93 North) • Brewster, Ohio
Region: Northeast Ohio (Stark County)
Handicapped access: Steps into plant

A CHIP COMPANY STARTED IN A GARAGE

I am happy to report that there are still many small potato-chip companies operating in Ohio. Places where you can go right to the factory and buy a fresh bag of hot potato chips.

Ballreich's Potato Chips have been a fixture in the Tiffin, Ohio, area since the company was founded back in the 1920s.

Fred Ballreich was looking for a job after serving in World War I. He decided to start his own business making potato chips. He started the operation in a garage, where he and his wife, Ethel, would peel the potatoes, chip them, and cook them in big kettles. Ethel would package the chips as Fred cooked. Eventually Fred's brothers joined the operation, and the company started to grow.

Now, 75 years later, the latest generation of the family, Tom Ballreich, Don Ballreich, and Andy Miller, still runs the business. It's mostly automated now, and they turn out an estimated 1.75 million pounds of potato chips each year! They run a large mail-order business, shipping to fans of their chips in all parts of the world.

(For nearby attractions, see Trip 23 in Book 1.)

Ballreich's Potato Chips   ☎ 800-323-2447 or 419-447-1814
186 Ohio Avenue • Tiffin, Ohio
Region: Northwest Ohio (Seneca County)
Handicapped access: Steps to the building.

Ballreich's Potato Chips

109 Cheese

It is claimed that cheese was first made by an Arab merchant riding a camel across the desert more than 4,000 years ago. For some reason he was trying to transport a container of milk (and no, I don't know if it was camel's milk). Thanks to the motion of the camel combined with the heat of the desert he found that evening that instead of milk, he now had curds and whey. Being in the middle of the desert with nothing else to eat or drink, he sampled the curds and found them tasty. He washed them down with the whey. As he spread the word of his discovery, new kinds of milk were tried, and various kinds of cheese were born.

I like cheese, but I especially like Swiss cheese. Not only because much of my heritage is Swiss, but because I grew up on Ohio's version of Swiss cheese.

Now I know they make good cheese in Wisconsin and, of course, in Switzerland, but the truth of the matter is that several of the best cheese makers in Switzerland came to this country years ago. They settled here in Ohio and started making the cheese that had made Switzerland famous, only I think they did it better in Ohio.

Maybe it's the climate, maybe it's our mix of cows, but I think that some of the best cheese in the world is made right here in the Buckeye State.

SWISS CHEESE MADE IN OHIO

It all started back in 1833 when a man by the name of Steiner moved from Switzerland to the rolling hills of Tuscarawas County in Ohio. He dragged along, all the way from Switzerland, a large copper cheese-making kettle, and as soon as he was settled in the tiny community of Ragersville he started making cheese. Wonderful, nutty-tasting Swiss, with large holes in it, just as he had back in Switzerland. It didn't take long for the cheese to catch on, and as its popularity grew, more and more Switzers made the move to this country. Soon the hills of Southeast Ohio became a "Little Switzerland" of cheese factories and chalets and cowbells. The Swiss fell in love with the area because it so closely resembled the hills of their homeland. Today they compete in world-class competitions with their cheese and bring home major awards.

For example, the Steiner Cheese Company, which is still in business now in nearby Baltic, Ohio, won the Ohio Grand Champion Cheese competition in 1987, '89, '90, '91, and '93. They have a small outlet store at the factory where you can buy fresh cheese when the factory is open. *(For nearby attractions, see Trip 60 in Book 2.)*

Steiner Cheese   ☎ 330-897-5505
201 Mill Street   ·   Baltic, Ohio
Region: Northeast Ohio (Tuscarawas County)
Handicapped access: No.

BABY SWISS CHEESE

There was another first for Ohio when Alfred Guggisberg immigrated to this country from Switzerland and started experimenting with smaller wheels of Swiss cheese. He found a process to make the holes smaller (the holes are caused by gas as the cheese ferments), and the end result was a miniature wheel of mild, tasty cheese that he called "Baby Swiss." Alfred is gone now, but his wife, Margaret, and her family continue to make the cheese that has made the Doughty Valley of Holmes County famous. They turn out an estimated fourteen 200-pound blocks of Baby Swiss cheese every day to ship all over the world. In their cheese house you can watch the cheese being made early in the morning. There is a retail store, where you can buy the cheese and many gifts imported from Switzerland. There is also a fine restaurant across the street where they serve Swiss- and German-style foods, including their cheese. You can try it on sandwiches or even in fondue (melted cheese that you dip cubes of bread in). Next door is an inn operated by the family, in case you would like to spend the night. *(For nearby attractions, see Trip 30 in Book 1.)*

Guggisberg Cheese   ☎ 330-893-3600
5025 State Route 557   ·   Charm, Ohio
Region: Northeast Ohio (Holmes County)
Handicapped access: Yes.

CHEESE IN BUNKER HILL

Don't let the name fool you. "Bunker Hill" is a local name for an area just outside the small town of Berlin, Ohio, the center of the largest Amish population in the entire world. It was to this area that John and Lilli Dauwalder came from Switzerland. It was 1935, the height of the Great Depression. They took over a small cheese factory, and John, using his cheese-making skills, began to make Heini's brand of Swiss cheese. Today his son, Peter, and Peter's family run the business, and what a business it is.

They have one of the largest Swiss-cheese operations in Ohio. In their retail store you can try free samples of over 50 different kinds of cheese. Everything from Swiss cheese to chocolate cheese (they really do make it; it tastes a lot like chocolate fudge). They offer to let you watch the Swiss cheese being made if you can get there very early in the morning. It's a fascinating process that turns the milk from surrounding area Amish farms into the world-famous Swiss cheese.

One of the things they do here that is different in making their cheese is that they use a microbial coagulant, or enzyme, instead of the traditional rennet (which is made from the stomach of a calf—the next time you have a cheeseburger keep that fact in mind). The enzyme works with the natural enzymes in milk and transforms the milk to a custardlike gel. Also, microbial coagulant does not induce food-allergy reactions. It is also permitted by most vegetarians.

The bottom line is that some of the best Swiss cheese is made here every day, and you can buy it right at the factory.

(For nearby attractions, see Trip 28 in Book 1.)

Heini's Cheese Chalet, Bunker Hill Cheese Company   ☎ 330-893-2131
6005 County Road 77 · Millersburg, Ohio
Region: Northeast Ohio (Holmes County)
Handicapped access: Yes.

CHEESE IN SMALL BATCHES

With a name like Hans Schindler, you just know he has to be a cheese maker. He is. He and wife, Nancy, are the owners of the Broad Run Cheese House on the eastern edge of the village of Sugarcreek in Tuscarawas County.

They have produced some prize-winning blue-ribbon cheeses down through the years. And because they work in smaller batches they make more than just Swiss cheese.

You can also find muenster and butter brick and even an "old fashioned full process" Swiss and Swiss curd. They also make a Baby Swiss and a sharp Swiss that is getting harder and harder to find in the cheese houses around central Ohio because of the high demand for Swiss cheese (to make sharp Swiss you have to let it age).

They also sell over 30 other varieties of cheese from around the world.

Another reason to visit Broad Run Cheese is Nancy Schindler's curtain shop. She has lace curtains from all over the country on display and for sale This is still pretty much a Mom-and-Pop operation. It's the way most cheese companies in the Amish area once were. A small neat plant that produces its own products, and the owners still have time to show you how they do it.

(For nearby attractions, see Trip 34 in Book 1, and Trip 60 in Book 2.)

Broad Run Cheese House   ☎ 800-332-3358 or 330-343-1092
Old State Route 39 • Dover, Ohio
Region: Northeast Ohio (Tuscarawas County)
Handicapped access: Yes.

AN AMISH FARMERS' CO-OP

If you want to try something a bit different from Swiss cheese, travel over to Middlefield in northeastern Ohio, in Geauga County. In recent years 200–300 small Amish dairy farmers decided to band together with some non-Amish farms to create their own co-op and cheese-processing plant. Realizing that the Swiss cheese market was already well saturated, they decided to go a different route and try making cheddar cheese their specialty. Today they make both yellow and white cheddar, as well as some Monterey Jack, yellow brick, and some pepper jack cheeses. Much of the cheese is sold wholesale, but they also have an outlet store at the cheese factory where the public is welcome to buy some of their products. However, remember, since Amish are involved in the business, they are not open on Sundays.

(For nearby attractions, see Trip 9 in Book 1.)

Middlefield Original Cheese Co-op   ☎ (no phone)
16942 Kinsman Road (Route 87) • Middlefield, Ohio
Region: Northeast Ohio (Geauga County)
Handicapped access: Yes, to store.

THE ORIGINAL OF THE ORIGINALS

Before there was a Middlefield Cheese Coop, most Amish used to sell their milk to the Middlefield Cheese Company, which, for years, was the only cheese manufacturer in Geauga County. Several years ago the Amish farmers decided to start their own cooperative (see story above), so Middlefield Cheese began importing much of their milk from farmers in nearby New York and Pennsylvania. They still make four kinds of Swiss cheese, which is their specialty. From Baby Swiss to mild, sharp, and no-salt Swiss. They also carry approximately 50 other types of cheese, some of it imported from all over the world. There is a small museum at their retail store that explains the story of how cheese was and is made, and there is a short movie showing the cheese-making process. If that doesn't satisfy you, you can contact them for reservations, and they will offer you an actual tour, early on a weekday morning, of the cheese-making plant in full production. This is only done on a reservation basis, no drop-in visits. The retail shop is open Monday through Saturday, closed on Sundays.

(For nearby attractions, see Trip 9 in Book 1.)

Middlefield Cheese Company   ☎ 440-632-5228
15815 Nauvoo Road · Middlefield, Ohio
Region: Northeast Ohio (Geauga County)
Handicapped access: Yes.

BEST IN THE WORLD

Speaking of award-winning cheese, I have already told the story of Alpine-Alpa of Wilmot, Ohio (see Amish Restaurants chapter). Besides operating a restaurant, owning the world's largest operating cuckoo clock, and running an imported food and gift store, Alpine-Alpa also makes and sells their own Swiss cheese. Their Swiss won an international award for "best in the world" a couple of years ago. By the way, this is one of the few cheese houses open on Sunday.

(For nearby attractions, see Trip 61 in Book 2.)

Alpine-Alpa Cheese Company   ☎ 330-359-5454
1504 U.S. Route 62 · Wilmot, Ohio
Region: Northeast Ohio (Stark County)
Handicapped access: Yes.

110 Spring Water and Bottled Water

Bottled water has been around almost as long as the United States has existed. Old Ben Franklin is said to have brought back the first bottled water from a spring in France. It just never caught on real big. Offices in plants and factories used it, but only the very wealthy had bottled water in their homes. My mother used to always keep a jug of distilled water to use in her early steam iron, but that was all the water was ever used for. You had to look real hard in a grocery store to find the distilled-water display, and it was usually just a few jugs stashed away near the cleaning supplies. Bottled water was just not very popular until the last couple of decades of the 20th century.

My Grandfather Currier was a farmer out in Henrietta Township in Lorain County. We never had city water. We had water wells and cisterns and creeks on the farm for our water supply. We had running water in the house, but it came from wells and cisterns and often wasn't good to drink, it was only for washing and flushing toilets and the like.

There was a well about 20 feet from the barnyard that our drinking water came from. One of us would go out to the well sometime during the day and pump a large pailful that would then be deposited on the kitchen counter with a large porcelain dipper hanging nearby on a nail. All members of the family used this common dipper to get a drink. In those innocent days of the 1930s none of us realized that we were probably passing germs back and forth between family and friends with our common drinking utensil.

As the years went by, running water from the well was finally installed in the house, but the water always had a strange taste. My grandfather decided that we would use bottled water for drinking. My grandmother cleaned out a few old glass, gallon-sized cider jugs, and we would set out for Amherst, Ohio, and "the Old Spring," located behind Amherst City Hall. A pipe stuck into the side of a hill constantly spilled out frigid water from deep inside the earth.

It was fun on a hot summer's day to climb down into the grotto formed by the erosion from years of water pouring out of the hillside and place your mouth over the end of the rusty pipe that jutted from the hill. Cold, clear water would shoot into your mouth and spray out of your nose, leaving you choking and coughing but wonderfully refreshed. When we had our thirst quenched, we went to work holding the open bottles under the ever-flowing stream.

It only took a few minutes to fill a half-dozen gallon bottles and then lug them back up the stone steps to the road up above, where we filled the truck of my grandmother's 1938 Plymouth and started home. The cost: nothing. Water was free. In fact, water was about the freest thing in life. At least in Ohio.

My father was an insurance salesman, and when I would travel with him as a youngster and wanted a drink of water, we would start looking for a roadside spring. It seems like they were everywhere. Dad would spot a pipe sticking out of the ground near the highway with water running freely. He would stop the car and take a sheet of paper from his briefcase, fold it quickly into a paper cup, walk to the pipe, draw a glass of water and sip it, and unless it had an odd color or some foreign objects in it, we would both have a refreshing drink. Again, water was free.

My father and grandfather would both probably roll over in their graves if they knew that today water is sold, like milk or soda pop. They would be even more amazed to see it available in plastic bottles in every service station or corner store, sometimes selling for more than a popular soft drink.

Those free springs along the road have probably been condemned because of surface runoff from all the chemicals on the roads and in the fields. Or if it was a truly good, deep spring, the farmer has capped off the free pipe and built a water building nearby where he now sells the water. If not a retailer himself, he is probably wholesaling the water to some big bottling company.

How big a business has it become? In 1997, according to the Beverage Marketing Corporation, bottled water sales increased to nearly 4 billion (that's with a "b") dollars.

Back in 1981 bottled water consumption represented only 1.8 percent of U.S. liquid consumption. By 1996 it had leaped to nearly 7 percent and continues to grow. In fact, in 1997 bottled water growth stood at nearly 10 percent, while soft drink growth was only 3.3 percent and fruit beverages 2.5 percent.

Baby boomers, they say, are responsible. As they mature and become more health conscious, they tend toward low-calorie beverages. Exploding suburban communities whose aging water systems have problems keeping up with growth have also contributed to the popularity of what people perceive to be "pure" water. Problem is, with all that money out there to spend on water, some unscrupulous bottlers put a fancy spring label on bottles and fill them with tap water. How do you know if you are getting the real thing, pure water? Always check the label to make sure it's from a reputable company; even better, if you live near a spring and can go to the source, you know exactly what you are getting.

We are pretty lucky in northern Ohio to have several great natural springs whose water is offered to the public (at a cost). But in most cases what you are getting is checked constantly for purity and taste.

"ANNE'S FOUNTAIN"

Newton Baus was a Lorain County farmer in 1956 when he decided to build a new home near the corner of State Route 113 and West Ridge Road on the west side of Elyria. Water for a home in the country in those days meant digging a well. There were no city water lines outside of city limits. So Baus had a well dug on the lot where he was building his home, never realizing that that well was going to change not only his life, but the lives of his children and grandchildren. Baus hit water, but the source he hit was unlike those of most farm wells. He hit an artesian well, a source of large quantities of water under so much pressure that the water shoots up like a geyser when tapped.

Not only did he have a practically unlimited source of water for his home and farm, the water tested out as pure as water can be. It was a marvelous stroke of luck for Baus. He decided to share the water with others by building a quaint little sandstone house over the well. On the roof there was a small waterfall, and the inside of the building was equipped with drinking fountains and two faucets that accepted coins from people who wanted to take five or ten gallons home with them. He really didn't make much money off the water; it was just to help offset the cost of building the little sandstone structure and for its upkeep.

But when his son, Wayne, got out of the service in 1959, he had an idea. Why not bottle the water and sell it to places like offices and plants that wanted some really pure water? They bought a couple of trucks and built a small bottling building to the rear of the property, and the White House Artesian Springs water company was born.

Today they pump more than three hundred thousand gallons of artesian well water a day from the wells, which have never gone dry since they were first discovered back in 1956. The little stone house is still there, and a traveler can still stop to have a free drink of artesian spring water at the drinking fountain inside or bring a bottle and take home a few gallons. And they have added another feature, Anne's Fountain.

Anne was Wayne's high-school sweetheart, who became his wife and partner through the years when the water business was being formed. Anne lost a long battle with cancer and died in 1990. Wayne wanted to do something special as a memorial to their love, so one night he sat down and—although he had no background in design—drew a fountain, which he decided to build in Anne's memory, a fountain unlike any he had ever seen. It took months of experimentation, but it was a work of love and when it was done it was indeed special.

The fountain has 111 lights and 42 nozzles, which can be programmed to do dozens of different things to change the way the fountain sprays water. It becomes a magical scene at night as the lights come on and turn the water all the colors of the rainbow. The fountain is open to the public each summer. There is a simple plaque on a pedestal that proclaims it "Anne's Fountain."

(For nearby attractions, see Trip 58 in Book 2.)

White House Artesian Springs   ☎ 440-322-1317
8100 West Ridge Road • Elyria, Ohio
Region: Northeast Ohio (Lorain County)
Handicapped access: Yes.

White House Artesian Springs

ANOTHER SOURCE

At the intersection of state routes 113 and 58 in Amherst Township is an area called Whiskeyville. It got its name more than a century ago, when there were several taverns located near the four corners, as well as a stage-coach stop.

There has always been local suspicion that there was some illegal whiskey-making in the area before the turn of the last century, which also may have contributed to the name. I've always believed this to be true because of the ready source of water in the area, a necessary ingredient in "moonshine."

Today the area is much more respectable; only local folks and old-timers still call it Whiskeyville. The discovery of springs on the northwest corner of the intersection many years ago has given northern Ohioans another source of pure springwater. I've always thought it would have been poetic justice to call it "Whiskeyville Springs" or "the Springs at Whiskeyville," but the owners opted for the more mundane name of "Cherry Knoll Spring," probably because of the number of cherry trees on the site.

Like its neighbor to the east, White House Artesian Springs, Cherry Knoll Spring has been available to local folks for years. A small brick building near the intersection houses spigots and coin machines where you can fill your own jugs with cold, clear springwater. Today, water from Cherry Knoll Spring is also sold commercially throughout northern Ohio.

(For nearby attractions, see Trip 58 in Book 2.)

Cherry Knoll Spring Water   ☎ 440-986-2197
8470 Leavitt Road (State Route 58) · Amherst, Ohio
Region: Northeast Ohio (Lorain County)
Handicapped access: Yes.

WATER WITH AN INDIAN NAME

It was just over a hundred years ago, in 1896, that Abbey and Earl Wright discovered a spring in a cherry orchard near downtown Cleve-land. Seeing the possibilities of selling water to downtown offices and wealthy Clevelanders, they started bottling the water. They called their firm the Minnehaha Water Company. The name derived from Longfel-low's poem, "Hiawatha's Song." In the poem, the maiden Minnehaha would bring fresh springwater to her lover, Hiawatha.

In the last century the Minnehaha brand has become the best-known brand of bottled water in northern Ohio. In the 1920s the original spring began to slow, so a search was started to find a new water source. They located another spring in the now-exclusive East Side suburb of Hunting Valley. A deep-rock spring there has provided the company with all of their water ever since and today still provides the cold, fresh springwater many northern Ohioans drink.

(For nearby attractions, see Trips 5, 15, and 16 in Book 1.)

Minnehaha Spring Water ☎ 216-875-5132
1906 East 40th Street • Cleveland, Ohio
Region: Northeast Ohio (Cuyahoga County)
Handicapped access: Yes.

111 Festivals

I am often asked, "Why don't you visit all those wonderful festivals in Ohio? They would make great 'One Tank Trips.'" The problem is that we always travel on two days in the middle of the week, usually Wednesday and Thursday, and most festivals occur on the weekends.

Also, when we visit a destination our report sometimes does not get on the air for a week or more. By the time it was featured, a festival would probably be over, and people would be disappointed that they missed it.

Finally, we once did reports on festivals and discovered that later in the year, when I might be on vacation or on special assignment and the station would air the segment again—announcing that it was a repeat—some people just didn't listen. Invariably I would get an angry phone call or letter from a viewer who saw the rerun, loaded the family into the car that weekend, and drove a couple of hours to find the small town where the festival was held. Only problem: the festival was six months ago. One angry letter I received from a family stated, "We drove for two hours, and all we found was a dog sleeping in the middle of the main street."

However, I have visited many of the festivals over the years as a general assignment reporter (and I even had a small role in creating the Woollybear Festival, Ohio's largest single-day festival), and I heartily recommend them as fun, family-type entertainment.

I include them here because one thing all these festivals has in common is usually an array of delicious foods.

It's been said that Ohio has more festivals than any other state in the nation. I don't know how you prove that, but it seems that every one of Ohio's 88 counties has at least one, and often several festivals at various times of the year. In fact, I don't think there is a month in any given year when there isn't something going on somewhere in the state.

So, while this is in no way a complete list of Ohio Festivals (you might want to give 1-800-BUCKEYE a call for that), here are some of the ones I have known and loved.

WHAT'S A WOOLLYBEAR?

I'm starting with this one because it's the one closest to my heart. It was begun back in the 1970s by my longtime colleague, Dick Goddard—Mr. Northern Ohio Weather himself. Dick had long wanted to pay honor to the Woollybear caterpillar, that little brown-and-orange worm that is so prevalent on trees and roads in the late summer and early fall. At that time my former wife, Gay, and I lived in Henrietta township in Lorain County. I arrived home from work one night to find the local Birmingham Elementary School P.T.A. officers, of which my wife was one, meeting in my living room. As I walked across the room, one of the ladies asked if I had any fundraising ideas for them. I nonchalantly suggested that if they started a "Woollybear Festival," Dick Goddard would not only publicize it on television, he would probably be the host and come to it.

They were skeptical but agreed to try it. The rest is history: the festival was held, and Dick has been the backbone of it for nearly three decades, as it has grown into an event that today attracts upwards of two hundred thousand people to the tiny Erie County town of Vermilion each October.

It is still run entirely by volunteers, all concessions are operated by non-profit charitable groups, and admission is free. As for food there have been "Woollybear Cakes," fanciful cakes with orange and chocolate frosting, and some of the local restaurants have even tried "Woollybear chili" (I'm not sure what all the ingredients were, but I doubt it contained any real Woollybears). One year there was even a booth that sold "Woollybear hot dogs," consisting of a quarter-pound hot dog wrapped around the middle with orange cheese, with brown chili sauce over each end of the hot dog.

It's just fun to see what new ways people will come up with each year to incorporate the Woollybear into their product. My personal favorites are much more mundane. The area around Vermilion is studded with lots of apple orchards, and by the time Woollybear Sunday rolls around each year, the first fresh pressing of cider is available. To me, that is the true taste of autumn.

The only problem with the Woollybear Festival is when it's held. It is always on a different date, either in very late September or the first couple of weeks in October. The reason: Dick Goddard is the official statistician for the Cleveland Browns, so each year he has to wait for the Browns to set their schedule before he can decide on the date for the festival. To find out when it is, either watch Fox 8 TV in September (Dick mentions it frequently during his weather broadcast), or call the Vermilion chamber of commerce.

(For nearby attractions, see Trip 20 in Book 1.)

The Woollybear Festival ☎ 440-967-4477
The Vermilion Chamber of Commerce • Vermilion, Ohio
Region: Northeast Ohio (Erie County)
Handicapped access: Yes.

THE GREAT PUMPKIN SHOW

One of the oldest festivals in Ohio, the Pumpkin Festival in Circleville was begun way back in 1903 when mayor George Haswell started a small exhibit in front of his office on West Main Street. It was a collection of cornstalks and pumpkins, many carved into jack-o'-lanterns. People started calling it "the Pumpkin Show." The next year some of the neighborhood merchants got into the act, adding more pumpkins and cornstalks and putting up decorations in the main street. In 1905 a merry-go-round was brought in, adding to the festivities. The festival kept growing until finally a formal organization was set up to promote the agricultural items of the county and, especially, the growing of pumpkins.

Today the Circleville Pumpkin Festival is the sixth-largest festival in the U.S. and attracts an estimated 300,000 people during its four-day run.

Also, it is still a free-admission type of attraction. The food is dominated by pumpkins. There is, of course, pumpkin pie. In 1998 they set a world record by cooking the "World's Largest Pumpkin Pie," which weighed 350 pounds and measured five feet in diameter.

There is also pumpkin ice cream, pumpkin fudge, pumpkin candy, pumpkin cookies, pumpkin bread, and just about anything else that can be made with pumpkins.

It is usually held for four days in late October. The 1999 dates were October 20 through October 23.

By the way, the largest pumpkin in the 1998 show weighed in at a whopping 429 pounds! That is a lot of pumpkin pie.

(For nearby attractions, see Trip 26 in Book 1, and Trip 62 in Book 2.)

The Circleville Pumpkin Festival   ☎ 740-474-7000 or 740-474-4224
159 East Franklin Street • Circleville, Ohio
Region: Central Ohio (Pickaway County)
Handicapped access: Yes.

A FESTIVAL COVERING COVERED BRIDGES

This festival is usually held the second full weekend in October. Ashtabula County has just completed building its sixteenth covered bridge—the fourth new covered bridge in the past 20 years. The festival celebrates these bridges with a huge parade through downtown Jefferson, the county seat, to the Ashtabula County fairgrounds, where only community-sponsored food wagons and attractions are allowed. One of the favorite foods here is bean soup, cooked each year by a local service club in a large kettle over an open wood fire. People line up for this, and they can't usually make enough to keep up with the demand. You can also take a self-guided tour of all the covered bridges in the county with maps the festival committee has prepared.

(For nearby attractions, see Trip 9 in Book 1.)

The Ashtabula County Covered Bridge Festival   ☎ 440-576-3769
25 West Jefferson Street · Jefferson, Ohio
Region: Northeast Ohio (Ashtabula County)
Handicapped access: Yes.

OHIO CELEBRATES SWISS HERITAGE

This one is held on the first weekend in October or the last weekend in September each year to celebrate the Swiss cheese that is made here, as well as the Swiss heritage of many of the residents. There is always yodeling, Swiss music, lots of people running around in Swiss costumes, and even a "Steinstossen" (stone-throwing) contest. Wait until you see the size of the stone you are supposed to throw! The highlight of the festival is, of course, Swiss cheese. You can buy some of the best made in Ohio and the world at the festival, as well as many other food products based on Swiss cheese. Lots of food and lots of entertainment. Also lots of people.

(For nearby attractions, see Trip 33 in Book 1.)

Ohio Swiss Festival, Inc.   ☎ 330-852-4113
downtown Sugarcreek · Sugarcreek, Ohio
Region: Northeast Ohio (Tuscarawas County)
Handicapped access: Yes.

SAUERKRAUT FESTIVAL?

I like this festival because it has absolutely nothing to do with the town, the community, the county, or the area of the state in which it is held. It was created strictly to help bring people to town. Back in 1970 the Waynesville Retail Merchants were planning to hold a sidewalk sale and discussing ways of attracting customers. One of the ideas was to tie in the sale with some sort of festival. But what kind? One of the merchants casually remarked that he had just had sauerkraut for lunch, so why not a sauerkraut festival? Now bear in mind, no one in Waynesville grows cabbage, nor is there any nearby sauerkraut-processing plant. Cabbage is not a big crop in this part of Ohio, and there aren't even a lot of people of German ancestry around these parts. But the sound of the words "Sauerkraut Festival" caught the imagination of the merchants, and they quickly voted to sponsor the event, featuring imported sauerkraut.

It's been going on 29 years now, and local folks still don't grow cabbage or make sauerkraut, but they sure have learned to come up with all kinds of adaptations of sauerkraut for the festival. The best-known product is the sauerkraut candy one merchant developed. It was so good that the chamber of commerce passes out samples to visiting delegations. Of course, there is sauerkraut on hot dogs or sausage, and cabbage rolls, and they even used to make a sauerkraut ice cream. For some reason, they stopped selling that at the festival, and chamber officials won't discuss why. But it's believed that the mixture of fermenting cabbage (for that is what sauerkraut is) with milk and cream didn't set well in some people's stomachs. They do still make a sauerkraut pie that people who have tried it say is very tasty.

Today the festival attracts upwards of a quarter-million people to Waynesville, which is also known as "the antique capital of the Midwest." The festival is usually held on the second weekend in October, but, as with all festivals, always check to confirm the dates before driving there.

(For nearby attractions, see Trip 40 in Book 1.)

Ohio Sauerkraut Festival ☎ 513-897-8855
Waynesville Area Chamber of Commerce
downtown Waynesville • Waynesville, Ohio
Region: Southwest Ohio (Warren County)
Handicapped access: Yes.

A HONEY OF A FESTIVAL

Certainly one of the sweeter festivals held each year is the Honey Festival in the college town of Oxford, Ohio. Here you can see such marvels as a "living bee beard." That's when some person allows bees to swarm all over his or her face, creating a living beard of bees. There will be the obligatory Honey Festival Queen contest, only these will be young women and not honeybees. Mix in a classic car show and lots of crafts and food. That's food made with honey, which ranges from ice cream to turkey breast. The festival is usually held in the first week or two of September each year. Call for exact dates.

(For nearby attractions, see Trip 39 in Book 1.)

The Honey Bee Festival ☎ 888-53-HONEY
downtown Oxford • Oxford, Ohio
Region: Southwest Ohio (Butler County)
Handicapped access: Yes.

A BERRY FUN FESTIVAL

The Norwalk Jaycees have proven that a good idea doesn't have to die. The city of Norwalk had a Strawberry Festival that started in 1960 and ran annually until 1984, known primarily for its musical attractions and huge parade. As with many volunteer efforts, some of the prime movers either grew tired or moved on, and the festival was allowed to stop with the 1984 event. But in 1997 the Norwalk Jaycees decided to revive the festival and did such a good job that the new festival drew an estimated 15,000 people the first year! There are some changes in the festival, which is traditionally held during the Memorial Day weekend. They now offer such attractions as a strawberry bakeoff, a strawberry ice-cream social, a strawberry pie-eating contest, and even a "berry" cute baby contest. Of course the big parade is still held. The event is held at the Huron County Fairgrounds in Norwalk.

(For nearby attractions, see Trip 50 in Book 2.)

The Norwalk Jaycees Strawberry Festival   ☎ 419-663-4062
Huron County Fairgrounds • Norwalk, Ohio
Region: Northeast Ohio (Huron County)
Handicapped access: Yes.

GEMÜTLICHKEIT

It's been 14 years since some residents of German Village in Columbus recognized the obvious, that this is the perfect place to hold an American-ized version of Oktoberfest. The spirited three-day festival has lots of German music, dancing, and German food, as well as an arts and crafts show. They expect an annual crowd of upwards of 75,000 people who come to share in the spirit of *Gemütlichkeit* with everything to eat from strudel to bratwurst, from funnel cakes to shishkebobs, and, of course, lots of beer.

The festival is usually held in early September, call for dates.

(For nearby attractions, see Trip 26 in Book 1, and Trip 62 in Book 2.)

German Village Oktoberfest   ☎ 614-224-4300
624 South Third Street • Columbus, Ohio
Region: Central Ohio (Franklin County)
Handicapped access: Yes.

112 Unusual Markets

It has to be the zaniest grocery store in Ohio, if not the world. Four acres of food under one roof! The owner sometimes can be found wearing a cowboy suit and roller skates, rolling up and down the aisles of his store, a holster strapped around his waist, but instead of a six-shooter, he has a large leek (an onionlike plant) stuffed in the holster.

There is a six-foot-tall animated gorilla dressed like Elvis Presley that periodically breaks into some of Elvis's songs. There is an old 40-foot-long cabin cruiser renamed the SS *Minnow*, where a group of animated cereal-box characters serenades customers.

A giant mushroom seems to hover in midair over a display of mushrooms from around the world. Tucked away against a back wall is a movie theater, the marquee proclaiming the only movie they show, *The Jungle Jim Story*.

Welcome to Jungle Jim's International Market in Fairfield, Ohio.

It all started back in the 1960s when Jim Bonaminio was working his way through college by selling produce from the back of his pickup truck along Ohio Route 254, near his hometown of Lorain, Ohio.

When he transferred to Miami University, he moved his operation south to some of the highways in and around Cincinnati. He was successful, but officials hassled him because some of the places he chose to set up business were literally on the edge of the road.

He started renting vacant lots along the highway and parking there. Then he added a tent and finally purchased a location in Fairfield, where he erected a large garage with roll-up doors. Thus was born Jungle Jim's International Market.

Over the years that original garage has been enlarged many times, until today there are over four acres under its roof, making up a store that looks like a cross between a grocery warehouse facility and what a Hollywood set designer might think a grocery store should look like.

There is a giant cake suspended from the ceiling that serves as a roof over the made-from-scratch bakery department. A neon "Sushi" sign points to a department where three Japanese chefs are busy turning out the beautiful fish-and-vegetable creations that make up sushi. All of it made daily for carryout.

A larger-than-life Amish buggy containing mannequins portraying an

Amish family and pulled by a large fiberglass horse trots through the air above the international cheese department. Display cases overflow with cheeses from foreign lands as well as from American cheese makers. Cases of beer from nearly every land in the world climb toward the ceiling next to a cappuccino bar where you can sample imported exotic coffees. Nearby are stacked bag after bag of aromatic coffee beans. The fresh produce section of the store is an entire acre in size. The usual lettuce, celery, apples, and oranges are joined by exotic things like fresh sugar cane and cactus leaves as well as produce many native-born Americans have never seen—vegetables and fruits with strange names and shapes usually seen only in other lands, like prickly kiwi melon from Australia or unusual green vegetables flown in from Japan and Asia.

Jungle Jim has also given new meaning to the term "fresh fish." He has just installed a series of salt- and freshwater tanks so he can stock live, farm-raised fish in more than a dozen varieties. When you want fresh fish, you just point to one, and, as Jim puts it, "we catch it, bing, bang, bang, we process it, and hand you a package with fresh fish ready for the stove." It can't get any fresher than that.

Two large wooden elephants, gifts of the Indian embassy, mark the entrance to an aisle that sells nothing but food manufactured in and imported from India. The next aisles are a veritable United Nations of foodstuffs.

There is a Japanese aisle where you can even buy Japanese ice cream or canned water from a spring at the base of Mount Fuji.

Jim pays tribute to his own heritage with the largest import area, which features Italian food and is presided over by Luigi, a larger-than-life animated Italian chef who breaks into song every five minutes. Here you will find pastas and sauces like you have never seen outside of Italy.

The pets in your household have not been forgotten. In another department called Pet World, two large animated crows periodically break into rock'n'roll music to entertain customers as they search through the dozens and dozens of different food items for Fido.

There is a walk-in cigar humidor, a full-service state liquor store, and even a penny-arcade fortune-telling machine that features a cranky old professor, who, after you feed him a couple of quarters, will insult you and offer some "lucky numbers" for playing the lottery.

Persons meeting Jim Bonaminio for the first time come away with the feeling that they have just met a very savvy businessman with the personality of a mischievous 10-year-old who just doesn't want to grow up. "Business is a serious thing," Jim Bonaminio says. "I'm a very serious guy, but I also like to have fun. I work hard, my people work hard, but there is no reason we can't take time out for a smile or a chuckle." He says that is the reason for the crazy costumes, the roller skates, the animated figures—to make what otherwise would be just a grocery store a fun place to come.

Jungle Jim's International Market

"Give the people what they want," Jim says. "If you do, if you have something for all the members of the family, it encourages them to shop as a family, it makes for togetherness, it encourages family values." It also isn't bad for business. Jim's success has not gone unnoticed by big business. An internationally known company has recently asked Jim to speak to their "think tank" members about his marketing ideas.

The number of tour buses that keep arriving at this most unusual grocery store reflect the status of Jungle Jim's International Market as the second most popular tourist attraction in Butler County.

And he is not done yet. Jim Bonaminio calls his place "a work in progress." He recently purchased about 50 acres of land surrounding his market, and now plans a huge expansion to create a Disneylike "Food World."

He already has begun construction on a monorail that will carry visitors around the 50-acre campus, to pavilions where food specialists will give cooking demonstrations. There will be a conference center and an inn with 30-plus rooms for visitors, restaurants, and, of course, a much larger market.

What else is ahead? "I'm not sure, but I've got some ideas. Just wait until I get some more money. Heh, heh, heh!" A chuckle comes from that 10-year-old boy who never grew up. Open seven days a week, 8 a.m. to 10 p.m.

(For nearby attractions, see Trip 39 in Book 1.)

Jungle Jim's International Market ☎ 513-829-1919
5440 Dixie Highway (Ohio Route 4) · Fairfield, Ohio
Region: Southwest Ohio (Butler County)
Handicapped access: Yes.

HEALTH FOOD SUPER STORE

Near Akron, in the suburb of Montrose, is another grocery store that falls into the "different" category. Mustard Seed Market and Cafe is unique in the fact that owner Philip Nabors has decreed he will sell no products that contain artificial ingredients, chemicals, additives, and preservatives. Philip notes, "Most conventional supermarkets have more preservatives in one can of beans than we have in the whole store."

What this all means is that when you wheel your cart up and down the aisles in this 31,000-square-foot market, you do not see labels for familiar breakfast cereals, nor do you see stacks of well-known brands of soft drinks.

Throughout the store you will find similar products, but the labels are usually from companies you have never heard of, companies that make foods without additives, preservatives, or even artificial sweeteners. This is good news for those folks who want more control over what they eat or who have dietary problems and must eliminate fat, salt, or sugar from the diet—also for those who suffer from allergies to milk or wheat.

For people like these, a trip to a conventional supermarket is usually an exercise in frustration. They roam up and down aisle after aisle checking the nutritional labels on products, only to find that the vast majority of the products have large amounts of salt, sugar, fat, milk products, or other common ingredients they can no longer use. Many supermarkets give little attention to this growing population with special diet needs and have only a small corner of the store set aside for "health foods."

In the past that term, "health foods," has often been a synonym for "bland, tasteless products," but that is changing. Today many of these breakfast cereals, vegetable products, and even soy-based items have become flavorful, filling foods that compete well on the dining-room table.

The problem, says Philip Nabors, is that too many major food corporations control what goes on supermarket shelves by using their economic clout to reward grocers who push their products, and they ignore the smaller, Mom-and-Pop companies who provide similar, but perhaps more health-conscious products.

Nabors said he believes that with the ever-growing concern by average Americans about eating healthier foods, coupled with growing awareness of diet-related medical problems, there is a growing segment of our society looking for a store just like his.

And it isn't just groceries here at Mustard Seed Market and Cafe.

There is the restaurant on the mezzanine level of the store. It started out seating about 45; today it seats 135.

The food is carefully prepared by a team of several chefs trained in nutrition and alternative cooking methods. They offer everything from a hormone-free steak to farm-raised fish that have not been swimming all their lives in a polluted river or lake, to wonderful vegetable entrées that are attractive as well as flavorful and filling.

Some of his customers drive over 200 miles weekly to eat at the grocery store-restaurant. All dishes are prepared from scratch using food that comes from the grocery store.

There is more. The store also runs a cooking school where you can learn how to make great-tasting dishes that do not require large amounts of salt, fat, or sugar, and how to use the many products they sell here that might not be familiar to some customers.

Nabors, who is a musician, also invites artists in to entertain his customers several times each week in his upstairs cafe.

Several popular-music celebrities make it a point to stop for lunch or dinner when they are in the northern Ohio area. Nabors says that entertainer Jimmy Buffet has been a repeat customer, as has rocker Neil Young. And his reputation among these entertainers has created another business for him: catering.

When they play northern Ohio, many musical groups put in a call to Mustard Seed Market and Cafe for all of their food needs while in the area.

Philip Nabors says it all started years ago when he and his wife, Margaret, were first married. They bought two cooking pots and started a vegetarian catering service out of their home, with a $60 initial investment. That investment is about to pay off once again in late 1999 as they open a second and even larger store and cafe in nearby Solon, Ohio. Plans, he says, are already on the drawing board for a third store and restaurant on the west side of Cleveland. Open seven days a week.

(For nearby attractions, see Trip 14 in Book 1.)

Mustard Seed Market and Cafe ☎ 330-666-SEED
West Market Plaza • Akron, Ohio
Region: Northeast Ohio (Summit County)
Handicapped access: Yes.

TWO SPECIAL FOOD MARKETS

For those who like the unusual—the upscale products usually found in small specialty stores—West Point Market brings it all together in a large, marvelous market that makes shopping almost fun.

It began a little over 60 years ago a neighborhood market, but down through the years the consistently high quality of the food and the effort to find new and unusual items have taken out of the ordinary grocery-store mold and carved a niche in the northern Ohio grocery business.

For openers, not many grocery stores have a first-rate cafe in their midst. The Beside the Point Cafe is a warmly lighted island in the midst of the store that allows diners to watch the store's kitchen in action, preparing not only meals for the cafe but also some award-winning prepared dishes for those who are too busy to cook when they get home, or can't cook as well as the folks do here.

The chefs here at West Point Market are all graduates of the Culinary Institute of America, and nothing in the prepared foods display case comes from jars, buckets, or other containers. Everything possible is made fresh each day, using fresh ingredients. Their potato salad won the *Akron Beacon-Journal's* "Best Potato Salad" contest, and when they say "ham salad" that's exactly what they mean—no ground-up lunch meat, it's made from 100 percent ham.

Just a glance down the take-home menu can start my mouth watering. From Veggie Stuffed Grape Leaves to Plum-Glazed Chicken, from Marinated Bocconcini to Teriyaki Chicken and Spring Rolls, from Oven-Roasted Tomatoes to Individual Meat Loaves and Chicken Loaves. There is always something new and different being prepared in the kitchen. No tired old menus here.

But the cafe is just one of the secrets here.

There is the cheese shop with cheeses from all over the world. A seafood shop with truly fresh fish flown in from both coasts. Two of my favorite spots are the chocolate shop and the bakery shops, where they offer some of the most decadent desserts known to humankind. The butcher shop offers only the best grade of meat, cut to your specifications, and it goes on and on. The specialty shop is the spot where you can find dozens of gourmet mustards from around the world, and sauces and seasonings rarely found in other food stores. It's no wonder that customers drive here every week from all over northern Ohio to shop.

And they have now entered the computer age.

They suggest that you e-mail them before coming to be sure they have the specialty items you want. Or, if you prefer to do it the old-fashioned way, you can phone them. West Point Market is open Monday through Saturday; they are closed on Sunday.

(For nearby attractions, see Trip 14 in Book 1.)

West Point Market   ☎ 330-864-2151 or (800) 838-2156
1711 West Market Street • Akron, Ohio
Region: Northeast Ohio (Summit County)
Handicapped access: Yes.

West Point Market

THE SPECIALTY STORE

Like many other businesses in this book, the Dorothy Lane Market in Dayton had humble beginnings. It was back in 1948 that Calvin Mayne and Frank Sakada opened a fruit stand at the corner of Dorothy Lane and Far Hills Avenue. As with other successful businesses, it just grew and grew and grew.

In 1953 the fruit stand, which had now grown to be a market, was moved to 2710 Fair Hills Avenue but kept the name "Dorothy Lane Market." In 1958 Frank Sakada sold his interest to Calvin Mayne, beginning a family ownership that goes on today, even though Calvin died in 1972.

Today the market is a far cry from the little fruit stand. It now offers all kinds of premium foods and specialty items. Among the signature items are Euro Breads, breads baked in the store's bakery that are hand-kneaded and made from longtime recipes. They also offer a honey-glazed ham and multilayered brownies they call "Killer Brownies" that weigh up to a third of a pound!

(For nearby attractions, see Trip 38 in Book 1, and Trip 64 in Book 2.)

Dorothy Lane Market   ☎ 937-299-3561
2710 Fair Hills Avenue • Dayton, Ohio
Region: Southwest Ohio (Montgomery County)
Handicapped access: Yes.

SOME OTHER SPECIALTY FOOD PLACES, CO-OPS, AND SUCH

Co-ops have been around almost since the country began. At one time or another, all kinds of people have probably belonged to a co-op, whether it be an association of condominium owners or a group of farmers who form a grain elevator co-op to mill and sell their corn and grain. This is certainly nothing new, but food co-ops got a boost in the late 1960s and early 1970s from student activists in colleges around the country. The driving force is a little hard to sort out. Social concerns for the poor and environmental concerns about chemicals in food and pollution of the sea, land, and air all had their impact. I think that students trying to stretch a dollar also saw the benefits of cooperative buying of food and materials. Food cooperatives are still usually found near universities and colleges. With the increasing number of people concerned about health and dietary needs, the cooperatives have survived and even flourished in some places. Some are closed, some are open to the public. All have some sort of membership fee or work-exchange program that allows low-income people to trade their work to offset the cost of membership, which then gives them discounted prices on the food they buy from the organization. For example, the Oberlin College Good Food Coop charges a monthly fee to either households or individuals and a smaller fee to senior citizen households, or if members agree to work a certain number of hours each month in the co-op, then they get a free membership for that month.

Here are some co-ops that specialize in organically grown foods and specialty items you won't find in the corner chain-grocery store. However, please note that I have not visited these places and do not have a firsthand opinion about them. They have been recommended to me, but because of time constraints or other reasons, we have not visited any of the establishments listed below. Some have very limited hours of operation or operate only seasonally, so be sure you call before going.

(Co-ops are all over the state. For nearby attractions, see Books 1 and 2.)

Co-op on Coventry
216-791-3890
1807 Coventry Road • Cleveland, Ohio
Region: Northeast Ohio (Cuyahoga County)
Handicapped access: Yes.

Cleveland Food Co-op
216-791-3890
11702 Euclid Avenue • Cleveland, Ohio
Region: Northeast Ohio (Cuyahoga County)
Handicapped access: Yes.

Kent Natural Foods Co-Op
330-673-2878
151 East Main Street • Kent, Ohio
Region: Northeast Ohio (Portage County)
Handicapped access: Yes.

Good Food Co-Op
440-775-6533
Wilder Hall, West College Street • Oberlin, Ohio
Region: Northeast Ohio (Lorain County)
Handicapped access: Yes.

Phoenix Earth Food Co-Op
419-476-3211
1437 W. Sylvania Avenue • Toledo, Ohio
Region: Northwest Ohio (Lucas County)
Handicapped access: Yes.

Wooster Food Co-Op
330-264-9797
247 West North Street • Wooster, Ohio
Region: Northeast Ohio (Wayne County)
Handicapped access: Yes.

Good Food Co-Op
440-747-9368
62 Pyatt Street • Youngstown, Ohio
Region: Northeast Ohio (Mahoning County)
Handicapped access: Yes.

Cooperative Market
330-869-2590
1596 West Market Street • Akron, Ohio
Region: Northeast Ohio (Summit County)
Handicapped access: Yes.

Bexley Natural Food Co-Op
614-252-3951
508 North Cassady Avenue • Columbus, Ohio
Region: Central Ohio (Franklin County)
Handicapped access: Yes.

A EUROPEAN-STYLE MARKET

Okay, so you don't really relish the idea of getting up early in the morning and heading out to the field to sweat under a hot summertime sun while you stoop to pick fresh strawberries, or swat off bees while trying to pick blueberries or raspberries. You say you would rather let someone else do the picking, but you would still like to have fresh produce. That's the beauty of farmer's markets. Here you will usually find the freshest from the fields, piled high, just waiting to be transferred to your basket for the journey to your dining table. The best part: not only is it probably fresher than some of the produce you will find in your local grocery store, since you cut out some of the middlemen, chances are it will probably cost less, too.

For openers, you can't beat the West Side Market in Cleveland. It has been a favorite shopping spot of thousands of Clevelanders since it opened in 1912. This huge auditorium and the food stalls outside house almost 200 venders of every delicacy imaginable. From fresh fruit from around the world to ethnic meats and cheeses to baked goods and spices. A visit to the West Side Market is a cultural experience, especially on weekends, when the place almost reaches gridlock. There are the smells of different foods and spices and the melody of a dozen foreign languages all being spoken at the same time. Here you will often find the rich and the famous rubbing elbows with the poor, and even the homeless, as they search for food. The West Side Market is open Monday, Wednesday, Friday, and Saturday, year round.

(For nearby attractions, see Trips 5, 15, and 16 in Book 1.)

West Side Market   ☎ 216-664-3386
1979 West 25th Street (at Lorain Avenue) • Cleveland, Ohio
Region: Northeast Ohio (Cuyahoga County)
Handicapped access: Yes.

A FARMER'S MARKET, PLUS

The city of Toledo has come up with a plan to make their marketplace even more unique than Cleveland's.

A couple of years ago the old Civic Auditorium was given a new mission in life. The building that had served the city for years as both theater and exhibition hall was converted into an indoor marketplace.

Other buildings in the complex were leased out, one to an antique mall, the other to the Libbey Glass Company, which moved their popular glass outlet store from their factory to the market complex. Some open-air stands outside were refurbished for the traditional farmer's market.

The result has been the keystone to the renewal of a part of downtown Toledo that had been sliding into shabby disrepair for the last decade. While it is presently home to only about three dozen vendors, it's a good mix, ranging from fresh fish to fresh bread, several food stands, and a dozen gift shops. The Toledo bus service, TARGA, runs a free shuttle from the downtown each business day at noon to allow office workers a chance to wander the market while shopping for lunch. Weekends are very busy as farmers set up outside to sell their produce and busloads of tourists pull in to wander the market complex.

There are all kinds of bargains to be had here, from the fresh food and bakery items to the antique gallery that packs more than 80 antique dealers into a long adjoining hall. And then there is the Libbey Glass Outlet Store. Here you can purchase discontinued styles, overrun merchandise, and even seconds at a significant savings. And don't forget they also have a closeout section with even further bargains.

(For nearby attractions, see Trip 23 in Book 1.)

The Erie Street Market   ☎ 419-936-ERIE (Market);
419-243-1800 (Superior Antique Mall); 419-254-5000 (Libbey Glass Outlet)
237 South Erie Street • Toledo, Ohio
Region: Northwest Ohio (Lucas County)
Handicapped access: Yes.

114 **Picnic Spots**

HAVE LUNCH WITH A COUPLE OF HUNDRED FAMOUS PEOPLE— EVEN THOUGH THEY'RE DEAD!

Would you like to have lunch with a former president of the United States? How about the man who founded the Standard Oil Empire? Throw in a secretary of state and some famous law-makers, movie stars, and sports heroes. You can do it. But don't expect much conversation from them. They are all dead. What we are talking about is probably one of the most unusual places to have a picnic lunch: in a cemetery.

Lake View Cemetery in Cleveland has scattered picnic tables throughout its huge grounds which stretch from Euclid Avenue to Mayfield Road. The idea is to encourage people to realize that a cemetery is for the living as well as the dead. The parklike burial ground has over five hundred varieties of trees that are marked and identified and thousands of perennial plants that bloom throughout the spring, summer, and fall.

You will find picnic tables in the shadow of the imposing tomb that contains the remains of former president James A. Garfield. Nearby are the tombs of oil millionaire John D. Rockefeller; John Hay, President Lincoln's private secretary; Charles Brush, inventor of the arc lamp, which helped light our cities; and a host of other famous people from all walks of life. Other picnic tables are placed throughout the cemetery, like the one near the Wade Chapel on the edge of a small lake.

There is no charge to take a picnic basket and have your lunch in the beauty of this historic last resting place. Cemetery officials do ask that you remember where you are and that everyone buried here was once dear to someone. Please show respect for the graves and clean up after you have finished your picnic. Wastebaskets are located near the picnic tables, and no cooking is allowed inside the cemetery.

(For nearby attractions, see Trips 5, 15, and 16 in Book 1.)

Lake View Cemetery   ☎ 216-421-2665
12316 Euclid Avenue • Cleveland, Ohio
Region: Northeast Ohio (Cuyahoga County)
Handicapped access: Paved roads, some grassy areas near picnic tables.

Lake View Cemetery

OHIO RIVER OVERLOOK

This is one of my personal favorites, and it doesn't even have an address, you just have to follow the directions. Keidaish Park, part of the Monroe County Park System in Southeast Ohio, offers this tiny picnic area on a hilltop that overlooks the Ohio River. They say on a clear day you can see 20 miles in all directions. There are only a couple of tables, so it is usually not crowded. There are no restrooms, and the nearest public facilities are several miles away, so be forewarned. It's a difficult park to find, but if you follow the directions you'll be rewarded with a scenic vista that only the birds usually enjoy.

Here are directions from the county seat in Woodsfield, Ohio: Go east-southeast on State Route 78 to State Route 536. Turn right on Route 536 and follow it two and a half miles to County Road 43, follow 43 north one and a half miles to Township Road 419, which is also known as Short Ridge Road. From this point there should be signs that will take you to the top of the hill and the parking lot of the park. If you would like more information about this little-known picnic area, write to the park district office in Woodsfield. While no cooking grills are located in the park, it is permissible to bring portable grills in to cook on.

(For nearby attractions, see Trip 35 in Book 1.)

Monroe County Park District   ☎ 740-472-1328
105 West Court Street • Woodsfield, Ohio
Region: Southeast Ohio (Monroe County)
Handicapped access: Gravel parking lot, park is on an incline, no restrooms.

Monroe County Parks

A SPRINGTIME WATERFALL

The Paine Falls Reservation of the Lake County Metroparks system gets my vote as one of the most beautiful picnic spots, especially on a warm, early spring day when the river is high and the roar of the falls drowns out the noise of nearby traffic.

Paine Falls is one of the lesser-known Lake metroparks, as well as one of the smallest. Just 58 acres, it sits at the junction of Paine Creek and Paine Road. There are hiking trails that will take you to a lookout just across the creek from the falls. The water flow over the falls depends on the amount of rain that has fallen recently. In dry periods the falls shrink to a trickle, but in the spring it often offers a dramatic backdrop for a romantic picnic.

This spot is a little hard to find, but just follow the directions: From I-90 in Lake County, east of Painesville, take the Vrooman Road exit. Go south on Vrooman 5.5 miles to Carter Road. Turn left (east) on Carter and follow it two miles to Paine Road. Turn left on Paine Road, and the falls are

on the left, about a half-mile down the road. For more information about other great picnic spots contact the park headquarters.
(For nearby attractions, see Trip 13 in Book 1.)

Lake County Metroparks   ☎ 440-639-7275 or 800-227-PARK
Concord Woods Reservation
1121 Spear Road • Concord Township, Ohio
Region: Northeast Ohio (Lake County)
Handicapped access: Limited. Restrooms available, cooking allowed on grills supplied in park.

SOME OTHER PLACES TO PICNIC

When I was a youngster during World War II, growing up in Vermilion, Ohio, my family, for entertainment, used to go to the local railroad station to watch the trains go by. My mother would pack some sandwiches and put Kool-Aid in a jug with ice cubes, and away we would go for an afternoon of watching troop trains steam through. It was a chance to wave to the soldiers heading off for war. Also there were the famous express trains that sped through, like the New York Central Mercury, which would give us a quick glance at a dining car full of men and women in suits and hats, staring out the window and eating, headed for who-knew-where. There are not many passenger trains to watch any more, and the ones that still run usually pass through our community very early in the morning. But there are airplanes. Years ago they even had a small parking lot near Cleveland Hopkins International Airport where families could sit and watch the airliners take off and land right over their heads. However, airport expansion took over that property for other things, and today you need to seek out a side street near the airport to watch the comings and goings of the airplanes.

I have also noticed at some small airports that there is frequently a picnic table near the office. I suspect it is for the employees' use on a nice day, but I called my friends at Griffing Flying Service in Sandusky and asked if their picnic table was for use by the public. They said employees come first, but if the table is not being used and someone wants to eat lunch there and watch takeoffs and landings, they are welcome, as long as they clean up after their lunch. (By the way, Griffing Flying Service has a lunchroom where one of the specialties is a milk shake so thick you have to eat it with a spoon, and it's made from real ice cream, not some soupy mix.)

(For nearby attractions, see Trip 18 in Book 1, and Trips 48 and 66 in Book 2.)

Griffing Flying Service   ☎ 419-626-5161
Route 6 • Sandusky, Ohio
Region: Northeast Ohio (Erie County)
Handicapped access: Yes.

PICNIC IN A FARM MEADOW

Okay, your idea of a real romantic picnic is in a farm meadow, far out in the country, a long way from traffic, cars, airplanes, people. Only you and a special someone lying on a carpet of fresh clover, watching lazy hawks circle in blue skies overhead. Feeding on stuffed squab, fresh chocolate-covered strawberries, toasting each other with wine . . . well, there is such a place, but it's not free. Jim and Vicky Goudy of Cambridge, Ohio, have turned their farm home into a unique bed-and-breakfast. Located at the end of a dead-end road up a hill, the hilltop acreage bumps into acres of nearby forest. There is a spring-fed lake with fish and a barn with the Goudys' many animals (everything from goats to horses).

Here's the deal. You book a night at their bed-and-breakfast. Each room is private with its own private bath. You also book a picnic at an additional cost. When you arrive in the early afternoon, Jim will take you on your own personal hayride in a wagon behind his tractor. At the end of the ride, you arrive at a hilltop meadow that is surrounded by trees for privacy. On a picnic table will be a hamper filled with delectable gourmet picnic foods and everything you need for a picnic dinner in the meadow, including a couple of candles (either for light or to ward off the mosquitoes). You tell Jim how long you and your special someone want to be left undisturbed in the meadow, and then he leaves you to your private meadow to do what you will. Picnic naked if you like. When he returns at the appointed hour, he discreetly makes a lot of noise with the tractor as he approaches, so you know it's time to head back to the house. But the fun isn't over yet. Back at the house there is a large hot tub located in the orchard next to the house, a great place to relax after a long picnic in the meadow before turning in for the night. The next morning Vicky Goudy prepares a real country breakfast for all of her guests. (P.S., she is a wonderful cook.)

(For nearby attractions, see Trip 36 in Book 1.)

Misty Meadow Farm Bed and Breakfast   ☎ 740-439-5135
64878 Slaughter Hill Road • Cambridge, Ohio
Region: Southeast Ohio (Guernsey County)
Handicapped access: Yes.

A CARRIAGE RIDE, A WATERFALL, AND A PICNIC

If you don't have time or are too lazy to make your own picnic lunch, here's a suggestion for a romantic afternoon with someone special. For about $85 per couple you get a two-hour experience. It starts with an old-fashioned horse-drawn carriage ride around a farm on the edge of the Cuyahoga Valley National Recreation Area. Then you switch to another form of horsepower, a vintage 1967 Plymouth Barracuda that transports you to the meadow by Brandywine Falls in the national park. There you will find a basket filled with your choice of three entrées (beef, shrimp, or chicken), freshly made potato salad, some fruit and sweets, a bottle of nonalcoholic champagne, and two glasses. You can either spread a large blanket (included) on the ground and watch the falls, or move to one of the picnic tables in the nearby park. Reservations are required for this one. Picnic available (weather permitting) mid-May through October.

(For nearby attractions, see Trip 14 in Book 1.)

Carriage Trade Farm   ☎ Cleveland 330-467-9000 or Akron 330-650-6262
8050 Brandywine Farm · Northfield, Ohio
Region: Northeast Ohio (Cuyahoga County)
Handicapped access: Steps into carriage, grassy area near falls.

Carriage Trade Farm

115 Pick Your Own

Every time summer arrives I start getting a spate of phone calls about where folks can go to pick (choose one) strawberries, peaches, apples, peas, cherries, you name it.

Sadly, the choice of pick-your-own fruits and vegetables seems to get smaller each year as farms give way to developers, or insurance costs force farmers to keep visitors out of their fields and orchards; or too many people who visit the farms are careless while picking their products and damage the remaining crops, prompting an end to "pick-your-own."

Some farms are trying to fill the gap by picking the crop themselves and placing the fruits or vegetables in large containers at the salesroom, where customers may pick through and select the ones they want.

Happily, there are a few places still left that not only welcome you into their orchards and fields, but make the visit a fun one for the entire family.

A JOHNNY APPLESEED FARM

If you have ever driven through Ohio's apple country in the autumn and smelled the fragrance of ripe apples hanging in the crisp evening air, you can probably thank a man by the name of John Chapman. He was better known as "Johnny Appleseed."

He was born in 1774 in Massachusetts. His mother died when John was just two years old. There is a legend that his father served in the Revolutionary War but was dishonorably discharged.

With this kind of beginning, it is not surprising that he began supporting himself at a very early age. By the time he was in his teen years he had caught the bug of being an adventurer and had heard of the Great Lakes to the west and the fertile land in the valley of the Ohio River. He set off on foot from Massachusetts, never to return.

He was an odd sight on the frontier. In winter he wrapped his bare feet in sacks and made snowshoes from young trees. He wore a hat that doubled as a cooking pot. No one is quite sure when John planted his first apple tree, but there is speculation that during the winter of 1797/98 he picked a spot in western Pennsylvania for his first apple orchard nursery.

He was not the first to bring apples into the Great Lakes region; many settlers would plant an orchard as one of their first acts when clearing the land. Apples were important not only as fruit, but also because of the cider, which could be converted easily into applejack. It helped pass the long, lonely winters for many a frontiersman.

Probably no pioneer did more to spread the apple through the Midwest than Chapman, who became known as Johnny Appleseed to the sturdy individuals who were carving a civilization out of the forests.

What John Chapman did was combine religion with his love of apple trees. John was a member of the new church founded by Emanuel Swedenborg, and he became a missionary of the religion, spreading the word along with appleseeds and trees as the frontier pushed to the west, into Ohio and Indiana.

His quirky but gentle ways were remembered by the frontiersmen, and stories about him began to spread—of how he had saved residents near Mansfield, Ohio, by running through the forest when he learned the Indians planned to attack, warning settlers that the British and the Indians were torching everything in their path. Or tales of how he would trade apple trees for land as he started orchard after orchard.

He lived in the Richland County area of Ohio for nearly 20 years before the frontier moved west and he traveled with it. His life ended in Fort Wayne, Indiana, on March 18, 1845. He had a nursery there of over 15,000 young apple trees. Even today you can find descendants of the original Johnny Appleseed orchards still producing apples.

I had my first taste of one nearly 30 years ago when I stopped at Mapleside Farms in Brunswick to do a story on the fall apple harvest. Bill Eyssen, the owner and patriarch of the family, happened to mention that a tree in front of his apple house was a descendant of an original tree planted by Johnny Appleseed.

I thought it would make a great closing moment for the piece if I stood by the tree and picked an apple from it, and took a bite. Sort of a bite of history. Bill agreed that I could pick one of his historic apples, and as the cameras were rolling I said something about how Mapleside Farms represented a historic tie with the past, that this very tree I was standing in front of had come to us from the legendary Johnny Appleseed himself. With that, I ripped a small apple off the tree and took a bite.

It was the sourest apple I had ever bitten into in my life. In fact, it was so sour it made my mouth pucker up, and I was unable to sign off. All the viewers saw was me spitting out the apple while Bill Eyssen rocked with laughter, as I gasped, "Ohhh, that's sour! That's sour!"

Fortunately, the rest of Bill Eyssen's apples are really delicious. In fact, Mapleside Farms is worth a One Tank Trip, especially in the autumn when the apples are ripe.

They not only have 6,000 apple trees scattered over a hillside, representing just about every type of apple there is, they also make fresh cider at their mill.

There is a bakery, where many of the apples end up in pies and cakes, and there is a horse-drawn wagon tour of the farm and orchards that gets you within touching distance of trees loaded with red and yellow apples. They have an ice-cream shop, a gift shop, and a restaurant that has one of the finest views in northern Ohio.

From their hilltop location on Pearl Road, it's said that on a clear day you can see all the apple trees spilling down the hillside and trailing off to the horizon, 40 miles away.

It's a pleasant place to have lunch or dinner. There is a wonderful balcony for outside dining in good weather and a huge wood-burning fireplace for those cold winter nights. The food is all homemade, and the restaurant is a popular spot with greater Clevelanders

By the way, Mapleside Farms also sponsors a Johnny Appleseed festival at the farm every autumn on the third weekend in September. There are craftspeople, music, dancing, barbecue, and of course apples, fresh from the orchard and some freshly dipped in caramel. I doubt that old Johnny Appleseed ever had an apple that tasted this good.

(For nearby attractions, see Trip 14 in Book 1, and Trip 58 in Book 2.)

Mapleside Farms   ☎ stores: 330-225-5577; restaurant: 330-225-5576
294 Pearl Road • Brunswick, Ohio
Region: Northeast Ohio (Medina County)
Handicapped access: Yes.

WAGON RIDES, SING-ALONGS, AND PICK IT YOURSELF

John Bergman started his farm near Port Clinton, Ohio, back in 1947.

It's grown to a couple of farms today, and he carries all kinds of fruits and vegetables that he grows, ranging from strawberries in the early summer to peaches and apples in the autumn.

On certain days, he still allows customers to pick their own apples and peaches. He even has wagon rides for the kids, with sing-alongs and free samples. There is fresh cider made from his apples, as well as a host of other fresh vegetables and fruit filling not one, but two farm markets in the Port Clinton area.

(For nearby attractions, see Trip 21 in Book 1.)

Bergman Orchards ☎ 419-734-6280 or 419-734-4272
4562 East Bayshore Road • Port Clinton, Ohio
or, 600 SE Catawba Road • Port Clinton, Ohio
Region: Northwest Ohio (Ottawa County)
Handicapped access: drive into orchards, grassy areas around trees.

PICK CHERRIES AND MORE

In Lake County, in Perry, Ohio, near Painesville, the West family farm still offers almost summerlong pick-your-own fruit and vegetables.

They start in June with strawberries, then cherries ripen. There's a couple of weeks before the first batch of sweet corn is ready to pick, and then come peaches and finally the apple crop.

While they do a lot of pick-your-own, some of the things, like corn, they pick and sell at their farm market.

The West brothers, who operate the farm, are the fifth generation of their family to raise fruits and vegetables. When the picking starts, especially the pick-your-own crops, they carefully watch the fields and only allow so much picking each day to give the not-yet-ripe fruit a chance to ripen. It's possible that they may have to close down a field if it gets over-picked by eager customers determined to have some of the first-of-the-season fruit. For example, by being careful in strawberry season, they are usually still picking at the end of June.

The West farm is one of the few in Lake County that has pick-your-own for other things, like cherries. However, in strawberry season, just on a drive along U.S. Route 20 from Perry into Geneva I counted four places that allowed you to pick your own. Some advertise on the radio and in newspapers, but some just stick a sign out in front. Most growers supply containers to pick into.

(For nearby attractions, see Trip 13 in Book 1.)

West Orchards ☎ 440-259-3192
3096 North Ridge Road (US Route 20) • Perry, Ohio
Region: Northeast Ohio (Lake County)
Handicapped access: drive into orchards, grassy areas around trees.

ORCHARD FOR THE GROCERS

When peaches or apples ripen it's a tradition in some families to head out toward Berlin Heights in Erie County to this neat roadside market and orchards.

Chances are if you live in northern Ohio you have probably, at one time or another, eaten some of Burnham's fruit.

Their main customers are some of the largest grocery store chains in this part of the state. But with all their business they still have time to run a small roadside market where they sell their freshly made cider, as well as apples, peaches, and other fruits and vegetables, most of them grown by Burnham or in the local area.

And they still allow customers to pick their own peaches and apples during certain times in the fall. My family is still eating some of the giant peaches we picked in their orchard last year and froze.

Burnham's is usually open from the first of August through the end of March. They are usually open from 9 in the morning until 5:30 p.m., but hours can vary, especially during the busy harvest time. It's always a good idea to call first if you are driving any distance.

(For nearby attractions, see Trip 28 in Book 1, and Trips 56 and 61 in Book 2.)

Burnham Orchards Inc.   ☎ 419-588-2138
8019 State Route 113 East · Berlin Heights, Ohio
Region: Northeast Ohio (Erie County)
Handicapped access: drive into orchards, grassy areas around trees.

ORCHARD, MARKET, AND PUMPKINVILLE

Apple Hill Orchards is directly across the road from where I grew up, in Henrietta Township in Lorain County. So I have been eating these apples for most of my life.

Roger Miller, the current owner, still lets customers enjoy the fall harvest at his farm. You can pick your own apples, ride a wagon into the orchards, let the kids crawl through a maze made of bales of straw, and enjoy "Pumpkinville," consisting of painted pumpkins with whimsical faces.

They have a farm market here that also sells bulk foods and fresh cider, as well as their apples and other fruits and vegetables. They also carry plants and baked goods and are open year round. The apple-picking, of course, is in the autumn. This is a good place to bring along the kids when it's time to pick apples.

(For nearby attractions, see Trip 58 in Book 2.)

Apple Hill Orchards ☎ 440-988-3572
8716 Vermilion Road • Amherst, Ohio
Region: Northeast Ohio (Lorain County)
Handicapped access: drive into orchards, grassy areas around trees.

BERRIES GALORE!

If breakfast isn't complete without some fresh berries, here's the place to pick your own, located just off U. S. Route 2, west of Lorain. Keep your eye peeled: there are no large signs and only a small utility building on the property. Most of the berry bushes are located quite a ways back from the road and are not easily seen as you drive by. Blueberries, raspberries, and blackberries are what they grow. They are usually open from late June through most of August, Tuesday through Saturday, when berries are available. They have a recording you can call that tells you when berries are ready to be picked.

(For nearby attractions, see Trip 20 in Book 1.)

Baumhardt Road Berry Farm ☎ 440-246-7983
Baumhardt Road • Vermilion, Ohio
Region: Northeast Ohio (Erie County), half-mile south of State Route 2
Handicapped access: drive into orchards, grassy areas around trees.

STRAWBERRIES AND PUMPKINS

This is another large farm that allows you to pick your own strawberries and pumpkins in the fall. They also offer hayrides, a straw maze, and other Halloween activities in October. Their farm market also carries other fruits and vegetables. Usually open from June to October daily.

(For nearby attractions, see Trip 58 in Book 2.)

Red Wagon Farm ☎ 440-236-3007
16081 East River Road • Columbia Station, Ohio
Region: Northeast Ohio (Lorain County)
Handicapped access: drive into orchards, grassy areas around trees.

PICK VEGETABLES, TOO

Hilgert's probably offers more pick-your-own products than any other farm in northern Ohio.

Starting in June they let customers in to pick their own strawberries. Then as they ripen, the fields are opened up to pickers for beans, greens, peas, peppers, raspberries, and tomatoes. They also offer apples and a whole lot of other fruits and vegetables, including sweet corn. Hours here vary with the seasons.

It's always best to phone to see what's ripe, what they are picking that day, and what hours they are open.

(For nearby attractions, see Trip 14 in Book 1.)

Hilgert's Berry Farm and Market ☎ 330-325-1405
3431 Waterloo Road · Mogadore, Ohio
Region: Northeast Ohio (Summit County)
Handicapped access: drive into orchards, grassy areas around trees.

IN THE MOOD FOR BLUEBERRIES

My family and I were on our way to Dayton when we spotted the sign for fresh blueberries here. We stopped and in just a matter of minutes had filled three or four quart baskets with huge, ripe berries. The bushes cover a hillside, and the area is very well maintained, making picking very easy. If you aren't up to picking your own, they already have some boxed up and will sell you those, at a slightly higher price.

They also have a nice garden center here where you can buy everything from crafts to butterfly houses, annuals, perennials, and, yes, even blueberry bushes so you can pick your own in your own backyard. Open April through September daily.

(For nearby attractions, see Trip 59 in Book 2.)

Beilstein's Blueberry Patch ☎ 419-884-1797
1285 West Hanley Road · Mansfield, Ohio
Region: Northeast Ohio (Richland County)
Handicapped access: drive into orchards, grassy areas around trees.

PICK YOUR OWN ... TURKEY?

This isn't exactly a pick-your-own fruit or vegetable farm, What they raise here are turkeys. Thousands of turkeys. In fact, they are open to the public only a short time each year. They open up Thanksgiving week and run through Christmas time. This is strictly fresh turkey. No large processing plant and frozen birds with additives.

They say you can even point one out, and they will take care of the processing for you. But if you would rather skip that part, just go to their farm market during the weeks they are open, and a bird, ready to take home and put in the oven, will be ready for you.

They used to sell them "on the hoof," but the owner says some people just didn't understand how to go about the process of getting a live bird ready for the oven. (I'm trying to be delicate here—after all not too many homes have a chopping block and an ax in the backyard anymore.) In fact, if you call ahead and tell them how big a bird you need, they will have it waiting for you when you arrive. This is one of the last places you can still go "down on the farm" and select your bird for the holidays.

(For nearby attractions, see Trip 23 in Book 1.)

Britten Turkey farm   ☎ 419-874-6624
10700 Roachton Road · Perrysburg, Ohio
Region: Northwest Ohio (Wood County)
Handicapped access: Yes.

LARGEST PUMPKIN PATCH IN OHIO

This place claims to have the largest pumpkin patch in Ohio: 150 acres that produce an estimated 250,000 pumpkins each year. In October they put up a large tent on the edge of the pumpkin field and hold weekend festivals where kids can come in costume, have a hayride, and even play in a maze made of straw.

Of course the best part is that you and the kids can go into the field to find the perfect Great Pumpkin for your Halloween party. In fact, when school groups come out they give away any pumpkin the kids can carry out of the field by themselves.

(For nearby attractions, see Trip 23 in Book 1.)

Klickman Farms   ☎ 419-862-2859
16985 W. Portage River South Road · Elmore, Ohio
Region: Northwest Ohio (Ottawa County)
Handicapped access: some grassy areas.

116 Take Ohio Home with You: Local Products

I frequently get phone calls from viewers saying they want to send a gift package that fairly screams "Ohio" to a relative or friend who lives outside the state. I usually suggest things like a copy of any of my books (notice how I was able to sneak that plug in?). I also suggest things like Ohio maple syrup or a fruit basket of Ohio apples or some of the flour that is still ground daily at historic old mills around the state. Each Christmas a friend in Hawaii sends me some Hawaiian coffee and chocolate-covered macadamia nuts that are grown on the islands. As I savor a cup of the coffee or let a chocolate-covered nut melt in my mouth, it brings back wonderful memories of my visit to Hawaii several years ago. I often send them a jug of maple syrup and some freshly ground flour from the Clifton Mill in Clifton, Ohio, and hope that when they are having a breakfast of pancakes out there in paradise, they will remember the pleasant times they had when they visited the Buckeye State.

In my case, I am fortunate to travel the state repeatedly, and I can take my choice of the literally hundreds of businesses that sell Ohio-made or -grown products. But I realize that for some folks a week's vacation or a couple of weekend getaways are all they can manage each year. If that is you, and you need some ideas on how to find a choice of home-state products that you want to give as gifts, here are a few ideas from places I have visited and found to have some great choices.

FLAVORFUL OHIO

Gift baskets can be made up with everything from candies to zucchinis that come from Ohio. Chris Sancin says that what can be in the baskets is limited only by people's imaginations. She carries a great assortment of products grown and made in Ohio, everything from mustard and cheese to pottery to books about the state. She also carries jewelry, glass items, note cards, and even caramel corn made in Ohio. You can stop in at her store and pick out a ready-made basket, or design your own. She can also take care of shipping and delivery.

(For nearby attractions, see Trips 5, 15, and 16 in Book 1.)

The Flavor of Ohio   ☎ 800-755-6446
28879 Lorain Road · North Olmsted, Ohio
Region: Northeast Ohio (Cuyahoga County)
Handicapped access: Yes.

EVERYTHING MAPLE

If it's made from maple syrup, then it probably came from Richards Maple Products in Chardon. They have been around since 1910, making and selling maple products like syrup and candy and even the equipment to make your own syrup. One of my favorite things is to stop by when they are making candy in the kitchen and get a sample of fresh maple cream right out of the pot. Richardson's has a store that has maple syrup products from Northeast Ohio year round. They always have the syrup, maple spread, maple sugar candy, and gift boxes. They also will handle the shipping and delivery of your gifts.

(For nearby attractions, see Trip 9 in Book 1.)

Richards Maple Products   ☎ 800-352-4052 or 440-286-4160
545 Water Street · Chardon, Ohio
Region: Northeast Ohio (Geauga County)
Handicapped access: Yes.

SHOP AT THE STATEHOUSE

Inside the statehouse in Columbus is a great gift shop that specializes in all things Ohio. First you take the really informative tour of the recently renovated statehouse and poke your nose into the places where Ohio's laws are made. Then, before you leave, stop at the Statehouse Museum Shop. Here you will find things like Ohio-made pasta, cookies, and cheese, and a wonderful selection of Ohio-made wines representing many of the famous wineries from the Buckeye State. You can call them on their 800 number for a free catalogue if you can't make it to Columbus. They, too, will take care of shipping and delivery for you.

(For nearby attractions, see Trip 26 in Book 1, and Trip 62 in Book 2.)

The Ohio Statehouse Museum Shop, Ohio Statehouse   ☎ 888-OHIO-123
Broad and High Streets · Columbus, Ohio
Region: Central Ohio (Franklin County)
Handicapped access: Yes.

117 Wineries

I am not a wine connoisseur. I grew up in my grandmother's home, and she had been president of the Women's Christian Temperance Union in our local community. We were not even allowed to have any fermented juices in our home.

It was only after I had been in the marines that I really had my first glass of wine. I don't count the stuff they used to hand out in church for communion—I think that was usually grape juice, and the little thimble-sized communion glasses gave you hardly enough to wet your lips.

I have had friends who grew up in homes where wine was served with nearly every meal and was given to the children as freely as a glass of water. To the best of my knowledge, none of these friends grew up to be alcoholics or had their growth mentally or physically hampered in any way by the wine. In fact, many claim it was this early introduction to wine that has given them good health throughout their lives. And to be sure, there has been some medical research into the benefits of a glass of wine.

What all this is leading up to is that once I tasted wine, I loved it. Especially Ohio wines. In fact I was surprised to find out that some of the best wines in the world are produced right here in the Buckeye State.

I have never considered myself an expert on wines. Like many people who enjoy wine, I drink the ones I like, no matter what the label or origin. I probably wouldn't be able to tell you the difference between a French wine and one that originated in a vineyard in Ashtabula County. I just know that when I have served wines at my home, they have usually been Ohio wines, and friends and family have always enjoyed them.

Much of the Ohio wine industry can trace its founding to grapes that were grown on a hillside in Cincinnati nearly 150 years ago. The Longworth family vineyards were the first serious attempt at developing fine wines in Ohio. Nicholas Longworth is called "the father of Ohio wine."

He was a Cincinnati attorney who lived in a huge Greek-revival mansion that is now the home of the Taft Museum of Art. The Longworth Vineyards were planted where Eden Park is now in downtown Cincinnati. Longworth's wines became so famous that the whole river valley was called "the Rhineland of America." But the American Civil War came along and with it a manpower shortage, and the vines were not tended. In short order the vineyards were in shambles, and Longworth sold what winery assets he had to Meier's Wine Company, located about 10 miles north of Cincinnati in what is now Silverton.

Meier's continues to be the oldest operating winery in Ohio. It is also Ohio's largest winery. The chief plantings have been moved to the balmier weather of the Lake Erie islands. Today North Bass Island is one large vineyard, producing grapes that consistently win awards for the Meier's company. For example, in 1993 they won a Double Gold Medal for excellence in the highly respected San Francisco International Wine Competition.

Today Ohio ranks sixth nationally in the production of wine and fourth in the number of wineries. There are approximately 200 vineyards in Ohio, covering more than two thousand acres. The major areas for wine production in the state are the Lake Erie region, the Ohio River Valley region, and some other plantings around Akron and Central Ohio.

About 60 percent of the grapes grown in Ohio are American Concord and Catawba. These grapes are used for juices and jellies. Thirty-five percent are wine grapes; they include both European varieties and some American hybrid varieties. In case you are interested, Ohio produces more white wine than red. Premium varieties made in the state include Vidal, Catawba, Seyval, Riesling, Chardonnay, and Cabernet.

I have visited the wineries I am listing, and have sampled their wines.

There are so many wineries in Ohio that I am unable to visit all of them. The fact that I might have left one off my list means I just haven't been there yet. Most wineries offer tours, and certainly wine tastings. This is the best way to discover what wines you and your family like without buying a whole bottle and then being disappointed. It can be a lot of fun, spending an afternoon or evening at a winery, tasting the various wines. In fact, the fun increases with the number of people you have with you.

Some heated discussion can even erupt over the quality of the various wines being sampled. Just remember, if you are going to sample a lot of wines, bring along a designated driver. Wine does contain alcohol, and you don't want to ruin a fun day by getting arrested for driving under the influence. As always, call first before driving to any of these wineries to make sure that they are open during the hours you will be there, and to find out details about handicapped accessibility. Also ask about tours, and about food to go with a wine tasting. A phone call can save a lot of disappointment.

(Wineries are all over the state. For nearby attractions, see books 1 and 2.)

Meier's Wine Cellars, Inc. ☎ 513-891-2900 or 800-364-2941
6955 Plainfield Pike · Silverton, Ohio
Region: Southwest (Coshocton County)

Kelleys Island Wine Company ☎ (419) 626-4224
Box 747, Woodford Road · Kelleys Island, Ohio
Region: Northwest (Erie County)

Heineman Winery/Caves ☎ (419) 285-2811
Corner of Catawba and Thompson Streets · Put-in-Bay, Ohio
Region: Northwest (Ottawa County)

Lonz Winery ☎ (419) 285-5411
Middle Bass Island, Ohio
Region: Northwest (Ottawa County)

Buccia Vineyards/Bed and Breakfast ☎ (440) 593-5976
518 Gore Road · Conneaut, Ohio
Region: Northeast (Ashtabula County)

Cantwell's Old Mill Winery ☎
403 South Broadway · Geneva, Ohio
Region: Northeast (Ashtabula County)

Chalet Debonne Vineyards ☎ (440) 466-3485
7743 Doty Road · Madison, Ohio
Region: Northeast (Lake County)

Ferrante Winery & Ristorante ☎ (440) 466-VINO
5585 State Route 307 · Geneva, Ohio
Region: Northeast (Ashtabula County)

Old Firehouse Winery & Restaurant ☎ (440) 466-9300 or (800) UNCORK-1
5499 Lake Road, Box 310 · Geneva-on-the-Lake, Ohio
Region: Northeast (Ashtabula County)

Mon Ami Historic Winery and Restaurant ☎ (800) 777-4266
3845 Wine Cellar Road · Port Clinton, Ohio
Region: Northwest (Ottawa County)

Markko Vineyard ☎ (440) 593-3197
R.D.#2 South Ridge Road · Conneaut, Ohio
Region: Northeast (Ashtabula County)

Klingshirn Winery, Inc. ☎ (440) 933-6666
33050 Webber Road · Avon Lake, Ohio

Region: Northeast (Lorain County)

John Christ Winery   ☎ (440) 933-9672
32421 Walker Road · Avon Lake, Ohio
Region: Northeast (Lorain County)

Firelands Winery   ☎ (419) 625-5474 or (800) 548-WINE
917 Bardshar Road · Sandusky, Ohio
Region: Northwest (Erie County)

Breitenbach Wine Cellars   ☎ (330) 343-3603
R. R. # 1, State Route 39 · Dover, Ohio
Region: Northeast (Tuscarawas County)

The Winery at Wolf Creek   ☎ (330) 666-9285
2637 South Cleveland-Massillon Road · Norton, Ohio
Region: Northeast (Summit County)

Firelands Winery

118 Eight is Food

I invited my co-workers at FOX8 television to share some of their favorite places to eat . . .

DICK GODDARD

Dick Goddard is probably one of the most recognized people in all of northeastern Ohio. It's been a privilege to work at the same station with him for the past 32 years. He's a best-selling author, as well as dean of Ohio television weathermen, and his good deeds are legendary: his work with homeless animals, his charity appearances, and, of course, the biggest single-day festival in Ohio—the Woollybear Festival, which Dick co-founded. As I said, his good deeds are manifold.

However, 30 years ago one of those good deeds almost got him into trouble, and made him the target of a practical joke.

I had only been working at WJW-TV a short time when a school group in the Firelands School District, where I lived at the time, held a benefit auction. Unbeknownst to me, they had contacted Dick and asked if he would contribute some original artwork. Dick, an accomplished cartoonist with a degree in art, drew a caricature of me and sent it to the school. I did not learn of this until the night of the auction when, much to my surprise, they announced they were selling an original caricature of me drawn by Dick Goddard.

Now, I am no judge of artwork, but I thought the drawing more closely resembled a humanized Goodyear blimp than me. Nevertheless it went up for sale. Nobody offered a bid. I sat there trying to hide my head in embarrassment. Nobody wanted to offer anything for a drawing of me, a local son! Finally someone in the back of the room said, "You say that was drawn by Dick Goddard?" The auctioneer assured him it was, and that it was of local resident Neil Zurcher. The man responded, "I never heard of that Zurcher guy, but I guess I'd bid 75 cents for a Goddard drawing." He added that his wife watched Goddard all the time. The auctioneer swiftly brought my embarrassment to an end by hammering the table and shouting "Sold! For 75 cents!" and went on to the next item.

I was crushed. Here I was a reporter for a big-time television station, and the local folks didn't even seem to care. I slunk out of the auction without buying anything.

It took me a day or two to start seeing the humor in the situation, and by that weekend I found myself laughing about the incident. I was relating it to my longtime friend, Elyria attorney Jack Zagrans. Now Jack was a man who loved practical jokes. We both sat there in his office laughing as I related how the man had bid only 75 cents for the drawing, and Jack got a twinkle in his eye, looked at me, and said, "You are going to sue Dick Goddard." I almost choked. "For what?" I said.

"For holding you up to public ridicule and for defamation of character," Jack replied with a big grin. "He drew the picture without your knowledge, right?" he asked. I nodded my head. "People were laughing at you that night, weren't they?" he said. "Yeah," I responded, "but Dick didn't mean to embarrass me, it was the fact that people didn't want to buy the picture that was embarrassing."

"Doesn't matter," Jack said. "We aren't really going to sue him, we're just going to have some fun."

During the next few days, Jack had a real lawsuit transcript drawn up. He brought both the Lorain County recorder and the county sheriff's department into the joke. The recorder put official-looking seals on the suit, making it look as though it had really been filed, and an off-duty sheriff's deputy agreed to come to Cleveland in uniform to "serve" the bogus lawsuit on Dick.

On the appointed day, I had clued in everyone in the newsroom about what was going to happen. Anchors Doug Adair and Martin Ross were at their desks across from Goddard. Behind some curtains in the news director's office we had set up a camera to capture the scene. Jack Zagrans had requested this because he wouldn't be there to witness Dick's reaction to our joke. At 4:30 in the afternoon, when we were sure Dick would be in the newsroom, the deputy, in full uniform with a gun, walked in, came up to Goddard's desk, and asked, "Are you Dick Goddard?"

Goddard looked up, smiling curiously as the deputy placed the bogus lawsuit in his hand and said, "You have just been served with a lawsuit." With that he turned, keeping a straight face, and walked out of the newsroom, leaving Goddard with his mouth hanging open. He opened up the papers and read that I was suing him for $200,000. When he saw my name, he started to laugh, thinking it was some kind of joke; then he saw the official seals and the filing stamps and he stopped laughing.

At that point, on cue, I walked out of the news director's office right in front of Dick. He looked up and said, "What's this all about? Why are you suing me . . ?" I cut him off by replying, "Sorry, Dick, under instructions from my attorney, I cannot discuss the matter." And with that I swept out of the office into the hallway where the deputy was still waiting, with others who had been tipped off as to what was happening. We were all bent over with silent laughter. When Dick came running around the corner, apparently looking for me, he suddenly saw the crowd and realized he had just been "had."

Our joke really worked because, unknown to us, Dick had recently been served with an actual lawsuit, and he knew what the procedure was. He said later it was the deputy and the stamps on the suit that convinced him I was seriously going to sue him for drawing that caricature. We all had a big laugh, and I assured Dick the suit wasn't real, just payback for a caricature that no one wanted.

I don't think Dick was mad. Of course he has never asked me to be grand marshal of the Woollybear Parade, I haven't gotten a Christmas card from him in years, and he has never tried to give me a homeless cat or dog. And he has never drawn a picture of me since then.

In all seriousness, I meant what I said at the beginning of this chapter. It has been an honor and a privilege to work with a man like Dick for the last 32 years. I have always thought of him as both a colleague and a friend.

When I told Dick I was going to include my colleagues in a section about their favorite "comfort" foods, I learned we had already covered two of his favorite spots—Strickland's Frozen Custard, and Swenson Drive-in Hamburgers, both in Akron. Dick said that when he was young he really liked hamburgers. In fact, he said, his friends called him "Wimpy" because he ate so many burgers. (Wimpy, the hamburger-fixated character in the old *Popeye* cartoon strip, not "wimpy" implying weakness, as the term usually does today.)

Today, Dick says, he is trying to be a vegetarian, so he seeks out places that have sandwiches with meat substitutes. One he recommended to me was a place in Westlake where he found a nonmeat chili dog that, he claims, is hard to tell from the real thing. It's made with tofu, a soy product that in some forms resembles those plastic peanuts they use for packing materials. I guess it couldn't be worse than what probably goes into the meat grinder to make some hot dogs. I checked with the folks who run the Web of Life Natural Food Market in Westlake and learned that they have a variety of sandwiches made with natural products that are good, and good for you. While Dick is partial to their Coney Island non–hot dog, they also say they make a wonderful mock tuna sandwich. They carry many other things, like organic foods and gourmet kitchen items.

(For nearby attractions, see Trips 5, 15, and 16 in Book 1.)

The Web of Life Natural Food Market ☎ 440-899-2882
25923 Detroit Avenue • Westlake, Ohio
Region: Northeast Ohio (Cuyahoga County)
Handicapped access: Yes.

TIM TAYLOR

Tim Taylor and I have known each other for over a quarter of a century. Now, I don't want to mislead you—we know each other, but we don't socialize a lot. We do try to exchange Christmas cards each year, but Tim has been known to be a bit forgetful. Take Christmas of 1997. I received a Christmas card from "Mr. and Mrs. Tim Taylor." Then a few days later I got another Christmas card, this one signed "Tim and Kathy Taylor," then a few days later a third card, this one just signed "Tim and Kathy." I suggested to him that he must have "A," "B," and "C" card lists, and for some reason I was on all three. Last Christmas I only got one card from him, with a note, "Zurcher, this is the only card you're getting this year."

There are reasons we don't socialize much. Tim is a golfer. I am not. Tim is a fisherman. I am not. Tim is an anchor. I am not. But we do have one thing in common. Food.

Not fancy stuff, just "comfort food," like warm, fresh donuts just out of the fryer with the sugar still melting on top. Or like a good fish sandwich. Tim seems to know, instinctively, where good food can be located.

So when I was working on this book, I mentioned to him that I was going to have a section about big hamburgers. He said, "If you're looking for a really big 'quality' hamburger, then you'll want to visit the Gaslite Inn in Bedford." He described a truly huge hamburger that weighs more than half a pound, fairly swimming in mushrooms and cooked onions. I promised him that I would check it out but never got there.

I did talk with the owner of the Gaslite Inn, John Fetsko, who laughed when I told him about Tim's description. "First of all," John said, "it's not a hamburger like you get those at chain restaurants. This is a Steakburger." John went on to describe the 85 percent lean sirloin steak that is ground to make his burgers. He said they make it into a half-pound patty before they start cooking. When it's all done, with cooked onion, cheese, mushrooms, and anything else you want on it, John says it weighs upwards of one pound! That's a man-sized hamburger, I mean, Steakburger.

Stop in at the Gaslite to try one, and if you see Tim there, tell him thanks for the tip.

(For nearby attractions, see Trips 5, 15, and 16 in Book 1.)

Gaslite Inn   ☎ 440-232-0540
630 Broadway Avenue • Bedford, Ohio
Region: Northeast Ohio (Cuyahoga County)
Handicapped access: steps to entrance, restrooms inaccessible to wheelchairs.

WILMA SMITH

Now not too many people know this. In fact I think Wilma has forgotten it, or perhaps it never registered in her mind, but I confess I once "hit on" Wilma Smith. It was years ago, when Wilma had just returned to Cleveland from a job in Virginia. She was working at Channel 5, and she and I were teamed up at a charity putt-putt golf match. I had never met her before. Understand I was much thinner and younger at the time, and I think my initial reaction to Wilma was the same as that of hundreds of other men when they meet her the first time. This is one attractive woman. Not only that, in person she is also witty and obviously very intelligent. Now, I hate golf. I don't understand it, and I don't like it in any form—including putt-putt—and usually I do anything I can to avoid playing. But this one time I truly enjoyed the game and didn't want it to end. When it did, I made my clumsy "pass" at Wilma Smith.

I asked her if she would like to go have a drink. Perhaps I just don't choose to remember, but I honestly don't recall exactly how she said "No." But knowing Wilma, I am sure she did it in a way that didn't totally crush my ego. I do recall that it was said in a way that left no doubt she wasn't interested.

Now, I have been turned down by several beautiful women during my lifetime, and I can't honestly say that I dwelled on my failure to charm Wilma. But while researching the favorite foods of my colleagues, I discovered what Wilma's favorite "comfort" foods were and was tantalized by the thought, what if instead of proposing we go for a drink, I had suggested we travel over to Farkas Pastry Shop on Lorain Avenue and split one his famous napoleons? Who knows, maybe things would have gone in a different direction. Probably not, but napoleons and Farkas Pastry will always be something that Wilma and I have in common. Wilma says that Farkas's napoleons are "the best ever!" and I agree.

A napoleon, in case you're interested, is a dessert. You begin with a puff pastry, fill it with custard and whipped cream, and add another layer of dough. When it's finished it's a melt-in-your-mouth concoction that measures about 2–3 inches square, and it's about three inches high. Farkas Pastry has been making them on Fridays and Saturdays for years.

(For nearby attractions, see Trips 5, 15, and 16 in Book 1.)

Farkas Pastry Shop ☎ 216-281-6200
2718 Lorain Avenue · Cleveland, Ohio
Region: Northeast Ohio (Cuyahoga County)
Handicapped access: Yes.

ANDRE BERNIER

When Andre isn't doing the weather, he says he likes to treat himself to a vanilla malted milk shake. The very best that he has found, he says, is out in Chesterland, Ohio, at the Valley Villa Ice Cream stand.

(For nearby attractions, see Trips 5, 15, and 16 in Book 1.)

Valley Villa Ice Cream ☎ 440-729-4194
820 Mayfield Road · Chesterland, Ohio
Region: Northeast Ohio (Geauga County)
Handicapped access: Yes.

MACIE JEPSON

Macie, with her busy schedule as an anchorwoman and a mom, says nothing is more comforting than a big dish of Pierre's Moose Tracks Ice Cream. She says she doesn't keep it around the house because once she starts eating it, it's very hard to stop, and she has been known to finish off the whole carton. The ice cream is available at grocery stores in the Cleveland area.

(For nearby attractions, see Trips 5, 15, and 16 in Book 1.)

Pierre's Ice Cream ☎ 216-432-1144
6200 Euclid Avenue (business office) · Cleveland, Ohio
Region: Northeast Ohio (Cuyahoga County)
Handicapped access: Yes, product available in grocery stores.

WAYNE DAWSON

Wayne says that he, like me, is partial to the wings at Quaker Steak and Lube in Sharon, Pennsylvania. But when he can't get up there, he can find some mighty good wings at Harpo's Sports Cafe on Brookpark Road in Cleveland. Wayne says they offer more than 20 different flavors of the hot wings, and he thinks their "Southern Sizzlers" are just about as good as those made in Sharon, Pennsylvania, or Buffalo, New York.

(For nearby attractions, see Trips 5, 15, and 16 in Book 1.)

Harpo's Sports Cafe   ☎ 216-267-7777
13930 Brookpark Road • Cleveland, Ohio
Region: Northeast Ohio (Cuyahoga County)
Handicapped access: Yes.

STEFANI SCHAEFER

Stefani Schaefer, or "Sissy" as her friends at the station and folks in
Alliance, where she grew up, still call her, agrees with my comments about
Doug's 57 Diner in Alliance (see Diner chapter). She spent a lot of her
youth there and says she still starts salivating when she thinks about their
apple fritters. "I ate an awful lot of Doug's apple fritters," she told me with
a big smile of remembrance. She also thinks their sandwiches can't be
beat. But she does have a local favorite: Tommy's in Cleveland Heights.
Stefani says you have not lived until you have one of their chocolate-
peanut butter milk shakes. I called Tommy's, and they said it's the homemade peanut butter that makes it special. It's made with Pierre's vanilla ice
cream, Hershey's chocolate syrup, homemade peanut butter, and fresh
milk. They said the amount of the ingredients varies, but they always use
enough to make it thick, and have it taste like a Reese's peanut butter cup.
(For nearby attractions, see Trips 5, 15, and 16 in Book 1.)

Tommy's   ☎ 216-321-7757
1824 Coventry Road • Cleveland Heights, Ohio
Region: Northeast Ohio (Cuyahoga County)
Handicapped access: Yes.

JON LOUFMAN

Jon tells me he and his family are hooked on the French fries you get at
national burger chains, but that he is also fond of a "comfort food" that is
local. When he wants a special treat, he and the kids head for Swings-N-
Things in North Olmsted. They make their own ice cream, and Jon says he
hasn't found a flavor yet that he doesn't like.
(For nearby attractions, see Trips 5, 15, and 16 in Book 1.)

Swings-N-Things Family Fun Park   ☎ 440-235-4420
8501 Stearns Road • North Olmsted, Ohio
Region: Northeast Ohio (Cuyahoga County)
Handicapped access: Yes, to dining area.

JOHN O'DAY

John O'Day, who has been around almost as long as I have, says he gets "Lizard Lips" about noon every day. The only place, he says, that knows how to fix them is the Winking Lizard, a sports bar in Independence, Ohio. Actually, John says he is partial to all of their "Repitizers." I checked the place out. What he is talking about is a fancy name for chicken fingers that you dip in barbecue sauce. "Repitizers" turns out to be a list of appetizers they serve, which includes "Lizard Lips."

(For nearby attractions, see Trips 5, 15, and 16 in Book 1.)

The Winking Lizard   ☎ 216-524-2226
6901 Rockside Road · Independence, Ohio
Region: Northeast Ohio (Cuyahoga County)
Handicapped access: Yes.

BILL MARTIN

My friend Bill Martin is a man who does not easily forget his roots. He was born and raised in Tonawanda, New York, a suburb of Buffalo and Niagara Falls. He says when he was growing up there was only one hot dog, and it came from Ted's Hot Dogs. Today you can buy Ted's Hot Dogs at many outlets in the Buffalo area. Bill says if you ever go to Niagara Falls, be sure to stop at his favorite Ted's Hot Dog stand on Niagara Falls Boulevard at Exit 50 on I-290. He also has a local pizza favorite: Angelina's Pizza in North Olmsted. He says he likes pizza so much that he even has it for breakfast, and Angelina's makes a "killer" breakfast pie. I gave Angelina's a call and asked what makes it so special. They said at breakfast time they replace the tomato sauce with scrambled eggs, cover them with three different kinds of cheese, and add whatever toppings you desire. Bill likes crumbled bacon on his. It's like having a good breakfast all in one dish. They also make regular pizzas.

(For nearby attractions, see Trips 5, 15, and 16 in Book 1.)

Angelina's Pizza   ☎ 440-734-3700
30594 Lorain Road · North Olmsted, Ohio
Region: Northeast Ohio (Cuyahoga County)
Handicapped access: Yes.

Index—Alphabetical

Index—Geographical

NORTHWEST OHIO